2826 $11.70

Christine Smith
Bernice Newton.
Beryl Glendinning
L Miller.
Stan Newton.
Hugh McCord
Fay McCready
Helen [illegible] Spargo -
Amy & Melvin Taylor.
[illegible] [illegible].
K R [illegible]
Ngaire Williams
Reginald H Knight
[illegible] Medland
Garry [illegible]
Ivan J. Medland
Myra C. Medland.
Glenis Cross.
[illegible] Hutson Joan Hutson
A Cross
Y. M. Cresswell
W. R. Warring
B J Millar

The Armoury Commentary

THE NEW TESTAMENT EPISTLES

The Armoury Commentary

THE NEW TESTAMENT EPISTLES

edited by
General Frederick Coutts

HODDER AND STOUGHTON
LONDON SYDNEY AUCKLAND TORONTO

Preface

This volume on the New Testament epistles is a companion to the earlier volume on the four gospels, and what was there said about the editors of *The Soldier's Armoury* since its commencement in 1955 applies here also.

F.C.

Contents

THE EPISTLE TO THE ROMANS

INTRODUCTION

This letter is a carefully planned essay upon the Christian faith written by the Apostle Paul and sent in advance to Rome to prepare the way for his arrival in the imperial capital on his proposed journey to Spain (15:24). First of all, however, he had to return to Jerusalem with the collection which he had organized for the mother church (compare 1 Corinthians 16:1 ff., 2 Corinthians 9:1 ff. and Romans 15:25–28), and for that mission besought the prayers of his brethren in Rome (15:30, 31).

A. M. Hunter has described the Epistle as 'a deliberate exposition of the deepest principles of Christianity as Paul knew them', adding that 'whoever has mastered the theology of Romans has mastered Paul's gospel.'

Though the church in Rome was largely Gentile, the many references in the Epistle to the Hebrew faith presuppose a substantial Jewish element as well. Most encouraging of all, the effective witness of the church was already acknowledged throughout the Mediterranean world (1:8).

ROMANS 1:1–7

'He was declared Son of God by a mighty act in that He rose from the dead' (v. 4, N.E.B.).

NO ILLUSION. In ancient times the beginning of a letter was divided into three parts: the sender's name, the name of the recipient, and a greeting. As was his usual practice, Paul expands this conventional framework into a statement of Christian truth. It is worth noting that he describes himself as 'set apart for the service of the gospel'. The word 'pharisee' meant 'separated' and the apostle recognizes that he is now 'set apart', not for the service of the law, but for the gospel.

This gospel, which is to be the main theme of this lengthy letter, hinges upon a unique event—the resurrection of Jesus Christ. It was in this mighty act of God that Jesus was disclosed as Son of God, the fulfilment of the hopes of the prophets.

This dependence of Christian faith upon the resurrection of Jesus may be felt as a weakness in an age when men demand that truth must be open to scientific verification. But we need to be clear what the Church actually believes in this respect. As D. W. D. Shaw has written: '"What actually happened" that first Easter, we shall never know, if by "know" we mean some sort of neutral, allegedly objective account either of the mechanics of the resurrection or how we in the twentieth century would have described what the disciples saw, or what a candid camera might or might not have revealed. But what we do maintain and have good grounds for maintaining is that the cry of astonishment, "Jesus lives!" was no illusion'. The 'how' of the resurrection is beyond our verification: the spiritual experience of the risen Christ in our lives is not. It is for us—Sebastian Moore has said—to 'bring into creative relationships the upheavals of the present time and the upheaval that took place in Palestine two thousand years ago when the stone was rolled away'.

ROMANS 1:8–17

'God knows how continually I make mention of you in my prayers' (v. 9, N.E.B.).

THE PRIDE THAT IS HUMBLE. Having complimented the Roman Christians on their faith, Paul told them how much he longed to see them, not only that he might impart some spiritual gift, but that he himself might be enriched by them. Their fellowship together was to be mutually helpful. He then confessed his sense of evangelical obligation to the whole world and his pride in the gospel of Christ, the one basic answer to human need.

Pride in the gospel is always related to profound personal humility. There is an evangelism which is rude, insensitive, and arrogant. It claims to know all the answers, asks embarrassing questions and attempts to bully people into the Kingdom. It shouts when whispered understanding is required. Paul's pride in his message expressed itself in his intercessions. He prayed consistently for the people he was trying to help. D. T. Niles asked a searching question in his book *The Preacher's Calling To Be Servant*: 'Can you mention the names of the people—two or three perhaps—who are to you a cause of real sorrow because they are not Christians? They are good people, they are your friends, but always when you think of them there is a pain in your soul because they do not serve Jesus Christ. Are there such people in your life? If not, you are not an evangelist however much may be the evangelistic work which you do.'

ROMANS 1:18–25

'The anger of God is being revealed from heaven against all the impiety and depravity of men who keep truth imprisoned in their wickedness' (v. 18, Jerusalem Bible).

NOT INDIFFERENT. Before prescribing the divine remedy for man's moral and spiritual sickness, Paul gives us a fairly detailed diagnosis of the disease. Turning first to the pagan world, then to the Jewish, he portrays man's universal need of salvation.

God's intention for man is partially revealed in His 'anger' against all wickedness. The apostle's use of the term 'wrath of God' needs careful understanding for it is both open to grave misunderstanding and yet at the same time is indispensable. First, we must try to detach the idea of divine anger from its normal human associations. Self-concern and vindictiveness play no part in God's reaction to sin, nor is there any trace of personal animosity. God's wrath is His ceaseless, unrelenting opposition to evil in every shape and form.

We must also remember that God's wrath is a part of His love. If God were indifferent to us He would be indifferent to our sin. F. F. Bruce comments: 'Paul would certainly have agreed with Isaiah in describing the execution of God's wrath as His "strange work" (Isaiah 28:21), to which He girds Himself slowly and reluctantly. Indeed he sets forth the revelation of God's wrath here as the background to His "proper work" of mercy, which is so congenial to His character that He speeds with joyful haste to lavish it upon undeserving penitents.'

ROMANS 1:26–32

'Since they refused to see it was rational to acknowledge God, God has left them to their own irrational ideas and to their monstrous behaviour' (v. 28, Jerusalem Bible).

PERVERSE WORSHIP. Paul's indictment of pagan society does not make pleasant reading but the colours he uses for his picture are no more sombre than those used by the historians of his day. Moral decay and corruption were widespread, though we have no reason to doubt that, as always, there was undoubtedly goodness and decency in the world as well.

In contrast to our reading it might be helpful to remember the well-known story of William Temple's attendance, when an undergraduate at Oxford, at a meeting addressed by a famous American evangelist. The preacher quoted Isaiah's description of sin as 'scarlet'. Temple recalled, 'Though I went to the meeting in a serious, inquiring spirit. I found myself quite unmoved, for, alas, my sins were not scarlet, they were grey—all grey. They were not dramatic acts of rebellion and violent self-affirmation, but the colourless, tired sins of omission, inertia and timidity.'

The abiding truth behind Paul's diagnosis of pagan society is his assertion that wrong worship leads to wrong conduct. In his view, it was idolatry that led to moral corruption. Can we not apply his analysis to our sins—those 'colourless, tired sins of omission, inertia and timidity'. If our worship were truly focused upon God in Christ these sins would be as unthinkable as the flagrant lawlessness which Paul here portrays. Thomas Merton accurately defined sin as 'our refusal to be what we were created to be—sons of God, images of God. Ultimately sin, while seeming to be an assertion of freedom, is a flight from the freedom and responsibility of divine sonship.'

ROMANS 2:1–11

'Now if you feel inclined to set yourself up as a judge of those who sin, let me assure you, whoever you are, that you are in no position to do so' (v. 1, Phillips).

UNIVERSAL CONDITION. Having exposed the corruption of pagan society, Paul now turns to charge the Jews with being similarly in bondage to sin. His style at this point is one which the ancients called the *diatribe*, in which questions or objections are put into the mouth of an imaginary critic in order that they may be dealt with by the writer.

In a society as degenerate as that of the Roman Empire in the first century, it was all too easy for the Jew to feel morally superior. But, says the apostle, if the essence of sin is unfaithfulness to our knowledge of truth, the Jew has no grounds for pride. Pagans flouted the natural law written in their hearts: Jews disobeyed the law of God given to them by special revelation.

Because sinfulness is a universal human condition we need to acknowledge our inevitable involvement in this, as well as our personal and particular faults. Specific confession of our individual failures is necessary for growth in self-understanding but all too easily we fall into the error of assessing the degree of our guilt, and of comparing ourselves with others. This we can never do correctly. In God's eyes the measure of our guilt depends, not upon the particular sin committed, but upon how much light we have received and whether unconscious compulsions have lessened our responsibility. The use of such prayers as the General Confession and the Lord's Prayer frees us from futile comparisons with other people and helps us to accept the truth that, for better, for worse, we are bound up in the bundle of life.

ROMANS 2:12–16

'It is not familiarity with the Law that justifies a man in the sight of God, but obedience to it' (v. 13, Phillips).

SPIRITUAL PRIVILEGES, 'When we open our eyes as babies,' wrote William Temple, 'we see the world stretching out around us; we are in the middle of it; all proportions and perspectives in what we see are determined by the relation—distance, height and so forth—of the various visible objects to ourselves. This will remain true of our bodily vision as long as we live. I am the centre of the world I see; where the horizon is depends on where I stand.' As the late Archbishop of Canterbury went on to point out, this is also true of our mental and spiritual vision. Each takes his place at the centre of his own world. Yet we are not the centre of the world, and God is. Our 'original sin' consists in our taking the place that belongs to God alone. We are not 'guilty' on this account for we cannot help it. This is the universal human condition. But only as we escape from this state can we avoid spoiling our own lives and the lives of others.

This radical selfishness is nowhere more apparent than in the way in which religion itself becomes tainted by it. Addressing his fellow Jews, Paul tries to strip them of the smugness and complacency which many of them felt in being the custodians of God's special revelation. What should have been a spur to moral effort had become for some simply an excuse for spiritual pride.

Self-centredness can assume a religious guise as well as a rebellious attitude of defiance. Christ aims to lead us away from both attitudes towards self-forgetful love.

ROMANS 2:17–24

'You are convinced that you are a guide to the blind, a light to those in darkness, a tutor of the backward, a teacher of infants. . . . Well then, you who teach others, do you never teach yourself?' (vv. 19–21, Authentic New Testament).

BRINGING RELIGION INTO DISREPUTE. As a great deal of first-century Jewish writing indicates, many Jews living in a pagan environment felt called to be 'a guide to the blind, a light to darkened souls' (v. 19, Moffatt). Unfortunately, their lives often fell so far short of their ideals that they brought their own religion into disrepute. Paul refers to Isaiah 52:5—'My name continually every day is blasphemed.' The sad plight of the exiled Jews centuries before had made the Gentiles scoff at Jehovah, imagining He was impotent to help His people. 'Now it is not His people's misfortune, but their misconduct (commented F. F. Bruce) that causes the Gentiles to conclude that the God of such a people cannot be of much account'.

Here we find ourselves in something of a dilemma. To be oversensitive to what unbelievers think about our lives can lead to a complete loss of spontaneity, to being 'other-directed' instead of 'inner-directed'. This is the worst form of bondage. Yet the danger that our lives may give the lie to our faith is too real to disregard.

If we keep our eyes fixed upon Christ we shall not bring our religion into disrepute, not because we shall become suddenly perfect, but because we shall be saved from insincerity and self-righteousness, the two forms of moral failure which, more than anything else, make religion repugnant to unbelievers. We could be helped by using the prayer of the Taizé office: 'Almighty God, accept the repentance of Thy servants whose lives are not in accordance with their faith; may we begin again through the life-giving breath of Thy Spirit, the Comforter.'

ROMANS 2:25–29

'The real Jew is the one who is inwardly a Jew, and the real circumcision is in the heart—something not of the letter but of the spirit' (v. 29, Jerusalem Bible).

INWARD REALITY. Paul here continues his attempt to save his fellow Jews from the spiritual conceit which imagines itself exempt from universal human sinfulness. For unless we recognize our sin we cannot hear the word of the Gospel. So the apostle points out that being a Jew by birth is not enough. True religion is an inward experience of the heart. This is a reminder we all need and one that will invariably keep us humble. The externals of religion can so easily be used as an evasion of the need for inner reality. It was Søren Kierkegaard who said that he meant 'to labour to achieve a far more inward relation to Christianity; hitherto I have fought for its truth while in a sense standing outside it.'

Thomas Kelly, a Quaker, wrote some 'Reflections' while briefly staying in a monastery. He described an evening conversation in a quiet, friendly garden where two priests and himself discussed the sacraments. In terms of Catholic theology he, an 'unbaptized' Quaker, was not a Christian, except for the saving provision which allowed one to be a Christian 'by desire'. But he adds, 'As the conversation moved to the love of God, to the need of Christ being formed in us, to the outgoing love of the Nazarene, to the blind and lame and wounded in body and soul in these days, the conversation became a sacrament where the Presence was as truly in our midst as He is in the Mass within the chapel walls.'

The externals of religion, whether membership of 'the people of God', or the observances they practise, are of value only as they correspond to, and facilitate, an inward experience. They become a positive hindrance when they become substitutes for the reality they represent.

ROMANS 3:1–8

'God must prove true to His word, though all men should play Him false' (v. 4, Knox).

PRIVILEGE IS AN OBLIGATION TO WORK HARDER. Paul is arguing with an imaginary objector, who wants to know, in the light of the Apostle's claim that the true Jew is one inwardly, what advantage, if any, there is in being born of God's chosen people. Paul replies that the Jews enjoyed the privilege of being entrusted with the Law, a privilege, however, which did not exempt them from God's judgment. In that case, continued the objector, the disobedience of the Jews gave God an opportunity to reveal His justice; their faithlessness actually emphasized His faithfulness, so why condemn them? The Apostle replied that such an argument was a piece of very special pleading and unworthy of serious consideration.

He had no wish to under-value the role of the Jew in the purposes of God, but wanted to underline, above everything else, that privilege meant responsibility. In the words of Jesus, 'Much will be expected from the one who has been given much, and the more a man is trusted, the more people will expect of him' (Luke 12: 48, Phillips). We do well to ponder such words, for we take so much for granted and are tempted to whimper at the slightest inconvenience. The privilege of being chosen by God places upon a man the obligation to work harder. This is always the outlook of the saint. Far from lauding it over less favoured individuals, or thinking himself superior to them, he translates every privilege into the thanksgiving of service.

ROMANS 3:9–20

'We have already formulated the charge that Jews and Greeks alike are all under the power of sin' (v. 9, N.E.B.).

NOT WITHOUT HOPE. Paul has almost completed his grim survey of universal human sinfulness. The condition he analysed is one with which many of our current dramatists and novelists agree. As the late C. E. M. Joad (of Brains Trust fame) believed, 'strands of evil are woven into our fundamental make-up.' In contrast to some scientific humanists, who seem to have a naïve faith in human perfectibility, many contemporary artists are keenly aware of man's plight. They do not use the word 'sin' but speak rather of alienation, loss of meaning and estrangement.

Having built up his case from the observable facts of the life of his times, Paul rounds it off with a chain of six quotations from the Psalms and Isaiah. This is surely the way that modern evangelism must usually proceed—from life to the Bible and back to life again. When we start from the Bible we all too often fail to meet modern man where he is.

If the Apostle's survey of the human condition seems depressing, we need to remember that it is not pessimistic but realistic. 'To be able to deal hopefully with men', D. E. Jenkins has written, 'one has to face the fact that men are alienated from themselves, from one another and from God. This is their fallen condition which is, when so understood, a potentially hopeful condition. For to be fallen is to be neither what it is intended to be nor what it is necessary to be.'

ROMANS 3:21–31

'Both Jew and pagan sinned and forfeited God's glory, and both are justified through the free gift of His grace by being redeemed in Christ Jesus' (vv. 23 and 24, Jerusalem Bible).

FROM DIAGNOSIS TO CURE. This is one of the great passages of the New Testament. Having established that all are equally needy, Paul returns to the original thesis of 1:17.

Laying down some lines of guidance for the dramatists of his day, the Roman poet Horace criticized those who too easily brought in a god to solve problems in the plot of their plays. 'Do not bring a god on to the stage,' he said, 'unless the problem is one that deserves a god to solve it.' Luther applied these words to the sinfulness of man. Here is a situation only God can unravel.

At this point in his letter Paul begins to explain how God has dealt with this insuperable problem. He turns from diagnosis to cure. God purposes to justify sinners on the basis of their faith.

'Justify' does not mean 'make righteous': it means 'declare righteous'. So God does what would be unthinkable in a court of law—He acquits guilty men and treats them as righteous. Of course, while we think in terms of a law court, this is problematic. In family relationships, as Jesus showed in His parable of the Prodigal Son, it is not at all unusual.

Nothing that Jesus said or did altered God's attitude to man, but rather revealed it. He did not die to placate an angry God, for the Father and the Son are one. Jesus is that 'image' of the Godhead (Heb. 1:3) we have been privileged to see. The life and death of Jesus teach that God Himself bore the cost of man's redemption.

ROMANS 4:1–8

'And Abraham believed God, and it was reckoned unto him for righteousness' (v. 3, Phillips).

RESTFUL TRUST. No sooner has Paul introduced the theme of God's justification of the sinner than he makes what is to non-Jewish readers a rather tedious digression. Having claimed that the Gospel was the fulfilment of Old Testament expectations the apostle felt he must relate this to the one whom all Jews most highly revered—Abraham. When the Bible narrative says that the patriarch's faith was 'reckoned unto him for righteousness' it implies that he had no righteousness of his own. Paul draws out the implications of this by distinguishing between a wage, which is a man's rightful due, and a gift which is entirely unearned. God's justification is sheer gift.

The apostle then adds the example of David to that of the patriarch Abraham. Neither of these men was without sin. Their happiness consisted in the fact that they had unreservedly thrown themselves upon the mercy of God. As Pascal said: 'Jesus Christ is the God whom we can approach without pride, and before whom we may abase ourselves without despair'.

'Just now,' wrote one person who had entered into this kind of restful trust, 'I am happy again, because I have entrusted the worst and the best of myself to God, including everything that still resists Him.' Here is true assurance, not based upon our own goodness, or even upon the fulness of our own surrender (of which we can never be certain), but solely upon the love of God. This is the way to spiritual growth and joy.

ROMANS 4:9–16

'The promise was made on the ground of faith, in order that it might be a matter of sheer grace' (v. 16, N.E.B.).

GOOD NEWS. Paul Tournier, a Christian psychotherapist, describes two ways in which he has tried to help people who are obsessed and humiliated by the vulgarity or the cruelty of their thoughts. One way is to suggest that such ideas are not a true part of their personality since actually they fight against them and deplore them. Yet he found that this rarely pacified his patients. It therefore seems better to say to them, 'Of course you have horrible thoughts, because evil is woven into the heart of man, and he is utterly powerless, by himself, to subdue it. This is in fact what the Bible teaches. Everyone has thoughts of which he is ashamed.' Paul Tournier then goes on to speak of God's acceptance of us as we are. To suggest that we must first conquer the evil in our hearts is a denial of the Gospel of grace.

This approach is firmly grounded in Paul's teaching. The apostle was also anxious to show that this was rooted in Old Testament religion at its best. We in turn may well reflect that it is firmly based upon the facts of human nature. If 'love is the fulfilling of the law' it is also true that we cannot love to order. Love is evoked by being loved. It has been said that this situation would spell frustration unless there was a universal resource of love available. There is! This is what we mean when we speak of the grace of God which, like His peace, passes understanding.

ROMANS 4:17–25

'Abraham, when hope was dead within him, went on hoping in faith, believing that he would become "the father of many nations". He relied on the word of God' (v. 18, Phillips).

HOW ZEAL COULD DESTROY FAITH. When Abraham received the promise that all the families of the earth would be blessed through his descendants, he was childless and 100 years old. Sarah, his wife, was only ten years younger. Yet the old patriarch never doubted God. He acted on the assumption that what the Eternal had promised he was able to perform. Paul used this incident to illustrate his argument that it was Abraham's faith, his readiness to take God at His word, that was counted unto him for righteousness and thereby brought him into a living relationship with God.

The patriarch believed that God was able to accomplish the impossible. We tend to imagine that everything depends upon our efforts, which hard experience so often proves to be futile. So we get depressed and either give up altogether or wear ourselves out in feverish activity. Work (often involving great sacrifice) is essential if God's purposes are to be fulfilled, but unless the worker is content to reflect God's light, and not try frantically to generate it, he allows his own zeal slowly to destroy his faith. The balance is preserved in a sentence of William Barclay's: 'A man may well hesitate to attempt a great task by himself; there is nothing which he need hesitate to attempt with God.'

ROMANS 5:1–5

'These sufferings bring patience, as we know, and patience brings perseverance, and perseverance brings hope' (vv. 3 and 4, Jerusalem Bible).

CHRISTIAN ENDURANCE. In the book *This Stranger, My Son*, Louise Wilson tries to assess some of the gains wrested by her family from the tragedy of her schizophrenic son. 'I believe', her daughter once said, 'in a special way we've all acquired a kind of toughness. You think, well, one of the worst things imaginable has happened, so maybe we'll be able to manage anything else that comes along.' To which Louise Wilson adds, 'Toughness, yes . . . and along with it—really a part of it—discerning compassion, too.'

Having described God's way of justifying sinners, Paul now turns to set out the blessings of those who have entered into this new relationship of grace. Although Paul felt called to give detailed treatment to justification, because it was this aspect of his teaching which met most opposition, his deepest interest seemed to lie in the new life which followed justification.

One of the blessings of this new life was that even the believer's trials were not without some compensation, resulting in a quality best described as 'testedness'—a maturity of character or, in the words of Louise Wilson's daughter, a 'toughness'. This is the very opposite of the hardness and bitterness that can result from suffering for it combines strength and endurance with compassion and deeper insight. Such a union is not sterile but fruitful. As Martin

Luther King declared: 'I will go on with the faith that unmerited suffering is redemptive.'

ROMANS 5:6–11

'If, while we were His enemies, Christ reconciled us to God by dying for us, surely now that we are reconciled we may be perfectly certain of our salvation through His living in us' (v. 10, Phillips).

PENITENCE DOES NOT MERIT FORGIVENESS. Christ died for us, not when we were good, but when we were bad. And this is the final proof of His love, but not of His love only. The death of Christ reveals the eternal love of God. Some people appear to believe that Jesus died to persuade God to love us, to offer Himself a sacrifice for sin to avert the wrath of God. But God was in Christ reconciling the world unto Himself. He did not need to be reconciled. His love for mankind was no greater after the Crucifixion than before; it was always infinite.

There are individuals who imagine that their repentance enables God to love them. But does a mother ever stop loving her prodigal son or reject him until he is suitably penitent? She loves him ceaselessly, and it is as he realizes the depth and suffering of this love that his heart is broken and he returns home to seek her forgiveness. Only when a man knows himself to be loved by God does he learn the true meaning of repentance, and this explains the humility of the saints. Neither their love nor penitence earns God's forgiveness. His loving acceptance of them 'while they were yet sinners', love wholly unmerited and unwavering, drives them to their knees in shame and sorrow. They are forgiven not because they love; they love because they are forgiven.

ROMANS 5:12–21

'As by one man's disobedience many were made sinners, so by one man's obedience many will be made righteous' (v. 19, Jerusalem Bible).

ADAM OR CHRIST? One relevant comment on this passage is that 'in God's sight there are two men—Adam and Jesus Christ—and these two men have all other men hanging at their girdle strings'.

Dealing with the view of man held in the Eastern Orthodox churches, A. M. Allchin has written that 'if we had asked the Fathers of the church whether or not they believed that the Genesis story was historically true, they might have been at a loss what to reply, for neither they nor their contemporaries made the precise distinction between historical and other forms of truths which we make. Certainly they would have held that that narrative is true; but they would I think, for the most part, have held that its main significance lay in what it told us about all men, about mankind as a whole, rather than in what it told us of an original pair, historically considered. What matters is that Adam is the type of every man that is to be saved.'

It is this view of the solidarity of mankind, which Western man has largely lost, that Paul expounds in this passage. The Hebrew word for Adam means 'mankind' and the apostle sees him as far more than the father of the race: he is simply man, every man and all men.

But if we are bound together in a solidarity of mankind in evil, it is also true that we are bound together for good. So the obedience of Christ has an even vaster potentiality for good than the sin of 'Adam'. It is for each man to decide which fact—the old solidarity in evil or the new unity with Christ in grace and life—shall determine the way he lives.

ROMANS 6:1–11

'Look upon yourselves as dead to the appeal and power of sin but alive and sensitive to the call of God through Jesus Christ our Lord' (v. 11, Phillips).

NEITHER LAXITY NOR LEGALISM. At the close of the last chapter Paul declared one of the most gracious truths of the Gospel, 'Where sin abounded grace did much more abound.' Yet it was a word not without danger. Again and again in Christian history it has been perversely interpreted as meaning, 'Since to multiply sin is to increase God's grace, let us go on sinning.' So in Southey's life of Wesley we read, 'There were members of the society who spoke in the most glorious manner of Christ, and of their interest in His complete salvation, and yet were indulging the most unchristian tempers, and living in the greatest immoralities.' And from a very different tradition we have the notorious example of the Russian monk, Rasputin, who taught and lived his version of salvation through deliberately repeated sin and repeated 'repentance'.

Libertinism—living without any restraint—stands at the opposite pole of legalism—ordering life by rules and regulations. It is the easiest thing in the world to flee from one extreme to the other. Paul refused to do this. Even when his doctrine of justification by faith was abused into an excuse for moral laxity, he stood firm. He had known the toils and strains of legalism and had now discovered in Christ a more excellent way.

His advice therefore was, 'Become what you are.' The believer's standing in Christ is utterly incompatible with indifference to moral values. We must therefore make real in daily life that status as children of God which has been given us freely as an act of grace. This new reality cannot be earned but it must be lived out.

ROMANS 6:12–19

'Sin shall no longer be your master, because you are no longer under law, but under the grace of God' (v. 14, N.E.B.).

RESPONSIBLE LIVING. Many of Paul's opponents could think of no way of opposing sin except by the Law. Once invalidate the Law and what could you expect but the chaos of moral anarchy? Yet from his own personal experience the apostle knew the futility of the Law in making a man righteous and he therefore reversed the arguments of his opponents. It is when a man is no longer under the Law, but under grace, that sin ceases to be his master.

To feel the force of his argument we need to widen the concept of law to embrace, not only the Jewish Law, but all rules, conventions and expectations imposed by other people. Not that a man can live without law in this sense, but when his life is determined wholly by external regulations he loses all sense of freedom and responsible choice. In terms of a distinction already made, he is other-directed instead of inner-directed.

The Gospel calls man into a life of loving relationships and these in turn lead to responsible living. This is to live 'under the grace of God'. Thomas Merton has pointed out the danger that we may always slip back into legalism. 'If we forget that the laws and organization of the church are there only to preserve the inner life of charity, we will tend to make the observance of law an end in itself. Then the Christian life becomes externalized . . . And this makes genuine holiness impossible, since holiness is the fulness of life, the abundance of charity and the radiation of the Holy Spirit hidden within us.'

ROMANS 6:20–23

'For sin pays a wage, and the wage is death, but God gives freely, and His gift is eternal life, in union with Christ Jesus our Lord' (v. 23, N.E.B.).

CONTRASTING SERVICE. We need not be unduly disturbed if the word sin is out of fashion. Modern writers and artists certainly acknowledge its existence though, lacking the religious dimension, they are compelled to use different terms. 'Mankind today is in poor shape,' wrote the Italian novelist Ignazio Silone. 'Any portrait of modern man, if at all faithful to the original, cannot but be deformed, split, fragmentary—in a word, tragic.' This is not far removed from the description of the human condition in Paul's letter to the Romans.

The apostle claims that the Christian is like a slave who has changed masters. Slavery being a much more exclusive relationship than the modern master-servant relationship, his analogy is far more powerful. A slave has no obligation whatsoever to any previous master, nor is it possible to have more than one master. However, the change of master, from sin to God, is no more striking than the vastly different results of such service. Sin pays a wage, and it is this wage that is documented so fully by Paul and by many modern novelists. God, however, extends to man a free gift and in consequence the whole nature of our service is transformed.

It has been well said that 'since gratitude may be regarded as the most ethical of all the emotions (a man who has known no gratitude is morally dead), justification which must, when appropriated, issue in gratitude, contains within itself the power of moral renewal.'

ROMANS 7:1–6

'But now we are rid of the Law, freed by death from our imprisonment, free to serve in the new spiritual way and not the old way of a written law' (v. 6, Jerusalem Bible).

LAW AND LOVE. 'Do you know what frees one from this captivity?' asked the artist Vincent van Gogh in a letter to his brother. 'It is every serious, deep affection. Being friends, being brothers, love, that is what opens the prison by some supreme power, by some magic force. Without this, one remains in prison.'

Having used the analogy of master and slave to illustrate the Christian's freedom from sin, Paul goes on to use that of marriage to underline his freedom from the Law. The death of a woman's husband sets her free from the obligations of her marriage. So, too, the Christian is liberated from the life of submission to an external code by the death of Christ.

This analogy is not one of Paul's best, but the point he makes is clear enough. The whole nature of morality has changed for the Christian. Like Vincent van Gogh in a different context, the believer knows that the prison house of unwelcome obligation and constraint has been opened by love. This does not mean that his morality will be less reliable, or less sensitive, than that of man who orders his life by an external law. On the contrary, his morality has a completely different motivation which increasingly lifts him above the dangerous conflict between desire and obligation. More and more he finds that what he *ought* to do is what he wants to do.

ROMANS 7:7–13

'The commandment which should have led to life proved in my experience to lead to death' (v. 10, N.E.B.).

FAILURE OF MORALISM. That Paul should follow up his illustration of the believer's freedom from sin with an analogy of his freedom from the Law would seem almost blasphemous to Jewish readers. Surely sin is evil and the Law good. Yet the fact was that these two opposites were closely related in Paul's experience, as they are in the lives of many. It is undeniable that prohibition all too frequently stimulates desire. Several commentators use Augustine's illustration of this process. Describing how he and some youthful friends raided a neighbour's orchard to steal some pears, he wrote, 'It was not the wretched pears my soul coveted, for I had plenty better at home. I picked them simply because I wanted to be a thief. What was it I loved in the theft? Was it the pleasure of acting against the law in order that I, a prisoner under rules, might have a maimed counterfeit of freedom by doing with impunity what was forbidden?'

As C. H. Dodd has pointed out, it is highly significant that Paul chooses the one commandment in the Law—'Thou shalt not covet'—which deals with inner disposition and not overt action. Usually we can regulate outward conduct to conform to rules but we are powerless to order our desires according to some ideal pattern. This is where moralism becomes utterly impotent.

Only a way of life which transforms our nature at depth can resolve this tension, and Paul had found this in Christ.

ROMANS 7:14–25

'What a wretched man I am! Who will rescue me from this body doomed to death? Thanks be to God through Jesus Christ our Lord!' (vv. 24, 25, Jerusalem Bible).

NO ABSTRACT ANALYSIS. The famous Scottish preacher, Alexander Whyte, asserted that whenever his attentive bookseller sent him on approval a new commentary on Romans he turned immediately to the seventh chapter. 'If the commentator sets up a man of straw in the seventh chapter,' he said, 'I immediately shut the book. I at once send the book back and say, "No, thank you. That is not the man for my hard-earned money."'

This chapter is no abstract analysis of the psychology of human sin: it is the description of Paul's personal anguish and travail. But was this conflict past or present? It is described in the present tense yet reflects what seems to be a pre-conversion experience without any trace of moral victory. Erudite scholars have lined up on both sides of this argument. To many readers the most attractive suggestion will be that of C. L. Mitton that Paul here describes, not only man's pre-conversion experience, but also the similar experience which befalls a Christian when he ceases to live in daily dependence upon divine grace. As C. S. Lewis wrote: 'Relying on God has to begin all over again every day as if nothing had yet been done.'

All too easily we slip back into a legalistic attitude to God. Then the old conflict between desire and duty erupts and we become people divided against ourselves. This wearisome turmoil is certainly not the experience of the Christian when he is relying on Christ, but at any time it may once again be true of the man who has temporarily ceased to live by God's grace.

ROMANS 8:1–8

'God has done what the Law, because of our unspiritual nature, was unable to do' (v. 3, Jerusalem Bible).

STRONG TO SAVE. In a play by the German poet Wolfgang Borchert, God appears in the guise of a weeping old man wringing His hands helplessly over the sufferings and stupidities of the human race. 'I can do nothing,' God says. 'Just so,' replies another character, 'you can do nothing. We do not fear you any more. We do not love you any more. You are not modern. The theologians have let you become an old man . . . You speak low at present, too low for the thunder of our time.'

This may summarize the feelings of many of our contemporaries, but it is not peculiar to our time. If we expect a magician god who produces the spectacular, or a tyrant god who forces men to do his will, then we shall certainly experience this disappointment. But the loving God of the Christian faith has acted and continues to act to the limits of love. That He does not choose some method other than love is not grounds for unbelief, but for rejoicing in His faithfulness.

Deep assurance of God's power comes when, with the apostle Paul, we experience liberation from the toils of sin or reluctant obedience into a life of free and loving fellowship. This results from taking seriously God's decisive action in Jesus Christ, and responding to His continued presence in our lives by His Spirit. Here is no God impotently 'wringing His hands' over the sins of the human race, but One who is strong to save those who trust Him.

ROMANS 8:9–13

'Your interests, however, are not in the unspiritual, but in the spiritual, since the Spirit of God has made His home in you' (v. 9, Jerusalem Bible).

SPIRIT OF CHRIST. Those zealous for doctrinal tidiness might wish that Paul had been here less free in his choice of words. 'God's Spirit', 'Spirit of Christ' and 'Christ within' are phrases which he uses interchangeably. This does not mean that the apostle identified Christ with the Holy Spirit in the strict sense, yet neither are we to think of him as merely careless in his description of the Christian life. The fact is that the Church has always needed the reminder that the Holy Spirit is the Spirit manifested in Jesus, and that 'experiences' of the Spirit must be tested by God's revelation in Christ. Without this there is always the risk that merely emotional or ecstatic experiences should be mistaken as evidence of the presence of the Holy Spirit.

A. N. Wilder once suggested that the first days of the Church were rather like the Falls of Niagara, in which the tremendous force of the water is obscured by its secondary manifestations of noise and foam and mists. The coming of the Holy Spirit at Pentecost, and His coming to believers in many later periods of history, was accompanied by many 'secondary manifestations'. These are not to be denied, or feared, or explained away, but neither are they to be confused with the primary work of the Holy Spirit which is to recreate in us the image of Christ.

ROMANS 8:14–17

'The Spirit Himself and our spirit bear united witness that we are children of God' (v. 16, Jerusalem Bible).

CHOSEN AND ADOPTED. In the first century A.D. an adopted son was in no whit inferior to a son born into the family. Indeed, chosen by his adoptive father to perpetuate his name and inherit his wealth, he might well be more highly regarded than a natural son. This should be kept in mind when we read Paul's assertion that we have received the spirit of adoption—which means, as Michael Keeling has observed, that 'God offers us the chance to be ourselves, to be sons, not slaves, and to be a son means to take the risk of being wrong, but in the confidence of God's ultimate love for us.'

It is only in and through Christ that the Christian enjoys the assurance of God's Fatherhood. Jean Paul Richter wrote a novel in which a character falls asleep on a hillside and has a terrible dream of a Christ who has lost His heavenly Father and who confesses that He has misled men into a false faith. 'We are orphans all,' says the dream-Christ, 'both I and ye. We have no Father.' This disillusioned Christ confesses that He has journeyed through the universe and found nothing but a dreadful emptiness, a dumb nothingness.

This terrible vision ends when the sleeper awakes to hear evening bells ringing and to find himself in a world which he believes rests in the hands of the God and Father of Jesus Christ. The stark contrast between the nightmare doubt and the awakening faith shows us the transforming effect of life in Christ. We know how mighty a thing it is that we can say 'Abba'.

ROMANS 8:18–27

'The created universe waits with eager expectation for God's sons to be revealed' (v. 19, N.E.B.).

ASTONISHING VISION. Michelangelo carved four sculptures for the tomb of Pope Julius. The figures look unfinished, said David Anderson, 'emerging from the rough stone as though they were tearing themselves out of it with tremendous effort and pain, drawing towards an assertion of triumph which yet includes within it the agony of the creative process'. In similar fashion Paul here portrays the whole universe travailing and agonizing for a consummation which will make sense of all that has gone before. And this fulfilment is the appearance of man; not man as we know him, divided against himself and his fellows, but man as God intends him to be.

The physical universe, then, is not merely the stage setting for the drama of man's redemption, after which it will dissolve. In the biblical view the universe will share in man's redemption. Obviously, this faith can be expressd only symbolically, not descriptively. Yet 'even now man, who by selfish exploitation can turn the good earth into a dust bowl, can by responsible trusteeship make the desert blossom like the rose, what then (asked F. F. Bruce) will be the effect of a completely redeemed mankind on the creation entrusted to his care?'

God's purpose in creation and redemption is vast beyond our conceiving, but even a glimpse of this purpose fills us with wonder and expectation.

ROMANS 8:28–39

'What can separate us from the love of Christ?' (v. 35, N.E.B.).

LYRICAL CONFIDENCE. Helmut Thielicke recalls a mother who was an unbeliever, long estranged from the Church. 'I met her again and again', he writes, 'at the bedside of her son, who was slowly dying in great pain, and I observed how she nursed him with quiet calmness, literally wrapping him in the cloak of her motherliness during his last agonies. She betrayed not a single sign of how much she herself was consumed by pain and anxiety.' When her attitude was admired by the German preacher-professor her reply was, 'Yes, attitude perhaps, but don't look underneath. I haven't a thing to hold on to.'

In this passage of lyrical confidence Paul asserts, not that he has something to hold on to, but that he is held unfailingly in the love of God. Two things can separate a man from God: sin and suffering. Concerning the first, the apostle asserts that the only one who could condemn us for our sins is Christ, and He in fact has become the Advocate for our defence. Concerning the second, Paul piles up all the awful and terrifying possibilities that can befall us. Some of them he has tasted at first hand, so he is no theorizing optimist. But he dares to assert that not one of them can take us out of that love which grasps us in Christ Jesus.

We can share Paul's confidence today, not only concerning the major trials that may befall us, but regarding the minor difficulties and irritations of daily life.

ROMANS 9:1–5

'For I could even pray to be outcast from Christ myself for the sake of my brothers, my natural kinsfolk' (v. 3, N.E.B.).

THE PROOF OF CHRISTIAN CARING. Chapters 9 to 11 wrestle with the question as to why God's chosen people should crucify God's Son. This was to Paul a source of indescribable anguish. Indeed, he confessed that he was even willing to be banished from the very presence of God if thereby his kinsmen would be saved. As we read these chapters, we may at times be mystified and possibly startled by some of the Apostle's arguments, but never shall we doubt the depth of his love for his own people. He longed that they should come to a knowledge of God's love in Christ, for he recognized that, despite all the privileges of their spiritual history, they were missing this one great essential. How sad that after all the long centuries of preparation for the advent of their Deliverer, the Jews should reject Him brutally!

Reflecting upon this heartbreaking development, the Apostle, far from being moved to criticize or condemn, felt only profound compassion for a people whose very religion had become a barrier against God. And his compassion was more than sentiment for sentiment is emotion without action, and Paul was anything but passive in giving expression to his compassion. He prayed for his people, pleaded with them, and sometimes rebuked them, but always because he cared so deeply.

The substance of one pertinent comment is that it was one of the ironies of history that so sincere a patriot should have been so implacably pursued by his fellow countrymen because of his vision of a world-wide commonwealth of God in which there would be neither Jew nor Gentile.

ROMANS 9:6–13

'Not all those who descend from Israel are Israel; not all the descendants of Abraham are his true children' (vv. 6 and 7, Jerusalem Bible).

WHAT IS GOD DOING? That the majority of Jews had rejected the Gospel did not mean that God's plan had miscarried or that God had broken His promise to Abraham. The history of Israel itself shows that not all the nation responded at any time to the call of God. The promises were not made to those who were Israelites by physical descent but those who are Israelites in their faith towards God.

It is along these lines that Paul first seeks to solve the problem of his nation's place in the plan of God. Elsewhere, he seemed to think of the obedient remnant as becoming progressively smaller until only in one Man, Jesus Christ, is the promise made to Abraham fulfilled (Gal 3:16). Then around that one Man the new people of God becomes established.

What has this to say to us who probably never give a thought to this particular problem? We can learn much from Paul's earnest searching for it indicates the scope of every true Christian's concern, which is never only the salvation of his own soul but what God is doing in the world. All movements which have had an impact upon the world of our time, such as Fascism and Communism, have offered a particular view of history. Christianity has its own daring and exciting philosophy of history, and the faith is diminished when it is reduced to nothing more than a message to individual people.

ROMANS 9:14–24

'Does it follow that God is unjust? Of course not' (v. 14, Jerusalem Bible).

MAN'S FREEDOM. One of the deepest convictions born of religious experience is the awareness that the good in us is there by God's grace. What then of the man who shows little evidence of this goodness in his life? Has he been passed over by the divine mercy? This, in essence, is the problem Paul is wrestling with in this passage.

In this dilemma, the apostle makes the assertion, 'When God wants to show mercy He does, and when He wants to harden someone's heart He does so.' This does not accord with the general tenor of his teaching, or with his evangelism. What led him to portray God acting in this arbitrary way?

The Hebrew mind frequently attributed directly to God events which we would ascribe to a subsidiary cause. Where we would say, 'God allows this,' they said, 'God wills this,' because of their insistence that there is only one supreme spiritual Being.

We would find the origin of evil in man's misuse of his freedom. It is not that God inspires some men to good and others to evil: rather is He present in every life seeking to elicit a response to His grace. But some choose to turn their back upon Him and then it is of His will that they remain free to pursue their own course. God is responsible for the gift of freedom which allows men to sin; He is never responsible for their sinning. As Chrysostom said: 'God having placed good and evil in our power, has given us full freedom of choice. He does not keep back the unwilling, but He embraces the willing.'

ROMANS 9:25–33

'Israel, following the Law of righteousness, failed to reach the goal of righteousness. And why? Because their minds were fixed on what they achieved instead of on what they believed' (vv. 31–32, Phillips).

A MARK OF HEALTHY RELIGION. We are back now to the two basic ways by which men seek a relationship with God. There is the way of law, represented by the Jewish religion, and the way of love, represented by Christianity. The former places the emphasis upon human achievement, upon the right to receive

His blessing; the latter upon receiving the love of God as an undeserved gift. One way is an attempt to place God under an obligation to bless, to warrant His support as a reward for personal worthiness. The other is a childlike acceptance of His unmerited love revealed in Christ. As Dr. Barclay comments: 'The Jew sought to put God in his debt; the Gentile was content to be in God's debt. The Jew believed he could win salvation by doing things for God; the Gentile was lost in amazement at what God had done for him.'

It follows from this that healthy religion is always marked by the believer's deepening wonderment at the unconditional, unending love of God. He does not wait for our repentance before loving us, any more than parental love for the prodigal son is regulated by his penitence or the absence of it. The incredible truth is that, 'just as we are', unashamedly rebellious or at best respectably second-rate, He loves us mightily; and this explains why He can neither let us go nor let us off, the theme of the final verse in this reading.

ROMANS 10:1–13

'If your lips confess that Jesus is Lord and if you believe in your heart that God raised Him from the dead, then you will be saved' (v. 9, Jerusalem Bible).

FUTILE QUEST. Paul's long and futile struggle to find salvation by obedience to the Law provides the background to this passage. There had been no lack of zeal in his religious life; simply a total misdirection of zeal. A. M. Hunter has observed that 'salvation is not a matter of achieving but of believing. We receive it—at Christ's hands; we do not earn it. No heroic attempts to storm the citadel of heaven or the kingdom of the dead are needed. Christ the Saviour is here, incarnate and risen, God's gift to every man with faith, be he Jew or Gentile'.

In Franz Kafka's novel *The Trial*, a competent bank official, Joseph K, is visited one morning at his lodgings and informed by the police that he is under arrest. The charge is not specified and the police depart without taking Joseph K with them. At first Joseph K decides to ignore this absurd charge but gradually he becomes obsessed with the need to vindicate his innocence. Yet when he begins to seek access to the Law through the judicial apparatus—courts, advocates, magistrates, judges—he is frustrated at every turn. The rest of the book concerns his agonized attempts to prove his innocence.

Kafka's parabolic novels are open to various interpretations. At one level *The Trial* illustrates the futility of the search for self-justification. It shows how essentially selfish such a request always is. Joseph K becomes increasingly thoughtless of other people as his obsessive need for self-justification grips him more firmly. This vicious circle can be broken only by grace, by freely offered forgiveness. This is what Paul discovered in Christ and it remains the heart of the Christian experience of God.

ROMANS 10:14–21

'Faith is awakened by the message, and the message that awakens it comes through the word of Christ' (v. 17, N.E.B.).

BY WORD AND DEED. Nothing but crass disobedience was responsible for Israel's rejection of the Gospel. This is Paul's assertion in this passage as he continues to wrestle with the problem of Israel's place in the purpose of God. For salvation to come to any one, what is needed is a preacher, sent by God, and also a message for him to proclaim. These conditions were fulfilled in Israel's case but the response was lacking.

The point in Paul's argument most worth our consideration is his claim that 'faith comes from what is preached' (v. 17, Jerusalem Bible). The Continental theologian, Gerhard Ebeling, is both an untiring champion and a sharp critic of preaching. Proclamation is for him 'the alpha and omega' of the Church's work. This is because Jesus, who in His life and death witnessed to what it is to have faith in God, has become, through His resurrection, the basis upon which we too may live in faith. Proclamation is much more, however, than a recounting of past events. It is always a relating of these events to the concrete circumstances in which man lives today. This requires imagination, skill and mental toil.

Does this mean that the man who never stands in a pulpit or on a platform is excused his part in this vital role of the Church? By no means. Proclamation is always by word and deed. Christians must therefore be engaged in demonstrating their faith, as well as in speaking about it. Indeed, there are occasions when the latter is not timely, but the former is our constant duty.

ROMANS 11:1–10

'Israel did not, on the whole, obtain the object of His [God's] striving, but a chosen few "got there", while the remainder became more and more insensitive to the righteousness of God' (v. 7, Phillips).

HARDENING OF SPIRITUAL ARTERIES. Paul, himself a Jew with a passionate love for his people, rejects the idea with horror that God has repudiated the whole Jewish nation. He points to an incident in Elijah's life to illustrate that, though the majority choose to turn from the truth, there remains a faithful remnant, individuals who walk humbly in the light. To explain the backsliding or empty religiosity of the rest, the Apostle says that they are in a spiritual stupor; their easy morals and self-satisfaction have made them insensitive of heart.

This dangerous condition of soul is helpfully illustrated in Donald Soper's definition of the opposite condition—sensitivity or tenderness. 'Before I travelled to America', he wrote, 'I was compelled to be inoculated and vaccinated, and penetrated in one way and another, and for some time I had an arm rather like a balloon. During the time when it was like a balloon, of the eight million people living in London, about seven million seemed to bump into it. I am an expert on what tenderness is. Tenderness is the capacity to be hurt.'

The degree to which we have this capacity is the extent of our spiritual vitality. Their name is legion whose souls have been corroded, not by one major failure, but by countless minor compromises; the result has been an imperceptible hardening of the spiritual arteries. The answer is to 'haunt Calvary' and then to act compassionately. For compassion (the capacity to be hurt) grows only as it is exercised.

ROMANS 11:11–16

'I am a missionary to the Gentiles, and as such I give all honour to that ministry when I try to stir emulation in the men of my own race, and so to save some of them' (vv. 13–14, N.E.B.).

CHRISTIAN LIVING AT HOME. The refusal of the Jews to accept the gospel of Christ was a terrible tragedy, but God turned it to good account. For He used it to open the door of salvation to the Gentiles. Indeed, the very fact of the Gentiles receiving the gospel was an added incentive for the Jews to do likewise. They would see the fruits of Christianity in the lives of the Gentiles and be moved—perhaps even by envy—to belief in Christ.

Paul was full of hope for the conversion of at least some of his fellow countrymen. This is the meaning of verse 16, which is a free quotation from Numbers 15:19–20—'If the dough offered as first fruits is holy, so is the whole lump; and if the root is holy, so are the branches' (R.S.V.). The Apostle meant—and we might find his reasoning strange—that just as the consecration of a part of something, a part symbolizing the whole, indicated that the whole was sacred, so the remnant of Israel, the faithful few, guaranteed that the whole nation was kept in a special sacred relationship with God.

It cannot be gainsaid that just as the remnant's knowledge of God was made possible by the faithfulness of parents, teachers, and the nation's spiritual leaders throughout the centuries (patriarchs and prophets), so we, having been made what we are largely by our Christian heritage, can never wholly escape the influence of our background and upbringing. In this sense, a father's dedication incorporates his son's, not by replacing it or making it unnecessary, but by putting the son more directly in the way of salvation. This in itself points to the crucial importance of Christian living at home and to the unconscious influence of parental or adult example.

ROMANS: 11:17–24

The Jews 'lost their position because they failed to believe; you only maintain yours because you do believe. The situation does not call for conceit but for a certain wholesome fear' (v. 20, Phillips).

CHRISTIAN DISCIPLESHIP IS NINETY-FIVE PER CENT OBEDIENCE. Thinking of the nation of Israel as the olive tree of God, Paul visualizes the Gentiles as wild olive branches being engrafted into the tree that is Israel, a tree stripped of some of its natural branches through the disobedience of God's chosen people. With such a picture, vivid and simple, the Apostle underlined that the Gentiles, once in a spiritual wilderness, were now able to nourish their souls from the same fertile roots that the Jews, in being trained as a missionary nation to the world, had known in part for centuries. In liberating the Jews from the bondage of the Law, and opening up the way for the Gentiles to enjoy a love relationship with God, Christ had revealed the eternal truth that all men, whatever their background or colour, were equally welcome in the family of God.

Paul also uses the illustration of the olive tree to give both a warning to the Gentiles and a word of encouragement to the Jews. He tells the Gentiles to guard against pride, against feeling superior and even secretly gratified that while they are being engrafted on, the Jews are being lopped off. The periodic emergence of anti-Semitism gives this warning a contemporary relevance. And it reminds us, too, that unless privilege deepens humility, it fosters pride and intolerance. The word of encouragement for the Jews, as for all backsliders and nominal believers, is that there is an open way back to God. He has not cut 'them off'; they have 'cut themselves off' by their disobedience. And this makes the one condition for their return unmistakably obvious. Indeed, Christian discipleship, based upon faith, is still ninety-five per cent obedience.

ROMANS 11:25–32

'God has abandoned all men to their rebellion, only to include them all in His pardon' (v. 32, Knox).

THE VOICE OF GOD IN ADVERSITY. Having argued, as we have seen repeatedly during this study, that God hardened the hearts of the Jews to open the door of salvation to the Gentiles, Paul insists that this hardening, this insensitivity to spiritual truth, was only partial and therefore not necessarily permanent. He was expressing the hope that, though Israel was for the moment the enemy of God, divine mercy would triumph in the end, winning the Jews back to their true soul allegiance.

This theme of God's mercy—His undeserved love and grace for sinful man—was central to the Apostle's faith. He even went so far as to say that God made 'all mankind prisoners to disobedience' that He might have mercy upon them all. In making this, to us, astounding statement, Paul was simply trying to emphasize beyond the possibility of misunderstanding that man's saving relationship with God was something he could never earn, merit, or demand by right. If the Jews had consistently obeyed, the Apostle seems to be saying, they might have argued that they had earned their salvation, that it was due to them. So God involved them in disobedience to make His mercy unmistakably clear.

We probably find this interpretation difficult, if only because, unlike the biblical Jew, we do not think solely in terms of primary causes; we think also of intervening cause and effect, the result of human freewill. But the essential truth remains—everything that happens in human affairs is evidence of the relentless love of God tracking down the sinner. Which means that in every experience, no matter how harsh, we are wise to ask, 'What is God trying to say to me in this situation?'

ROMANS 11:33–36

'What a fathomless wealth lies in the wisdom and knowledge of God! How inscrutable His judgments! How mysterious His methods!' (v. 33, Moffat).

UNREASONABLE FAITH. In these tender verses Paul's theology is translated into the murmurings of love. It seems as though, having stretched his mind to its capacity in wrestling with the paradox of God's sovereignty and human freewill, and with the place of his own disobedient people in the purposes of God, the Apostle's heart takes over. Not that his feeling replaces his thinking. Rather it is that Paul's faith in God transcends, as distinct from contradicts, his understanding of God's ways.

The Apostle is not making the language of devotion a substitute for the duty of thought. He is simply trusting God beyond, but consistent with, the point of his mind's understanding; and this is faith. Perplexity at the harsh mysteries of life undermines faith most easily when the believer, contrary to what Jesus taught, loves God with all his heart at the expense of loving God with all his mind. He needs to learn that faith and reason are not contradictory, that to have faith in something unreasonable is dangerously at variance with the mind of Christ. But when, in childlike trust, the heart takes a step beyond the point reached by the mind's strenuous probings, it discovers a foundation of rock, so that, though still denied understanding, it humbly testifies: 'I know Whom I have believed.'

ROMANS 12:1–8

'With eyes wide open to the mercies of God, I beg you, my brothers, as an act of intelligent worship, to give Him your bodies, as a living sacrifice, consecrated to Him, and acceptable by Him' (v. 1, Phillips).

WE ARE WHAT WE THINK. As is characteristic of Paul's writings, after the theology comes its ethical and moral implications. The Apostle obviously realized that it is easier to talk about God for five hours than to obey Him for five minutes. Hence this final section. It opens with the plea that the Christian should consecrate his body to God. Why? Because his body is obviously involved in everything he does. Let a man truly consecrate his body and he thereby, for instance, makes an offering to God of his daily work, his craftsmanship and industry. By writing of consecration in such terms, Paul related it to the ordinary affairs of daily life.

But he went a step further. He knew that the body was governed by the mind, that what a man did reflected only what he thought. So he advised, to quote Phillips' translation of verse 2: 'Don't let the world around you squeeze you into its own mould, but let God remould your minds from within.' We have often noticed that what we take into our minds we take into our lives. This being so, it follows that we best consecrate our bodies by guarding our thoughts—deliberately taking into our minds only those things which are consistent with the values of Christ.

ROMANS: 12:9–13

'Love in all sincerity, loathing evil and clinging to the good' (v. 9, N.E.B.).

KEEPING ZEAL AT BOILING POINT. As mentioned above we saw that we best consecrate our bodies by guarding our minds. But how do we guard our minds? Part of the answer is given in the verse at the head of this comment, a verse rendered by Phillips: 'Let us have no imitation Christian love. Let us have a genuine break with evil and a real devotion to good.' As Seeley has said that 'no heart is safe which is not passionate', and a passionate heart always loves good and hates evil. Christian love, which is goodwill on fire, proves its sincerity by drastically breaking with evil, both the evil itself and the cirumstances that give the seductions of evil their best opportunity. Little use praying for deliverance without fleeing from the place of temptation and burning behind us the bridges across which evil suggestion makes its appeal! Yet some of us do and then wonder why victorious living remains only a tantalizing dream!

As though with this possibility in mind, Paul further advised: 'Do not be sluggish in zeal. Keep your spirit at boiling point.' And if we again ask the natural question, 'How?', the Apostle's answer as given in today's verses is clear-cut: foster your love of the good and your hatred of the bad by enthusiastically treating every person and meeting every task in the Spirit of Christ; prayer will enable you to appropriate the necessary power. To live like this, not waiting to feel zealous or adequate, is, as William Carey said, to 'attempt great things for God' and to 'expect great things from God'.

ROMANS 12:14–21

'Don't allow yourself to be overpowered by evil. Take the offensive—overpower evil with good!' (v. 21, Phillips).

MORAL FRUITS AND SPIRITUAL ROOTS. Continuing his counsel, which, as we have seen, was the practical implications of his theology, Paul said that Christians should answer hatred with goodwill; congratulate the successful and sympathize with the sorrowful; maintain harmonious personal relationships, not least by refusing to stand in judgment, the very opposite of touchy self-defence; think of themselves humbly, without grovelling or straining not to be proud, and associate with unwanted, lonely people; guard their personal integrity; live in a spirit of reconciliation; and treat their enemies as friends, without patronage. Such a catalogue is enough to discourage the most ardent spirit. Then how best can we realize Paul's idealism, avoiding the equal dangers of trying too hard or accepting defeat before we even start?

The answer lies in the recognition that, paradoxically enough, we do not achieve Christian sanctity by seeking it directly. To seek directly to be humble, for instance, is to be secretly proud or snobbish. Christian virtue is always unselfconscious. It is an effect never a cause. In other words, far from being manufactured by human effort, it flows spontaneously out of something else, and that something else is maturing fellowship with God, the daily exploration of the mind of Christ. To think otherwise is to imagine, in keeping with arrogant human nature, that moral fruits can exist without spiritual roots. The fact is, however, that the realization of Paul's idealism is the by-product of a life centred in God and nourished by the Holy Spirit.

ROMANS 13:1–7

'There is no authority but by act of God, and the existing authorities are instituted by Him' (v. 1, N.E.B.).

THE CHRISTIAN AND SECULAR AUTHORITY. These verses make strange reading when we recall that Paul himself was to meet his death in the Neronian persecution, which was but the first of many. We need to remember that, up to this time, Paul had every reason to be grateful for Roman rule, which had facilitated the preaching of the gospel. When his own people would have killed him, Roman authority preserved his life. Shortly after writing this letter the Apostle was to make his famous appeal to Caesar—the right of every Roman citizen—feeling confident that in imperial Rome he would receive a fair hearing and a just verdict.

These verses should be read as a repudiation of the Zealot movement in Judaism which, at this time, was gathering strength for its final outbreak against Roman authority. Perhaps Jewish Christians were bringing into the Church their anti-Roman feelings, and Paul was anxious that the Roman Christians should not provoke and alienate the 'powers that be'.

Paul here enunciates a principle that cannot be applied to every situation, for there have been times when resistance to secular authority—indeed, sometimes religious authority as well—was a Christian obligation. If the state usurps God's place, obedience is betrayal. A. M. Hunter has pertinently said that 'while a Christian doctrine of the State may well start from Romans 13, it cannot stop there'.

ROMANS 13:8–10

'Keep out of debt altogether, except that perpetual debt of love which we owe one another' (v. 8, Phillips).

FULFILLING THE MORAL LAW. In the final verse of the above reading, Paul emphasized that no Christian should be guilty of tax evasion. He should pay all his dues, a standard prohibiting the exploitation of legal loopholes no less than the manipulation of expense accounts. But he should also avoid all private debts, that is, the owing of money for which repayment is uncertain, if not impossible without anxiety.

The Christian's only inescapable debt should be one of love; and if this characterizes his every personal relationship, everything else will fall naturally into its rightful place. Love, as Paul goes on to infer, makes impossible the use of another person for self-gratification, the removal of an enemy by killing, the stealing of someone else's possessions (money, wife, reputation) and the covetousness of self-love (another name for lust). Christian love is the fulfilment of the moral law, the fulfilment of its letter and its spirit. The common problem is to keep this love alive, for without it even moral living becomes pompously self-conscious and harshly vindictive. The Christian's only safeguard against such usually unrealized spiritual sickness is to concentrate upon his own unpayable indebtedness to the love of God, an indebtedness best perceived and nurtured at the foot of the Cross.

ROMANS 13:11–14

'Let us be Christ's men from head to foot, and give no chances to the flesh to have its fling' (v. 14, Phillips).

INESCAPABLE ROUTINE. Paul's motto could well have been: 'Do it now; tomorrow is too late.' He obviously realized the urgency of time and the insidious nature of procrastination—putting things off for a more convenient moment. Few lives are wholly unaffected by this deadly self-indulgence, the main reason for negative respectability.

The Apostle's aim was to live each day as though it were his last. But he avoided the pitfalls of indecent haste and frantic anxiety by seeing his temporal responsibilities in the light of eternal truth. This enabled him to look upon time as a gift from God, without mistaking feverish activity for progress or good intentions for sustained application; and the way to this end, he said, was to 'wake up to reality'—to bring every aspect of life to the touchstone of Christ's judgment.

Paul had particularly in mind the second coming of Christ, but his words are true for all the big issues of life and death. We best prepare for them by accepting each day, with its inescapable sameness, as a sacred trust, as an opportunity to prove our love for God. For it could be easier to die for Christ than to live for Him, especially when unsought circumstances restrict our personal usefulness and offer little in the ways of variation. It is then that we need, as Paul said, to be Christ's men and women from 'head to foot'.

ROMANS 14:1–12

'It is not for you to condemn someone else's servant: whether he stands or falls it is his own master's business' (v. 4, Jerusalem Bible).

CHRISTIAN LIBERTY AND TOLERANCE. When interviewed on television by John Freeman, Lord Russell was asked what he had learned about life that he would like to pass on to a future generation. He spoke about the search for truth and the need for tolerance. 'In this world, which is getting more and more closely interconnected, we have to learn to tolerate each other . . . If we are to live together and not die together we must learn a kind of charity and a kind of tolerance which is absolutely vital to the continuance of human life on this planet.'

Tolerance between people who think differently is immensely hard to achieve. Perhaps even more difficult is the kind of tolerance Paul wrote about the above passage—tolerance between people who in the main think alike. Some Christians observed special days and others had serious scruples about eating meat, perhaps because it was difficult to know whether it had been previously offered to some pagan deity. Other Christians did not feel bound by these rules.

Similar differences of Christian practice make heavy demands on our tolerance because they sometimes appear to call in question our own discipleship. The man who is more strict in his renunciations makes us feel less devoted: the one who is less strict causes us to wonder whether our own self-denial is little more than a fad. To know what Christ demands of us without seeking to impose our own discipline upon others: this is the one truly Christian way.

ROMANS 14:13–23

'So let us concentrate on the things which make for harmony, and on the growth of one another's character' (v. 19, Phillips).

TWO CONSIDERATIONS. Observing special days and refraining from eating meat obviously had little appeal for Paul. Christians with these kinds of scruples are referred to as 'weak' in faith. Yet the matter does not end there. Before asserting our own freedom, says the apostle, we must be sure of two things.

Our conscience as well as our logic needs to be liberated before we can set aside rules of conduct which were once valid for us. Otherwise we incur a sense of guilt which can greatly disturb our inner life. There is great insight in the apocryphal incident which tells how Jesus, 'seeing a man working on the sabbath, said to him, "Man, if indeed thou knowest what thou art doing, blessed art thou; but if thou knowest not, accursed art thou and a transgressor of the law"'. This does not mean we must be enslaved by ancient prejudices: it does mean that serious thought and consideration must accompany our assertion of freedom.

We must not selfishly disregard the influence our actions may have on others. To be concerned only about our own salvation is what Berdyaev called 'transcendent egoism'. 'One can be saved only with one's neighbour, with other men, with the world. Each one must take upon himself the sorrow and suffering of the world and of men, and share in their destiny.'

ROMANS 15:1–7

'In a word, accept one another as Christ accepted us, to the glory of God' (v. 7, N.E.B.).

LOVING ACCEPTANCE. Paul rounds off his examination of Christian liberty and Christian tolerance with an appeal to the example of Christ, the free Man who voluntarily bound Himself for others. Then he seems to summarize all he has said concerning Christian morality in one brief exhortation, calling believers to offer each other the acceptance they have found in Christ.

This is not an attitude which should be restricted to those in the Christian community. The most Christlike men and women have shown an astonishing, and sometimes shocking, acceptance of even the worst sinners. The truly holy have this ability. Only the self-righteous are censorious and condemning. Equally remarkable, the loving acceptance of the saints is not to be mistaken by sinners as condoning their sin. Rather it lifts them to new aspirations.

When Charles de Foucauld visited wounded legionnaires in North Africa he was warned that the visit of a priest would be nothing more than an excuse for foolish antics. When he entered the ward he was first ignored, then treated to one of the most ribald songs of the Legion. 'Thank you, my friends, for this musical welcome,' the priest said, 'though I'm afraid you must have mistaken me for your general.' Irreverent cartoons of devils, monks and angels had been drawn on the walls. Foucauld examined each one and made a few improvements. Lastly, he went from bed to bed showing keen personal interest in each man, yet never mentioning religion. Next Sunday, every man who could be in church was there.

ROMANS 15:8–13

'May the God of hope bring you such joy and peace in your faith that the power of the Holy Spirit will remove all bounds to hope' (v. 13, Jerusalem Bible).

GAY AND INDOMITABLE. Reading this letter, no one can charge Paul with superficial optimism about the human condition. The stark exposure of man's sin in the early chapters is uncompromising in its realism. Yet, because of what God has done in Christ, the apostle can describe the Christian life as marked by a boundless hope. No wonder this letter has proved such a beacon to lost souls.

Hope has been called the modern Cinderella in Paul's triad of Christian graces. Yet, together with faith and love, it is indispensable to Christian living. How else can we hold to the assurance of our faith amid all the ambiguities and contradictions of our existence? Only because we lay hold, albeit by parables and symbols, upon what God has in store for His creation.

Probably oppressed by the stifling piety of his own time, the English poet Swinburne wrote the well-known lines:

> Thou hast conquered, O pale Galilean;
> The world has grown grey from Thy breath.

But if Swinburne had studied the history of the Early Church, claims J. B. Phillips, he would have reached different conclusions. 'The surrounding world was indeed grey, sometimes black with corruption and all kinds of evil, but in the young Church there was gay and indomitable hope. Nothing could quench this hope ... While the pagan world had largely become sodden with self-indulgence and ridden by the fear of death, the brave, new fellowship of believers in Christ was a light and a flame in the darkness: it was a fellowship of hope.'

ROMANS 15:14–21

'My constant ambition has been to preach the gospel where the name of Christ was previously unknown' (v. 20, Phillips).

OUR PRIVILEGE TOO. 'All truly great apostles and evangelists look on everyone as potential Christians.' So claims Douglas Webster in his book *Unchanging Mission.* He also suggests that it is unfortunate, and in some respects unfair, to apply to those who are not yet in Christ, but who belong to the race for which He died, the negative prefix non-Christian. 'All humanity', he writes, 'is in some sense the latent church. To speak of those outside Christ as the not-church is to forget the scale of His triumph. Surely it is better to speak of them and the areas in which they live as the not-yet-church. This provides a more Christian perspective.'

Surely this is a view that Paul, courageous pioneer and restless evangelist, would have endorsed. Looking back over his missionary work, he could claim that he had made it an 'unbroken rule' (Jerusalem Bible) never to preach where Christ's name had already been heard.

Even if we possessed the apostle's daring and adventurous spirit, we may feel we are denied his privilege. Certainly most of our contemporaries have heard the name of Christ. Yet is not the distorted view of the Christian faith which so many of them hold worse than ignorance? By life and word we can make sure that those around clearly understand what it is to follow Christ. They may call themselves non-Christians, but they are among those for whom Christ died. Perhaps we should think of them as 'not-yet-Christians'.

ROMANS 15:22–33

'Now, my brothers, I am going to ask you . . . to stand behind me in earnest prayer to God on my behalf—that I may not fall into the hands of the unbelievers in Judaea' (v. 31, Phillips).

FACING DANGER. In the light of later events, Paul's sharing of his far-reaching plans with his readers takes on a note of tragic irony. He is setting out for Jerusalem with a collection for the poor Christians there: then he hopes to visit Rome on his way to more remote fields of missionary endeavour. In fact, he will arrive there as a prisoner who has appealed to Caesar for judgment. His request for his readers' prayers shows that he was aware of the dangers ahead. Just as his Master had craved the sympathy and companionship of His friends as He faced the Cross, so the apostle longs for the support of fellow believers as he approaches the crisis ahead.

Paul not only fell 'into the hands of unbelievers in Judaea': he encountered considerable misgivings and suspicion among Jewish Christians. Are we then to say that the prayers he requested were not answered? Perhaps we may be helped by the useful distinction once made by Leslie Weatherhead. 'Prayers may not be answered, but pray-ers, persons who pray, will always be answered . . . There are unanswered prayers, but no unanswered pray-ers.'

Paul would have been quick to point out that his prayer request was not primarily for his own safety, but for the furthering of God's work. In the event, this was probably accomplished as much by his captivity as it would have been by his freedom.

ROMANS: 16:1–5

'Give my greetings to Priscilla and Aquila, my fellow-workers in Christ. . . . Greet also the congregation at their house' (vv. 4–5, N.E.B.).

CHRISTIAN HOSPITALITY. Having urged the Christians at Rome to welcome and help Phoebe, a visitor from the port of Corinth, and one worthy of Paul's personal commendation, the Apostle sent his greetings to Priscilla and Aquila. These two, husband and wife, initially lived in Rome, but were banished from the city in a wave of anti-semitism (Acts 18:2). They then settled at Corinth, where they made a home for Paul. When he moved to Ephesus they went with him and settled there, eventually also providing hospitality for Apollos (Acts 18:26) and turning their home into a centre of Christian activity (1 Corinthians 16:19). The reference to them in this reading clearly indicates that they had returned to Rome, following the cancellation of the edict against the Jews, and characteristically made their home the Lord's house, a place where Christians met for worship and fellowship.

Wherever Priscilla and Aquila lived there was a practical expression of Christian caring. Their home was a haven, an open house to people in need. The same spirit inspired a retired social officer, Emily Berwick, who lived in London's East End during the Second World War, to place in the window of her home a notice which read: 'If you need help, knock here'. It is true that home must be the place to which, like everyone else, Christians can withdraw for guarded quietness and relaxation, but it should also be a centre of compassion, a place of sensitive hospitality where individuals otherwise unwanted and lonely find rest to their souls.

ROMANS 16:6–11

'Salute Andronicus and Junias, fellow-countrymen and fellow-prisoners of mine; they are men of note among the apostles, and they have been in Christ longer than I have' (v. 7, Moffatt).

OBSCURE FAITHFULNESS AND SPECTACULAR SUCCESS. Of the twenty-four people named in this chapter, six of them were women, an interesting commentary on the suggestion that Paul was anti-feminist. But perhaps more significant for us is the fact that, apart from this chapter, these people, men and women warmly commended by the Apostle himself, are virtually unknown. Their exploits for Christ are unrecorded, their heroic faithfulness is largely unsung.

This reminds us that the vast majority of Christians are called to serve, not on the centre of the stage, but in the wings or as members of the supporting cast. The trouble is that sometimes they seek the spotlight themselves, preferring the role of a Paul to that of one of his unheralded assistants.

There are certainly few more searching tests of character or Christian loyalty than to serve without recognition or appreciation, to contribute unnoticed to the progress of another, to sacrifice behind the scenes to the public success of a more gifted personality. Yet throughout the centuries multitudes of humble believers have done this, not only ungrudgingly, but with eager abandon, finding their complete satisfaction in contributing to the advance of God's cause. In the service of Christ obscure faithfulness is at least as vital as spectacular success. Indeed, to the eye of faith the two are indistinguishable.

ROMANS 16:12–16

'Salute that choice Christian, Rufus; also his mother, who has been a mother to me' (v. 13, Moffatt).

BIGNESS OF SOUL IN LITTLE TASKS. Paul's list of virtually unsung heroes of the faith continues, teasing the mind into all manner of romantic speculation. Was Rufus, for instance, the son of Simon of Cyrene, the man who was compelled to carry the cross for Jesus? For Simon, Mark's gospel tells us, was the father of Alexander and Rufus; and it seems reasonable to conclude that such information would not have been given unless the two brothers had been already well known within the Church when the gospel was written. However, we shall never know for sure, but there is something noteworthy about which we can be certain.

These humble believers at Rome earned Paul's commendation for their simple goodness. He mentioned specifically only such things as their hard work and the motherly interest shown by one of them to a comparative stranger. The Methodist Russell Maltby wrote of an imaginary preacher who spoke of great things and made them small, but the very opposite was the case with these obscure saints. They dignified and enhanced the ordinary with their quiet industry and strong compassion. Some people are only at their best, or try their best, on the big occasion, when they have an audience; but the man truly committed to Christ makes something big of every situation, certainly of the ordinary and even of the unpromising, not, however, by giving undue significance to the trivial, a favourite dodge of little-mindedness, but by bringing bigness of soul and mind to every task.

ROMANS 16:17–20

'It will not be long before the God of peace will crush Satan under your feet' (v. 20, Phillips).

GOD'S PEACE ON THE WARPATH. Paul warns the Christians at Rome to guard against those of their number who cause disunity and make it more difficult for the unconverted to find the truth. He knew that there were such people, individuals whose ostentatious piety was a cover for their scheming ambition. Their basic aim was personal notoriety, an end they served with a silvery tongue that played on the innocence or the vanity of unsuspecting believers. Having given the warning, the Apostle expressed his confidence that this strategy of Satan was finally powerless against the transparent sincerity of the truly committed. He knew that nothing was stronger than simple goodness. Hence his conviction that the peace of God would defeat the forces of evil, a truth sometimes forgotten or doubted by modern believers.

God's peace, however, does not mean the absence of conflict. It bears no resemblance to the tranquility that maintains itself by evasion—refusing to face explosive situations or make unpopular decisions. The peace of God takes the offensive against devilish intimidations and overcomes them. It fights, and fights unyieldingly, but only with weapons consistent with its own nature. For the battles of God's peace can never be won with the weapons of Satan.

Forgetting this, Christians have sometimes mistaken violence for victory, and evangelical techniques for spiritual power. The fact is that the warfare of God's peace is inspired only by love and sustained essentially by prayer, which means that in all our fighting for righteousness (with its sometimes hard hitting and possible giving of offence) these two factors should be clearly uppermost.

ROMANS 16:21–27

'Now to Him who is able to set you on your feet as His own sons . . . to Him, I say, the only God who is wise, be glory for ever through Jesus Christ, amen!' (vv. 25–27, Phillips).

HOW BURDENS BECOME BLESSINGS. 'One of the most interesting things in this whole chapter', wrote William Barclay, 'is the way in which again and again Paul characterizes people in one single sentence.' Sometimes, in fact, he has not room for a sentence and uses just two or three words. So Timothy is a fellow worker, Gaius is open-hearted and open-handed, and Quartus is a brother in the faith.

One-sentence tributes can be most rewarding. It was said, for instance, of Will Rogers that 'He never made anyone unhappy till he went away'; and of James Carmichael that 'He lit many fires in cold rooms'. Over the grave of a Chinese Christian were placed the words: 'He believed and he behaved the Bible.' Of Alexander Woollcott it was said that he 'was of such dimensions that he made New York into a small town'. One day someone will sum us up in one sentence. What will it be?

Paul unconsciously sums himself up by finishing his great epistle with a doxology. For people usually reveal themselves in the things for which they are truly thankful. The Apostle praised God for the gospel, with its promise to make the believer equal to every trial of strength, and for his (Paul's) privilege in being permitted to declare it. When a man is genuinely grateful for the opportunity simply to serve, a gratitude that turns burdens into blessings, and sacrifice into songs of thanksgiving, then, like the Apostle, he is centred in Christ and therefore free to live.

THE FIRST AND SECOND EPISTLES TO THE CORINTHIANS

INTRODUCTION

Because the contents of these two Epistles are so interwoven, any introductory notes had better consider them together.

It has to be remembered that the Apostle Paul's correspondence was probably not gathered together until about a quarter of a century after the traditional date of his martyrdom, and plainly more than two letters passed between him and believers in Corinth.

First of all, there was the letter mentioned in I Cor. 5:9, part of which may have been preserved in 2 Cor. 6:14–7:1.

Reports of internal dissension in the church had also reached Paul by word of mouth (I Cor. 1:11), and he sent Timothy on a mission of reconciliation (I Cor. 4:17). Meanwhile, the Corinthians themselves had asked Paul for guidance on specific points of doctrine and discipline (I Cor. 7:1) and this he gave at length.

Still uneasy about the welfare of the church, however, he seems to have paid them a flying visit. (If 2 Cor. 12:14 and 13:1 speak of a possible third visit, there must have been a second.) However, this seemingly accomplished little good, whereupon the Apostle wrote again in such stern terms that later he almost regretted having done so (2 Cor. 7:8). Scholars think that this letter may have been 2 Cor. chs. 10–13. But his anxieties were allayed by better news from Titus (2 Cor. 7:6), and a further letter followed judged to be 2 Cor. chs. 1–9. This concluded on a happier note, and conveyed his thanks to believers in Corinth for their generous support of the fund he was raising for the needy in the mother church in Jerusalem.

1 CORINTHIANS 1:1–9

'I am always thankful to God for what the gift of His grace in Jesus Christ has meant to you' (v. 4, Phillips).

HOW TO APPROACH DIFFICULT SITUATIONS. Paul commenced this letter to the Corinthian Christians knowing his task would be anything but easy. The situation in the church called for strong rebuke. The apostle's approach is most instructive for, in different situations, we also have problems of human relationships to meet.

Paul began by recognizing the genuine achievements of those he would have to rebuke. 'You possess full knowledge', he wrote, 'and you can give full expression to it' (v. 5, N.E.B.). Praise preceded rebuke. This is all the more noteworthy because the Corinthians suffered from an inflated sense of their own importance. Faced with such people we are tempted to try and 'take them down a peg'. Paul showed his appreciation of the Corinthians' many gifts, at the same time making it clear that God was the source of their enrichment. His praise aimed at awakening them to a sense of indebtedness, not at feeding their pride.

Every human problem must be approached in the spirit of love if we are to contribute to its solution. Paul's appreciation was not only tactful. His love for the Corinthians and his appreciation of their finer qualities was genuine. Love would solve many of our problems and eliminate the friction from many difficult relationships. Yet we must love for love's sake even when apparently it yields no rewards. Writing about the work of the West London Mission for delinquent girls Donald Soper affirmed: 'I have learnt by looking at Jesus crucified to be content to practise that love and not to demand visible and immediate proof that it works, and I am beginning to find that such love is its own reward.'

1 CORINTHIANS 1:10–17

'For the sake of our Lord Jesus Christ I beg of you all to drop these party-cries' (v. 10, Moffatt).

UNITED IN CHRIST. Without doubt the most dangerous problem in the church at Corinth was the existence of rival factions. These were a denial of the Spirit of Christ who is the

Spirit of love and peace. There will always be differences of opinion among people, of course, and it is no part of Christianity to abrogate a man's intelligence or to inhibit him from expressing his views. Christ wants people to be true to themselves. Within the context of the Christian Church there is scope for the exercising of the God-given freedom which is the essence of human personality and dignity.

Yet this must not, need not, lead to unloving divisions and cliques as it had obviously done at Corinth. The Apostle did not take sides in the disputes, however, but called the Corinthians to affirm their common loyalty to Christ in which harmful disunity could not exist. If they were for Christ, they could not be against each other. There are varied opinions and methods of procedure among Christian churches today, yet real ecumenism is possible when it is seen that the matters which divide are not together as important as the great fact which unites—a common allegiance to Christ. Nothing else really counts.

Said William Temple, 'The fundamental anomaly is that any two disciples of our Lord should not be in communion with each other'. How do we regard those Christians who do not worship in our particular way?

1 CORINTHIANS 1:18–25

'Our message is Christ the crucified' (v. 23, Moffatt).

THE REBUKE OF PRIDE. Partisanship of the kind which divided the Corinthian church is really a disguised form of self-assertion. This is why Paul moved swiftly from a rebuke of the Corinthian factions to expound the Cross of Jesus. The amazing humility of God is the best solvent of human arrogance. Wrote Bonhoeffer: 'We want a prouder God than He who became our brother in the cradle and on the Cross. But God veils Himself for our sake in sin and death so that faith alone should see what remains incomprehensible to the whole world.'

The divine humility is folly when we judge by worldly standards. In the palace of Septimus Severus at Rome a caricature has been found showing a man worshipping one on a cross—the crucified has the head of an ass. Under the drawing are the words, 'Alexamenos worships his God.' This picture, probably drawn by a pagan slave making fun of one of his fellows who was a Christian, shows how true was Paul's assertion that the Cross is 'folly to Greeks'.

The divine humility reverses all our standards when we make the Cross of Jesus central in our lives. Wrote A. E. Whitham, 'We all know of the rich man who can afford to wear an old coat and potter about with a tool box, whom you may easily mistake for the gardener. But if you do mistake him, he will soon let you know he has better coats indoors, and plenty of them. . . . But when Christ came, He was not merely like a carpenter, He was one. He only had an old coat in the whole of His wardrobe. He was not mistaken for a servant: He was one—a suffering servant.' Can we retain our conceit before such humility? As Gaston Deluz commented: 'At Corinth each sect wanted to prove itself right and the others wrong. But the Cross puts all of us in the wrong.'

1 CORINTHIANS 1:26–31

'God has chosen the things the world counts foolish to shame the wise' (v. 27, Barclay).

REBUKE TO OUR PRIDE. The majority of the Christians of Corinth were people of modest circumstances, and doubtless considered by many outside the church to be of little consequence. Yet they were the very people God had chosen, Paul asserted, so that it should be seen that what men might count worthless has value with God, and that it should be understood among the Christians themselves that they had nothing of which they could boast superiority, cultural or otherwise. 'If a man must boast, let him boast of the Lord.' The previous reading emphasized that the Cross was foolishness. We see that this is true also of the Church.

Accepting that humility is the distinctive Christian virtue, how rare it appears to be! A story is told of a famous Archbishop who was asked by a student, 'Your Grace, what is the best book on humility?' The Archbishop replied, 'There is only one. I wrote it myself.' In contrast, a tribute paid by a friend to Martin Luther King might be recalled. 'Few people knew how humble this giant was . . . Today when millions of portraits hang in simple cabins, in ordinary homes and in stately halls, it is hard to recall that he forbade his own organization to reproduce his picture. He did not want to be idolized; he wanted to be heard.'

Our conceits and excessive self-regard are rebuked by comments like that. But especially humbling is our recollection of Jesus, King of kings and Lord of lords, who for men's sakes 'made Himself nothing, assuming the nature of a slave' (Philippians 2:7, N.E.B.).

I CORINTHIANS 2:1–9

'When I came to you, I declared the attested truth of God without display of fine words or wisdom' (v. 1, N.E.B.).

CHRIST NOT SELF. When Paul went to Corinth he reminded the Christians there that his purpose was to preach Christ and His Cross. He said he would do this without high-sounding phrases or philosophical speculation. His approach was unlike that of the strolling orators with whom the Greeks were well acquainted, whose intention more often than not was merely to display their cleverness with words and amuse the crowds. Paul's high purpose was to present the crucified Christ, and this he did with a due regard for his own unworthiness and with a sense of utter inadequacy.

The Apostle's determination to 'think of nothing but Jesus Christ' (v. 2, N.E.B.) among the Corinthians is a reminder of the subtle temptation to which, in their concern to present the gospel to men, all Christians—and not only preachers—are exposed. Self-importance is out of place in the Christian. John Woolman, the Quaker saint, observed in his Journal, 'The natural man loveth eloquence. I was preserved in the ministry to keep low with the truth.' The advice given to a beginner in the art of fishing is applicable to those who would present Christ—'Keep yourself out of sight.'

Our *raison d'être* as Christians is to introduce men to Christ. While informed, reasoned argument and reinterpretations of the gospel in sociological terms may help to do this, the radiance of our own experience—proof that we have had a personal, dynamic encounter with Christ—is the best recommendation for our faith. Can we effectively introduce Someone whom we do not know very well?

I CORINTHIANS 2:10–16

'It is through the Spirit that God has given us the revelation of His truth' (v. 10, Barclay).

THE WISDOM OF GOD. The homespun philosophies of uneducated men are often full of wisdom. Many of the wise sayings that still guide and inspire us originated with men of little learning. Certainly, spiritual wisdom does not come with worldly knowledge but from God Himself. This is the point of this rather difficult passage. We have already noted that Paul admitted he did not deliver his message to the Corinthians with the oratory of a Greek philosopher. His was a simple message, delivered with simplicity. But that did not mean there is no wisdom in the gospel. For those who can receive it there is. This wisdom enables the Christian to see that there is sense and rightness in what might appear to others to be failure and tragedy. The history of the Church is full of examples of men of small education, as well as the scholar, with this kind of spiritual insight.

W. E. Sangster made this point in *The Pure in Heart*, his study of sanctity. He wrote, 'This is God's world. The saint believes it through and through. In the presence of what others would call "dire calamity" he says: "I believe that whatever happens to me is good to me." In fact, he believes more than this. He believes that in the grasp of faith evil becomes redemptive . . . Reason will serve him, for reason also is a servant of God. But he does not depend on reason. His normal road to reality is that of spiritual divination. In some strange way, he sees the inwardness of things.'

1 CORINTHIANS 3:1–9

'You are still unspiritual. Isn't that obvious from all the jealousy and wrangling that there is among you?' (v. 3, Jerusalem Bible).

LOVING GOD MEANS LOVING PEOPLE. When he first went to the Corinthians with the gospel, wrote the Apostle, he was not able to treat them as mature Christians. This is understandable. Newly-born Christians are babes, and babes must be fed with milk and not meat. But the party strife among them, in which their personal resentments and animosities, their jealousies and sense of superiority were shown, was an indication of their continuing childhood: the poverty of their spiritual life was proof they had not yet grown up.

It is tragic when, after years of discipleship, some Christians have made little spiritual progress, and exhibit signs of spiritual immaturity which should have disappeared years before. Human relationships, as today's reading shows, are an index to the quality of the spiritual life of the believer. We may be punctilious in our observance of the formalities required by the particular branch of the Church to which we belong: we may say our prayers devoutly night and morning without fail. But it is in our relationships with our family, our colleagues at work and with our neighbours that the depth of our spirituality is revealed.

Resentments (sometimes, maybe, deeply hidden), irritations, impatience, refusal to see another's viewpoint—these are evidence of lack of spiritual growth. It was this kind of attitude in the Corinthians that caused Paul such grief. We must never forget that our love for people is the measure of our love for God.

1 CORINTHIANS 3:10–23

'Everything is for you, whether it be Paul, or Apollo, or Cephas, or the world, or life, or death, or the present, or the future; it is all for you, and you for Christ, and Christ for God' (vv. 22 and 23, Knox).

WHY BE IMPOVERISHED? Partisan loyalty not only divides the Church, it sadly impoverishes its members. True, each party has something to offer to the whole but it also needs to receive from the whole. Inordinate loyalty to their separate cliques prevented the Corinthians from finding enrichment outside the boundaries of their own party. 'Instead of saying (commented Godet): "I belong to Paul", they should say, "Paul belongs to me." Ministers are only means to an end and that end is the Church. Peter has his personal memories of the life of Jesus, Apollos his knowledge of the Scriptures and his eloquence, Paul his deep understanding of God's plans and his unequalled apostolic achievements. But these men . . . are God's gift to the Church and they must be used but not looked down on or lauded to the skies'.

Being grasped by an over-riding loyalty dispels pettiness. In the lyrical phrases which conclude the third chapter the apostle moves swiftly from the short-sighted bickering of the local congregation to the transcendent reality of God. This is always the way to overcome pettiness. It is lack of spiritual vision which creates personality cults and personal rivalries.

Being grasped by an over-riding loyalty brings enrichment when that loyalty is directed toward God. For practical purposes our loyalty to God may be expressed within a narrow field—one particular denomination, a local congregation, one avenue of service—but the enrichment we receive from God knows no such limitation.

1 CORINTHIANS 4:1–5

'My conscience does not, in fact, reproach me; but that is not where my justification lies; it is the Lord's scrutiny I must undergoe' (v. 4, Knox).

THE QUALITY OF OUR SERVICE. Paul here uses two different words to describe Christ's servants—'underlings' and 'stewards' (v. 1, N.E.B.). The first was usually applied to an 'underrower', one who rowed in the lower bank of oars on a large ship. This word came to be used of service in general, particularly of a lowly kind. A steward, on the other hand, was an overseer of his master's estate and often carried considerable responsibility. In relation to his master, however, he was still a slave. Whether we serve in apparently lowly or exalted positions we are still God's servants.

God alone can assess the quality of our service. Judging others is sheer folly for we never have the necessary evidence. We are also incapable of seeing our own motives clearly, for our minds have depths which are inaccessible even to ourselves.

One day, when Dick Sheppard was preaching in St. Martin-in-the-Fields in London, he affirmed that he was unpleasantly pious and priggish as a child. The congregation were startled when a woman cried, 'You were nothing of the kind.' It was the vicar's mother, indignant at her son's misrepresentation of himself. It was a reaction we would expect from a mother, and actually the evidence does support her rather than her gifted son.

Certainly, we are all incapable of seeing ourselves objectively. Trying to judge ourselves all too often causes us to fall into self-righteousness on the one hand or despair on the other. Teresa of Avila discovered the happy medium when she wrote: 'It is a great grace of God to practise self-examination, but too much is as bad as too little . . . Believe me, by God's help, we shall advance more by contemplating the Divinity than by keeping our eyes fixed on ourselves.'

1 CORINTHIANS 4:6–13

'For it seems to me that God means us apostles to come in at the very end, like doomed gladiators in the arena!' (v. 9, Moffatt).

WHAT SORT OF PEOPLE DO YOU THINK YOU ARE? The Apostle continued to deal very faithfully with the factionalism in the church at Corinth, and turned the full force of his irony (v. 8) upon the consequent sense of imagined superiority which afflicted the various groups.

So far as he and his companions were concerned (he went on) they were like the miserable prisoners of war, doomed to die, who brought up the rear of a Roman general's victory parade. And yet, despite the slanders and privations they were called upon to endure, they were still able, by the grace of God, to return good for evil. 'Being reviled, we bless.'

A twentieth-century apostle, Albert Schweitzer, wrote from Lambaréné: 'In the middle of September we get the first rains, and the cry is to bring all the building timber under cover. As there is hardly a man in the hospital capable of work, I begin, assisted by two loyal helpers, to haul beams and planks about myself. Suddenly I catch sight of a Negro in a white suit sitting by a patient whom he has come to visit. "Hullo, friend", I call out "won't you lend us a hand?" "I am an 'intellectual' and don't drag wood about", is the answer. "You're lucky", I reply. "I, too, wanted to become an 'intellectual', but I didn't succeed".'

We must learn with Raymond Raynes that 'at the beginning we look at the Passion as a means of salvation but, as our life in Christ grows stronger, we look on it as something we must share with Him'.

I CORINTHIANS 4:14–21

'It is power that builds up the kingdom of God, not words' (v. 20, Knox).

WHERE POWER IS SEEN. Paul concludes his long appeal for Church unity, first by reminding the Corinthians of his unique relationship with them—he is their spiritual father in Christ—and then by warning the obstinate that he intends to visit them later. The self-importance of those causing party strife will then be tested, not by their clever argument, but by their spiritual power.

Forcefulness of personality is not the same thing as spiritual power, although the two are often confused. On the other hand spiritual power is not necessarily the possession of the unassertive, 'retiring' person, whose apparent meekness may simply be due to lack of confidence. Spiritual power is an elusive quality. Like happiness, or meekness, it is never found when sought for itself. The Christian concept of power must never lose sight of Calvary.

As J. A. T. Robinson wrote: 'God's self-definition of power is terrifyingly simple—as simple and as terrifying as the Cross. He has exposed the strong right arm by which He wills to curb the nations, and it is pierced with nails, stained with blood and riveted in impotence'.

When Dr. Mary Verghese was initiated into the medical sisterhood she was sprinkled with water from a hose-pipe and given a new name. 'I christen you Mighty Atom', pronounced a fellow student. It was only long afterward, when a road accident had paralysed Mary and she had wonderfully triumphed over her suffering, did it occur to someone that there was special aptness in the nickname—for an atom is broken before it reveals its power.

1 CORINTHIANS 5:1–13

'I wrote to you in my letter not to associate with immoral people. I obviously did not mean the people out in the world' (vv. 9, 10, Barclay).

DISCIPLINE IN THE FELLOWSHIP. The Corinthian Christians had no reason to be proud of themselves (v. 2). There was a shocking case of immorality among them such as even pagans would not tolerate, and with which they had neglected to deal. The Apostle did not hesitate to say that the sinning man must be severely disciplined, 'consigned to Satan'—that is, cast out of the church and into the world which was reckoned to be Satan's domain.

The woman in the case was not included in the discipline, presumably because she was not a believer. It was against the sinning Christian that action was to be taken. Paul is not saying that Christians should sever their associations with non-Christians. That would mean running away from the world; it is in the world, among the people of the world, that Christians must bear their witness. But refusal to condone wickedness among believers is the Church's duty, for it is essential that a high ethical standard be maintained within the Christian community.

This does not mean, however, that as individuals we have the right to set ourselves up as judges against our fellows. This would certainly lead to the self-righteous pharisaism which Christ condemned. Judgment and discipline will be exercised by the Church, through its leaders. We have the responsibility as individuals of disciplining ourselves—and 'the discipline of the outer life depends entirely upon the discipline of the inner life—that is, of the mind'.

1 CORINTHIANS 6:1–11

'If therefore you have such business disputes, how can you entrust jurisdiction to outsiders, men who count for nothing in our community?' (v. 4, N.E.B.).

HOW TO SETTLE OUR DIFFERENCES. Paul had already dealt with the problems of factions and immorality in the Church at Corinth. Now he has to address himself to another lamentable situation: Christians were taking to civil courts fellow Christians with whom they had some disagreement. Jews living in heathen countries were accustomed to settling their disputes among themselves. No doubt Paul expected Christians to do the same. To him it was inconceivable that any believer having a difference with another believer should seek to settle it by recourse to non-Christians.

The reality and depth of Christian experience are proved in personal relationships, and the strength and quality of a Christian group are shown by that group's ability to resolve difficult situations, which are bound to arise, involving personalities. Paul was concerned about the difficulties in this matter at Corinth because he knew that preoccupation with one's rights and privileges is a denial of the Spirit of Jesus. Differences among Christians should be resolved by love, toleration of the other's viewpoint and the willingness of individuals to sacrifice even that which they might justly account to be theirs.

A word of warning is necessary, however. It is Christlike to surrender our own privileges freely; it is wrong to expect others to forgo theirs on the ground that as Christians they should be ready for sacrifice! To contend for the rights of others is our Christian duty.

1 CORINTHIANS 6:12–20

'As a Christian I may do anything, but that does not mean that everything is good for me to do. I may do everything, but I must not be the slave of anything' (v. 12, Phillips).

LIBERTY NOT LICENCE. It needs only a moment's thought to see that, if liberty is interpreted to mean licence, ordered, harmonious living will be impossible. Laws are necessary in a democratic society so that freedom might be preserved equally for all its members. Yet it has sometimes been argued by Christians—the Corinthians had obviously argued it—that since in Christ there is liberty ('all things are lawful') there is no restriction on what a man might do; if he pleases he might indulge any bodily appetite to the full. Paul was dealing in today's passage with the moral and spiritual consequences of sexual indulgence. The Corinthians considered that no restraint was necessary on their desires, but the Apostle took quite another view. He would have no such unchristian reasoning. For one thing, actions must be judged not only by whether they are lawful, but by whether they are helpful and good. And again, liberty without restraint would lead in the end to enslavement. Liberty must be identified with responsibility.

Modern advocates of 'free love' would do well to ponder Paul's teaching on this, at least from a pragmatic, if not from a religious standpoint. But what the Apostle says must be applied not only to sexual desire; it concerns all our physical appetites. Gluttony and sloth, as well as lust, are among the seven deadly sins. God should be honoured 'in the body', said Paul, 'a shrine of the indwelling Holy Spirit' (N.E.B.). Any abuse of the body, therefore, is sin.

1 CORINTHIANS 7:1–7

'The husband must give the wife what is due to her, and the wife equally must give the husband his due' (v. 3, N.E.B.).

LOVE AT HOME. From the commencement of chapter 7 to the end of chapter 15 the Apostle deals with questions which have been addressed to him by believers in Corinth about the problems of Christian living in a pagan society. These ranged from domestic matters such as the marriage relationship to such basic theological questions as the doctrine of the resurrection.

In weighing up the Apostle's answers two facts must be kept in mind. One is that even in the first century the city of Corinth was a byword for vicious profligacy. In such a world strictness was a good fault. Undue care was better than undue laxity. The second is that in the mind of many believers—and without doubt in that of Paul also—the Lord's return was at hand. The Apostle might at times have altered his emphasis had he been concerned with long term planning, though this does not invalidate any of the principles which he laid down.

Though it may seem that celibacy was the Apostle's ideal and marriage but a second-best, what Paul had to say about marriage as a partnership will carry our judgment. Both husband and wife have their rights. Mutual consideration and mutual respect must be the order of the day. It might even be said that neither the bully nor the shrew will inherit a place in that kingdom of ideal relationships—the kingdom of God. As Elizabeth Fry, the Quaker prison reformer, wrote in her diary in the autumn of 1810: 'My beloved Joseph is a true helpmeet . . . The public service to which I have been called has very closely united us.'

1 CORINTHIANS 7:8–16

'Think of it: as a wife you may be your husband's salvation; as a husband you may be your wife's salvation' (v. 16, N.E.B.).

INFLUENCING OTHERS. William Booth was sixty-one when in 1890 his beloved wife Catherine died. They had been married for nearly forty years, and the influence of each on the other was incalculable. Theirs was a truly great love story. In a recently-published biography of Catherine Booth, her granddaughter, Catherine Bramwell-Booth observes: 'Their (William and Catherine's) eldest son Bramwell knew and loved them both better than any other being. He wrote of their love to each other: ". . . That love became a kind of element remote from the world, purer than the common air, in which they acted and reacted on one another to the comfort and joy of both."' How great may be the influence of a woman on her husband and a man on his wife! Paul suggests this in this reading and it is a thought we may extend to other human relationships.

In one of her books Rita Snowden reminds us that the Italian word for influence is *influenza*. 'We've all got influenza,' she says and tells the story of an old woman, a member of George Matheson's congregation, who lived in a cellar. One day she greatly astonished her neighbours by moving from her basement to a sunny garret. When they crowded round to question her, she simply said, 'Ye canna hear George Matheson preach and live in a cellar.' We must never underestimate our own influence on the people we meet.

1 CORINTHIANS 7:17–28

'Be sure in deciding these matters you are living as God intended' (v. 17, The Living Bible).

HUMAN DIFFERENCES. Believers in Corinth, as elsewhere in the Christian church, had to learn to live out their faith in a non-Christian setting. It is noteworthy that the Apostle's guidance was far from dogmatic. Naturally, he gave an answer to such questions as were addressed to him. But he was careful to distinguish between the clear command of Jesus and his own judgment on a specific situation. When he gave his own opinion he did not fail to make that plain (vv. 12 and 25).

Again, the Apostle was no revolutionary. He accepted many of the social and economic conditions of his day. His thought was that a slave—for that is what the word 'servant' in the Authorized Version means—however hard his lot, could be a follower of Jesus. We might ask today whether a first century master, converted to Christianity, could continue to keep slaves.

If Paul did not denounce the system on which the economics of his world rested, two facts should be remembered. One is that neither Greek nor Roman culture saw anything amiss with slavery. In the Roman empire of his day there could well have been sixty million slaves. The second is that slavery was acceptable to parts of the white world in the nineteenth century, and even now there are those who act as if people of a skin different in colour to their own are inferior to them.

These human tensions cannot be resolved without divine wisdom and Christian charity. We ourselves have no small part to play so that all men everywhere may live 'as God intended'.

1 CORINTHIANS 7:29–40

'I tell you these things to help you' (v. 35, Phillips).

PLEASING THE LORD. Certain principles guided the Apostle in his observations upon specific practices, peculiar to his own time, mentioned in this passage.

The first was that time was short (v. 29). The Lord was at hand. The second—that he had no taste for intolerant dictatorships. 'I have no wish to keep you on a tight rein' (v. 35, N.E.B.). The third—whatever a man's personal preferences, his main aim should be to please the Lord.

Scholars differ in their interpretations of vv. 36–38. Some suppose that v. 36 could have referred to an engaged couple who had decided to postpone marriage in view of the widely accepted assumption of the Lord's speedy return. If, however, they found this arrangement untenable, they had better marry than enter into any irregular union. The R.S.V. may be understood in this sense.

Another suggestion is that the passage refers to the practice of a man taking a young unmarried woman—both of them believers—into his care but each living a single life. So unusual a mutual agreement can perhaps be understood by us as a form of protest against the licentiousness of the age. However, the Apostle gave the sensible advice that if this plan, however well-intentioned, proved unworkable, the two had better marry. What was all important was that believers should 'please the Lord' (v. 32).

1 CORINTHIANS 8:1–13

'Be careful that this liberty of yours does not become a pitfall for the weak' (v. 9, N.E.B.).

CONSIDERING THE 'WEAKER BRETHREN'. In the pagan cities of the first century world the sacrifice of animals at the shrine of the various deities was commonplace. But only part of the meat was consumed at heathen altars. Some would find its way back into the butchers' shops, and believers could never be sure that the meat which they bought over the counter, or ate in the house of a friend, had not been dedicated to a heathen god.

Some would not give the matter a second thought. They could quite happily eat any meat, whether part of a pagan ceremony or not. That was the common-sense, mature Christian view which Paul himself shared. But not all the believers could think that way. They asked Paul for guidance, and in giving it he laid down a principle valid for all time.

In any course of action the 'stronger' Christian must always keep in mind the influence for good or ill he might have on his 'weaker' brethren—young people, perhaps, or the new convert. The lengths to which Christian liberty might be taken, the restrictions which for love's sake a Christian places on himself, are matters of vital importance. As believers we cannot ignore our personal responsibility for others. We cannot live and not love.

1 CORINTHIANS 9:1–14

'We do not mind any privations if we can only avoid putting any obstacle in the way of the gospel of Christ' (v. 12, Moffatt).

WHEN THE GOSPEL IS OBSTRUCTED. Although Paul had no doubts about an apostle's rights to financial support he voluntarily sacrificed that right and supported himself by his own labours. He implied, in this passage, that the Corinthians also should be willing, for the sake of 'weaker' brethren, to renounce their right to eat at banquets where sacrifice was offered. When Paul said he would rather suffer than hinder the gospel he used a word which literally meant 'a cutting into'. It was used of breaking up a road to prevent an enemy advance.

The gospel can be obstructed by Christ's own representatives. This can occur in numerous ways but most frequently through failure to love. During the early days of the Christian Church in New Zealand a Wesleyan mission was burnt to the ground by Maoris and the missionaries were fortunate to escape with their lives. Samuel Marsden, who pioneered the Christian cause in that land, was deeply disturbed when he discovered that because of this incident many missionaries were carrying weapons. At a very tense conference and despite strong opposition he threatened to dismiss any missionary who went about his work armed. 'We are here to preach the gospel of peace,' he affirmed. 'We cannot do it if we are armed.'

In very different circumstances we need to recognize that our Christian profession is a proclamation of the love of God. Nothing can serve to discredit our witness as much as our own lovelessness and indifference to the needs of others.

1 CORINTHIANS 9:15–23

'I have made myself every man's servant, to win over as many as possible' (v. 19, N.E.B.).

SERVANT OF ALL. Paul deeply cherished the privilege of preaching the gospel without expense to the churches and the original text of this passage reveals his strong emotion as he wrote of this principle. This involved no unfavourable comparison with the other apostles who were church supported. It seemed to Paul that their decision to follow Christ was freely made, whereas he had long resisted Christ and had to be taken into the Master's service almost by force. It was by his self-maintenance that he expressed his free consent and his deep gratitude to Christ.

Paul identified himself with every person he sought to win for his Master. There was no suggestion of 'take it or leave it' in his presentation of the gospel. He saw himself as every man's servant. The needs of his hearers, not his own prejudices or preferences, determined his approach. William Temple said that the Church ought to be the institution which existed 'primarily for the benefit of non-members'. This was the spirit in which the great apostle to the Gentiles served. His was the selfless identification which bears fruit.

When Archibald Fleming, first bishop of the Arctic, was due to take his first furlough, the Eskimos told him they had a new name for him. He was no longer to be called 'the young teacher' but *In-nook-tah-kaub*, 'one of the family'. 'Of all the honours given me during my life', he said later, 'none has been more cherished than this tribute from my children by adoption.'

1 CORINTHIANS 9:24–27

'Every athlete must keep all his appetites under control; and he does it to win a crown that fades, whereas ours is imperishable' (v. 25, Knox).

TWO KINDS OF SELF-DISCIPLINE. The present generation is not outstanding for its self-discipline. Partly this is due to an exaggerated reaction against the repressions of the last century. Its main cause is a deep and widespread uncertainty about the basic meaning of life. We must somehow make it clear to our contemporaries that Christian self-discipline is not negative and life-denying. As today's passage clearly demonstrates, it is a means to an end.

We need to distinguish two kinds of self-discipline. One form, like that of the Pharisees in the New Testament, merely imposes burdens which are 'grievous to be borne'. The other kind, which Jesus referred to when he invited people to accept His easy yoke, leads to fulfilment and moral achievement.

In his book, *The True Wilderness*, Harry Williams asks his readers to imagine a young man born into a family of scientists and expected to carry on the family tradition. His real interests are in literature. But in obedience to his father's wishes he goes to university and slogs away ten hours a day at the science syllabus. He makes no progress however, becomes depressed and eventually gives up. His work was a denial of his true self and left him utterly exhausted. But supposing the same boy enters the university to study English literature. His work would still require effort and self-control. Yet his labours would be an affirmation of his true self and would yield happiness and self-fulfilment. Christian self-discipline is of this latter variety: it aims to set us free to realize our true selves in love to God and man.

1 CORINTHIANS 10:1–13

'God keeps faith, and He will not allow you to be tested above your powers, but when the test comes He will at the same time provide a way out, by enabling you to sustain it' (v. 13, N.E.B.).

WATCHFUL BUT NOT ANXIOUS. If we ignore the artificial break at the end of chapter nine we see that Paul follows an illustration taken from the athletic stadium, a part of Greek life, with one from the life of the people of Israel. He was indeed 'all things to all men', clothing the unchanging truth in different garments to suit the varied needs of his hearers or readers. In both illustrations the need to guard against temptations which divert us from our course is stressed. In the stadium not all the runners who started completed the course: similarly, many Israelites perished before they reached the Promised Land. The Christian must be alert and watchful of the inducements to evil which spring from his environment.

Although watchful, the Christian need not be fearful, for God will support him in the hour of temptation or trial. Some believers anxiously speculate whether or not they could retain their faith in particular calamities. They forget that God matches His supporting strength with our need. Charles Peguy stressed this truth with a parable of a father teaching his son to swim. The father wants to support the boy all the time but he knows that if he does the lad will never swim. On the other hand, if he does not support him at just the right moment he may swallow a mouthful of sea water and lose his nerve.

This is the mystery of the liberty of man, God says,
And of my management of him and of his liberty.

If I support him too much, he is not free.
If I do not support him enough, he will fall.
If I support him too much I endanger his liberty.
If I do not support him enough, I endanger his salvation:
Two goods, in a sense, almost equally precious.

That which is a dilemma to a human father is no problem to an all-wise God.

1 CORINTHIANS 10:14–22

'My dear friends, have nothing to do with idolatry' (v. 14, Barclay).

POWERFUL ASSOCIATIONS. Gradually the apostle led his readers to the point where he faced them with an uncompromising command—'shun idolatry'. Was Paul guilty of inconsistency when he affirmed that one cannot have communion with Christ and with evil spirits? After all, he had already agreed that 'an idol has no real existence'. The answer is that in the minds of his Gentile converts idolatry was inseparably linked with evil associations. Therefore they must not see how near they could approach idolatrous practices and still retain their loyalty to Christ. Rather they must show their loyalty by seeing how far they could fly from such associations.

One commentator refers to a central African tribe where a goat's skin was believed to possess magical powers and was worn as a protection against evil spirits. When a tribesman was converted to Christianity he instinctively threw off his former dress because, while having no significance for a European, to the African it was impregnated with pagan beliefs.

We must wisely recognize the powerful associations, for good and evil, which certain situations and activities have for us. Our own personal history has created these associations and we rarely escape from them. If we are wise we make this psychological law work for us, rather than against us, avoiding those things which carry unhelpful associations and dwelling upon that which is inseparably linked in our minds with goodness and truth. As Dag Hammerskjöld observed: 'You cannot play with the animal in you without becoming wholly animal, play with falsehood without forfeiting your right to truth, play with cruelty without losing your sensitivity of mind. He who wants to keep his garden tidy does not reserve a plot for weeds.'

1 CORINTHIANS 10:23–11:1

'Each of you ought to study the well-being of others, not his own' (v. 25, Knox).

DO ALL TO THE GLORY OF GOD. The Christian possesses a liberty that is real, but it is a liberty that he should be prepared to limit, if needs be, for the sake of others.

Paul says that believers were quite at liberty to buy meat sold in the open markets at Corinth, and even to accept invitations to eat at the home of a non-believing friend where 'idol meat' might be served. They need ask no questions about what was placed before them.

But then the Apostle visualizes the situation arising in which the pagan friend might disclose to those assembled that it was 'idol-meat' they were eating. In this case, declares Paul, the Christian should refrain from partaking, not for his own sake but for his friend's.

Here is a principle that we can apply to our own leisure pursuits, our book-reading, radio-listening and television viewing. We do not live to ourselves, but are our brothers' keepers. Maybe at times we rebel at the restrictions this fact exerts upon us and cry, 'Why should my freedom to eat (or read, or listen, or view, or anything else) be at the mercy of someone else's conscience?' The answer is that the Christian's obligation is to 'do all to the glory of God', and this is sometimes achieved only by restraining ourselves in the exercise of our liberty. This is the principle which the Apostle himself follows, and this is why he can conclude his appeal by saying: 'Copy me, my brothers, as I copy Christ Himself'.

1 CORINTHIANS 11:2–16

'In Christ's fellowship woman is as essential to man as man to woman' (v. 11, N.E.B.).

MEN AND WOMEN. Even on the basis of today's reading it would be wrong to call the Apostle Paul an anti-feminist. We must not forget his approval of the ministry of women in the Early Church, and his declaration that 'gone is the distinction ... between ... male and female' (Gal. 3:28, Phillips).

This passage must also be considered in the context of the times in which it was written. Pagan women worshipped with uncovered heads. Paul favoured the traditions of Jewish worship, for which women covered their heads, and he urges all Christian women to observe the custom. The passage reflects Paul's rabbinic background, but does not support ideas of the inferiority of women.

The words 'woman's head is man' must be read in their context —'Every man has Christ for his head' and 'Christ's Head is God'; and we must also read 'for the man is the head of the woman' (Ephesians 5:22) with what follows: 'just as Christ is Head of the Church'. Christ does not dominate and exploit the Church. He gives Himself to it in love and His people bring to Him their trusting response. Similarly, the relationship between husband and wife must be based on love and trust. And this is true of all worthwhile human relationships. Mutual dependence is a fundamental law of life. We fly in the face of God's order whenever we try to 'go it alone'. As Dean Inge used to say: 'Christianity promises to make men free; it never promises to make them independent'.

1 CORINTHIANS 11:17–26

'Everyone keeps telling me about the ... divisions developing among you' (v. 18, The Living Bible).

MORE HARM THAN GOOD. The custom in the Early Church was to share a common meal for the purposes of Christian fellowship (see Acts 2: 46). Later this was to develop into a ritual act patterned on the Last Supper. Today's reading portrays a situation midway between early custom and later development.

Paul had felt it right to establish a fellowship-meal at Corinth, and doubtless elsewhere, and this was becoming a much abused custom. Instead of a delightful and natural 'love-feast' it was being turned into a 'a meeting of gluttons and unbrotherly men, where excess and hunger went hand-in-hand.'

The Apostle's word was therefore one of sharp rebuke. 'I cannot commend your conduct,' he writes, sternly, 'for it seems that your church meetings do you more harm than good!' The meal they shared—or did not share—was not the Lord's Supper, for its very purpose had been defeated.

These readings, revealing problems of worship within the first-century Church, should not be used for the purpose of self-congratulation. It is no comfort to say, 'They were no better than we are,' for we should be better than they, for they had been saved from a pagan background.

Let us examine the quality and effect of our own particular Christian fellowship. Does our worship bind us close to one another by stimulating our love? Does it build us up in the faith enabling us the better to work and witness for our Lord?

1 CORINTHIANS 11:27–34

'It is this careless participation which is the reason for the many feeble and sickly Christians in your church, and the explanation of the fact that many of you are spiritually asleep' (v. 30, Phillips).

THE PERILS OF THOUGHTLESSNESS. This passage has received various interpretations by different Churches. While most Christians observe some form of Holy Communion, there is all the difference in the world between, for instance, a Catholic Mass and a Baptist church observance of the Lord's Supper. Salvationists and members of the Society of Friends, believing that spiritual experience is not dependent on ritual, do not observe sacraments. They believe their witness has value for the whole Church in warning against undue dependence upon outward form. Today's reading has a lesson for sacramentalist and non-sacramentalist alike, for Paul was protesting at a thoughtless participation in Christian worship. So seriously did he view such insincerity that he believed it to be the cause of some kind of physical illness. Today a Christian doctor might say: 'Your careless attitude toward spiritual reality is producing emotional disorders which cause physical illness.'

Every Christian needs to guard against being thoughtless and casual in his attitude to spiritual things. 'The difficulty about religious experience', wrote L. P. Jacks, 'is not to get it, but to recognize it when it comes. It is always coming our way, always going on unnoticed in the deep and silent places of our lives.' What chance have we of perceiving the religious depths in everyday experience, if we are unaware of them even in our worship and prayer life? With General Orsborn we can pray that we 'may be always, increasingly, at home with our sacred work, but never familiar with it'.

1 CORINTHIANS 12:1–11

'And no one can say "Jesus is Lord!" except under the influence of the Holy Spirit' (v. 3, N.E.B.).

DIVERSITIES OF GIFTS. To some people the term Holy

Spirit introduces a note of unreality. This is due partly to false ideas of the word holy, and partly to a misunderstanding of how the Holy Spirit works in man. He is not to be associated only with the ecstatic and extraordinary. Though these have been a feature of Christianity, they are not the only signs that a Christian has received the Spirit.

Today's passage shows that Paul believed that the Spirit operates in different ways—through the wise speech of some, the works of healing of others (doctors and other agents of the Church's ministry of healing), as well as through ecstatic utterances. In *The Truth About the Early Church*, William Neil points out that though it was the dramatic evidences of the presence of the Spirit —speaking in tongues, miracles and prophecy—that first attracted the attention of the early Christians, 'side by side with them from the beginning went the recognition of the Spirit in less spectacular ways as a power that could change men's lives and build a Christian community.'

The man who honours Jesus as Lord is both impelled and empowered by the Spirit to do God's work in the world.

1 CORINTHIANS 12:12–31

'Now you are together the Body of Christ and individually you are members of Him' (v. 27, Phillips).

EACH A PART TO PLAY. George Eliot wrote that 'the growing good of the world is partly dependent on unhistoric acts: that things are not so ill with you and me as they might have been is half-owing to the number who lived faithfully a hidden life and rest in unvisited tombs'. This supports the above reading which makes it clear that no Christian should be over-concerned about what he might consider the smallness of the contribution he can make to the cause of Christ in the world. As part of the Body of Christ each believer has an important part to play, and the successful functioning of the whole body—the Church—depends on the faithfulness of each individual member. There is no reason for any of us to make unhelpful comparisons with our more talented fellow-Christians; this may so easily lead to resentment and discouragement. However small our gift, however restricted (humanly speaking) our sphere of influence, our own distinctive contribution counts. A commonplace truth? It is one of which we need to be often reminded.

George Seaver wrote of Edward Wilson of the Antarctic that he held 'with an unalterable conviction . . . that the worth of life is not to be measured by its results in achievement or success, but solely by the motive of heart and effort of will', which is another way of saying that it is faithfulness with what we have been entrusted that really matters.

1 CORINTHIANS 13:1–13

'There are three things that last for ever: faith, hope and love; but the greatest of them all is love' (v. 13, N.E.B.).

A PORTRAIT OF JESUS. Paul has sometimes been accused of showing slight interest in the earthly life of Jesus compared with his absorbing concern in Christ's death. Yet although the apostle rarely refers to specific incidents in the life of his Master he frequently reveals his thorough acquaintance with the story of Christ's life. What is this well-loved chapter if not a portrait of the personality of Jesus? Harnack said that this chapter is 'the greatest, strongest, deepest thing Paul ever wrote'. It is a passage to read, re-read and meditate upon.

True love overleaps all barriers of race or natural affinity. Alfred Starratt, a teacher in an Asian university, became an object of hatred and contempt when political revolution brought his work to an end. Although ordered to leave the country he was denied the use of a cross-river ferry which was his way out. His plight was desperate. Quite unexpectedly a man who owned a small boat, seeing what was happening, took Mr. Starratt on board and moved away before others could stop him. The police boarded the regular ferry to overtake and arrest the offending boatman on the other side. 'This will bring you much grief,' Mr. Starratt said to the old man. 'It is not important,' he replied. 'I also am a man.' On the other side the police arrested the boatman and led him away.

Greatly influenced by this incident Mr. Starratt later wrote, 'An unloving Christian is not really closer to God than a loving Hindu, and if one religion is more adequate as a path towards God than the other, the proof can only be demonstrated in terms of loving individuals who actually live in the love that was, and is, Christ.' As Hensley Henson once said: 'All extraordinary gifts are valueless without love; but love can exist in the absence of all extraordinary gifts'.

1 CORINTHIANS 14:1–12

'One who prophesies, preaching messages from God, helps the entire church' (v. 4, The Living Bible).

No believer need be in any confusion about what is called the gift of tongues. The guidance of the New Testament is clear and plain.

In the Early Church, as in some Christian communities today, there were those who spoke in tongues. This is not a language; it has no grammar; no dictionary has ever been compiled of the spelling and the meaning of the sounds uttered. The apostle declared, however, that he would not quarrel with any who claimed to possess this gift. He claimed to possess it himself—and that to a greater degree than most people (v. 18), but he much preferred the gift of prophecy.

Now the word prophecy, in this setting, had nothing to do with foretelling the future, but everything to do with what is elsewhere described as 'the whole counsel of God'. And this, said the Apostle most emphatically, is the gift which 'builds up the Church'. One's private raptures must take second place to what is for the public good.

The same principle applies to the whole range of Christian activity. Most of us have our personal preferences in Christian worship and work. This is quite understandable, but the overriding question is: what will most benefit the church (my corps) as a whole? To that end I subordinate my own likes and dislikes.

1 CORINTHIANS 14:13–25

'I will pray intelligently . . . I will sing intelligently' (v. 15, N.E.B.).

This passage begs believers to be grown-up in their thinking (v. 20, N.E.B.)—particularly in their corporate worship. Here they must behave like adults. Only one person must speak in a tongue at any one time, and not more than three persons in any one service. Furthermore, there must be someone who can interpret, and if no interpreter is available, then anyone who wishes to speak in a tongue must hold his peace. Otherwise an unconverted visitor might think he had entered a madhouse (v. 23).

Prayer, song and speech must all be intelligent and intelligible to the congregation. Otherwise what help would they be to any listener? He is transgressing the primary rule of Christian behaviour who is concerned only with his private exaltation of spirit. It is the declaration of Christian truth (vv. 24, 25) in speech that can be understood which will lay bare the secrets of the heart.

This rule applies today. It is truth which illumines the mind that can awaken the conscience and quicken the heart.

1 CORINTHIANS 14:26–40

'When you meet together, each of you has something which he wishes to contribute. . . . Everything must be done with the intention of building up the spiritual life of the congregation' (v. 26, Barclay).

OUR APPROACH TO WORSHIP. The form of worship followed by the first Christians has been described as having an 'orderly informality'. There was no professional ministry such as we know today—no cut and dried procedure in the services. Anybody who had a contribution to make was free to make it, the elements including the singing of hymns, teaching, extempore prayers and speaking in tongues (in Paul's view permissible only when an interpreter was present). How different was all this from much of today's public worship, where a stereotyped and lifeless procedure is often entirely in the hands of one man, and where joyous spontaneity is conspicuous by its absence!

As the ordering of public worship is not the responsibility of most believers how shall we personally engage in public worship? Evelyn Underhill had a wise word when she said: 'Coming to God we must be completely absorbed in the fact that He is; and rewards . . . them only who diligently seek Him for His own sake alone'.

With this in mind, we must never allow familiarity to breed, if not contempt, any carelessness in our worship. We must preserve a sense of its wonder and privilege. And we must worship with a due regard to the contribution we are required to make, even though we sit in the congregation. There are great gains from worship, but too often our chief concern is what we are going to receive, when every worshipper has the privilege and duty of giving also.

Perhaps we need to concentrate less on ourselves and more on God, worshipping Him for what He is.

1 CORINTHIANS 15:1–11

'I handed on to you the facts which had been imparted to me: that Christ died for our sins, in accordance with the scriptures; that He was buried; that He was raised to life on the third day . . .' (v. 3 and 4, N.E.B.).

THE CORNERSTONE. Following questions about marriage, church worship and spiritual gifts, Paul dealt with the problem of human destiny after death. He saved the biggest and most basic question until last. Writing about the modern conspiracy to convince us that there is no death, one American commentator writes, 'The procedures . . . of the mortician's trade in this country all revolve around one fundamental aim—the camouflage of the reality of death.' Such attempts can never wholly succeed; the transience of this life is too obvious.

Christ's Resurrection is the cornerstone of our faith that death is not the last word. Significantly, although the Cross of Jesus was the biggest stumbling block to the first hearers of the Christian message, it is the Resurrection which gives most difficulty to modern man. This sometimes causes a concentration on the Passion of Jesus without any attempt to relate this to its triumphant outcome. The result is a joyless gospel.

Christ's Resurrection is attested by history and personal experience. Most of those whom Paul lists as witnesses of the Resurrection were still alive when he wrote this letter. The Christian faith was first proclaimed by men who staked their lives upon the reality of the risen Christ. Ultimately, however, faith also rests upon our own experience of communion with Christ. The Christian 'knows the Christ who lives; therefore, he knows that Christ was raised'.

As Alice Meynell wrote:

> No planet knows that this
> Our wayside planet, carrying land and wave,
> Love and life multiplied, and pain and bliss,
> Bears, as chief treasure, one forsaken grave.

1 CORINTHIANS 15:12–19

'If it is for this life only that Christ has given us hope, we of all men are most to be pitied' (v. 19, N.E.B.).

UNBELIEF IS INCREDIBLE. Denial of life after death contradicts what we already know of God in Christ. This is the gist of Paul's argument in this passage. If faith is difficult, unbelief is incredible in view of our experience of God's grace. Life in Christ requires eternity for its fulfilment.

James Stewart says that, without the Christian hope, we 'have to believe that the spirit which was in Beethoven when he was working at white heat on the Ninth Symphony, or in Leonardo as he painted the "Last Supper", or in Martin Luther crying "Here stand I; I can no other; so help me God", or in Father Damien living the Christ life among the lepers—is of no more significance or ultimate value than the leaves which go flying down the street before the autumn winds, "cast as rubbish to the void".'

Both by His life and teaching Jesus taught the infinite value to God of every individual. This is the rock upon which Christian ethics are based and, incidentally, the foundation of the concern for social justice. But can the God who seeks the lost sheep until it is found, who watches tirelessly for the prodigal's return, who calls the individual soul into communion with Himself—can such a God allow the individual utterly to perish at death? Christian experience, reinforced by the Resurrection of Christ, answers with a resounding 'No'. Austin Farrar has well said that 'because Jesus is beyond the death we still have to face, our union with Him is union with an achieved immortality'.

1 CORINTHIANS 15:20–34

'Christ . . . must reign until God has reduced all His enemies to complete subjection' (v. 25, Barclay).

COMPLETE VICTORY. As has already been noted, the resurrection of Jesus assures us of the truth of the after-life. Death is not the last word; it is defeated for ever. Because of the Resurrection we can say joyfully with John Donne:

> Death be not proud, though some have called thee
> Mighty and dreadful, for, thou art not so . . .

One short sleep past, we wake eternally,
And death shall be no more; death, thou shalt die.

But this is not the whole or indeed the chief meaning of the Resurrection. It carries an even deeper message than the defeat of death and the promise of personal immortality. It is an assertion that all of life has meaning, that what we have entrusted to God is safe and true. The resurrection of Jesus points to the ultimate and complete victory of God over the forces of evil. In his book, *Weep Not for Me*, F. R. Barry puts it like this: 'Easter is the vindication of God. The power that runs the universe is committed to Jesus and therefore to the cause of man; and its ultimate energies are on his side . . . Here is a guarantee that the world is more than a closed system of determinants—though these, Christians hold, are on their own level a reflection of the faithfulness of God—that it is an open world, alive, purposive, organic to Spirit, with personal being its constitutive reality—a world in which personal life can grow.'

Because God is good and eternal, we may trust Him for the here and the hereafter.

1 CORINTHIANS 15:35–49

'As we have worn the likeness of the man made of dust, so we shall wear the likeness of the heavenly Man' (v. 49, N.E.B.).

GOD'S GIFT TO MAN. Greeks and Jews held different concepts of the nature of man. The Greek thought of him as an immaterial soul inhabiting a physical body. At death, the soul, the essential man, was released from the body which went into decay. The Jew, on the other hand, believed man was a unit with body, soul (animal life) and spirit (that which could know God), and his survival after death necessitated the survival of both body and spirit. This puzzled the Corinthians, and it puzzles some people today when they read and recite that part of the Apostles' Creed which affirms: 'I believe in . . . the resurrection of the body.'

Paul points out that after death man will have a different, spiritual body to suit his new environment. He illustrates this by the seed which, though it dies, lives on in a new and fruitful form. The new is different from the old, but essentially linked with it. This is a difficult subject, and it is as well to admit that no one can make a complete and detailed pronouncement of the nature of the future life. However, there emerge from the Apostle's teaching these two important points.

Firstly, though we may be doubtful about the details of our future life, of the fact of it, and therefore of the utter dependability of God, we may be absolutely sure. This leads to the second point. The Bible employs the term resurrection more frequently than immortality and underlines the truth that the life beyond of Christian expectation is the gift of God's love through the risen Christ, not simply a 'plus', an 'added gift', as it were, but a continuance of our life in Christ. Indeed, eternal life is the present reality, said Jesus, of those who believe in Him who sent Him (John 5:24).

1 CORINTHIANS 15:50–58

'Therefore, my beloved brothers, stand firm and immovable, and work for the Lord always, work without limit' (v. 58, N.E.B.).

THE GOSPEL IS MEANT FOR ACTION. Sally is a character in Walter Greenwood's *Love on the Dole*, a novel based on life in an industrial town in northern England in the bleak years of the early 'thirties'. Like most of the people in the story, Sally knows all about the struggle to survive, for jobs are few and money scarce. She is looking forward to some happiness when she marries Larry. Then Larry dies. To all the grim struggling is added this heartbreak. An older woman says to her, 'There's nowt for the like of us t' live for, Sal. Nowt! Religion, eh? Pah! Ah've no patience wi' it.' And Sally replies, 'No, not me neither,' adding bitterly, 'Ah've no patience wi' nowt nor nobody now.'

There is no hint in the story that the Church did anything to ease the lot of the depressed people. In real life there were in fact Christians who expressed their concern for the depressed areas in a practical way, but the author ignores this, reflecting the common complaint that religion has nothing to offer men but 'pie in the sky when you die'. The truth is that the gospel is meant for action here and now and that service to needy man is service to God.

At the end of his discourse on the Resurrection, Paul does not encourage his readers merely to look forward to some glorious future, he reminds them there is work to be done in the present. More than this, he indicates that the Christian's hope should provide a spur to his service, the word 'therefore' in verse 58 showing the link between belief and behaviour. It is the eternal dimension in the gospel that gives significance to all that a Christian does.

1 CORINTHIANS 16:1–12

'Now about the collection which is being made for the saints . . . Each of you should put aside, on the first day of the week, what he can afford' (vv. 1, 2, Knox).

OUR DUTY OF SHARING. After the high tone of the preceding chapter, Paul's appeal for money might at first thought appear to be somewhat mundane, anti-climatic and trivial. In fact it emphasizes a truth about which Paul had already written at some length in chapter 12: 'You are Christ's body and each of you a limb or organ of it' and 'if one organ suffers, they all suffer together'. The starving Christians at Jerusalem (had the 'all things in common' principle—Acts 4:32—failed?) shared with the Christians at Corinth a common membership of the Body of Christ. The Apostle's appeal provided the Corinthians with an opportunity of acknowledging in practical terms their acceptance of his teaching. It is a point for us to notice: as Christians we have a partnership with and therefore a responsibility to our fellow Christians regardless of the denominational label they wear.

Another important point emphasized by the Apostle's down-to-earth appeal is that the Christian gospel is not merely lofty ideals and beautiful thoughts, but is in every way concerned with the ordinary affairs of life. The gospel has to be lived and expounded in the world of the everyday, and the Church must use money; it would be impossible for the work to continue without it. This imposes obligations upon each of us to make systematic contributions according to our means. What we give, however, should be not only an exercising of our duty, but a reflection of our love for Christ.

1 CORINTHIANS 16:13–24

'Be on your guard, stand firm in the faith, live like men, be strong! Let everything that you do be done in love' (vv. 13, 14, Phillips).

STRENGTH AND LOVE. To the above verses J. B. Phillips gives the heading, 'A little sermon in a nutshell'. They are a summary of much of the Apostle's teaching in the letter as a whole, and it might be helpful to use them to recapitulate on what we have been considering during the past six weeks.

There is an appeal here for firmness amid uncertainty and unsettling doubts, the Apostle having in mind some of the problems on which he had already given counsel. His exhortation to the Corinthians to 'live like men' and to 'be strong' was, says James Moffatt in his commentary, 'a summons for church-life to be robust, intelligent and loyal, with an edge on the mind and will—anything but sentimentality and easy going. The Corinthians had been tolerant when they should have been strict, and intolerant when they should have been manly enough to make allowances . . .' It might be salutary to apply these words to our own relationships.

Moffatt goes on to say that 'the very effort to uphold strong convictions, to enforce discipline or to carry out active service, is beset by the temptation to be overbearing and impatient.' It was necessary, therefore, for Paul to add to his exhortation for vigilance and strength, 'Let everything that you do be done in love.' This was the warning he had given throughout his letter, and particularly in chapter 13. But note—being strong and loving are part of the same healthy Christian attitude. Strength is required not only to hold firmly to convictions, but also to show consideration for others.

2 CORINTHIANS 1:1–7

'He gives us comfort in our trials so that we in turn may be able to give the same sort of strong sympathy to others in theirs' (v. 4, Phillips).

THE COMFORTERS. A paean of praise follows the customary salutation in this letter. In severe trials, Paul and his fellow-workers had experienced the strengthening comfort of God. The nature of these trials we shall consider later. Sufficient now to recognize that affliction which could be linked with 'Christ's cup of suffering' was no trivial discomfort.

God comforts His children, claims the apostle, not to make them comfortable, but to make them comforters. Finding resources in God's love with which to transcend suffering equips us to help other sufferers. Is anything more reassuring to a person in anguish than the simple words, 'I know', spoken with sympathy and understanding?

In his account of life in the Buchenwald concentration camp, Pierre d'Harcourt describes some of the 'moral giants' who literally saved the lives of hundreds of their fellow-prisoners simply by sustaining their will to live. There was M., effeminate in appearance, grotesque in manner, but a genius in caring 'more for the most wretched and degraded sick human beings than for himself'. M., a Roman Catholic, became one of the legends of Buchenwald. There was Richard who, 'as though by some miraculous gift of telepathy', knew when a prisoner was touching the depths and would 'start whispering some ridiculous story which even at that stage would make one smile'. Invariably those men had a religious faith or were devoted to a cause greater than themselves. The strength they derived from this made them towers of strength to others.

2 CORINTHIANS 1:8–11

'We believe now that we had this experience of coming to the end of our tether that we might learn to trust, not in ourselves, but in God who can raise the dead' (v. 9, Phillips).

CREATIVE DESPAIR. What was the distress Paul suffered 'in Asia' which appeared to him a veritable 'sentence of death'? The Corinthian church evidently knew about this experience, though not of its full extent, and this is why we are left somewhat in the dark. A serious illness, mob violence, deep anguish at the estrangement between the Corinthians and himself: all these are possible. Whatever the trouble, it led the apostle through the dark night of despair to the dawn of simple trust in God.

We can often step out of despair if we recognize its positive implications. For instance, despair is sometimes the 'No through road' sign erected upon a false path we are treading, an indication that a totally new approach to our problem needs to be made, perhaps with another person's help. Antony Bloom has reminded us that 'despair is conducive to a new spiritual life when we have the courage to go deeper and farther, realizing that what we are despairing about is not the final victory but the means we have employed to reach it'.

Despair can be creative, as Paul discovered, when it leads us to seek a more reliable ground of confidence. So David Gascoyne wrote of 'kissing the hand' that had consigned him to—

where I must learn
The revelation of despair, and find
Among the debris of all certainties
The hardest stone on which to found
Altar and shelter for Eternity.

2 CORINTHIANS 1:12–14

'There are no hidden meanings in our letters besides what you can read for yourselves and understand' (v. 13, Jerusalem Bible).

RESPECT FOR WORDS. Reading this letter we shall find increasing evidence that Paul had some highly vocal opponents at Corinth. Against their charges, he here defends his own sincerity and straightforwardness. The Greek word for sincerity meant 'examined by the light of the sun' and found pure. Paul related this particularly to his use of words. His letters (and, we may infer, his speech) meant what they said—no more, no less.

George Eliot warned us to 'watch your own speech, and notice how it is guided by your less conscious purposes'. Our integrity may be the victim of our speech. Robert Adolfs, a Dutch Catholic theologian, reminds us that Plato charged some of his contemporaries with 'corruption of the word', using words no longer to communicate truth. 'This resulted in the other person ceasing to be a real partner in dialogue and becoming merely an object—human material—to be used by the speaker.'

In the modern world Boris Pasternak, Russian author and poet, was an example of one prepared to pay dearly for his respect for words. Edward Crankshaw has remarked that 'while others were fighting with more or less integrity the battle for survival, the battle to be heard and yet to preserve a remnant of their private vision (as though vision were divisible), Pasternak was fighting the battle for truth. When he could speak the truth as he saw it, he spoke; when it was physically impossible for him to speak the truth he was silent'.

2 CORINTHIANS 1:15–22

'He is the Yes pronounced upon God's promises, every one of them' (v. 20, N.E.B.).

NO AMBIGUITY HERE. In a modern parable composed by the Oxford philosopher, Basil Mitchell, a member of the Resistance in an enemy-occupied country meets a Stranger who deeply impresses him. The Stranger reveals to the partisan that he himself is in charge of the Resistance and urges him to trust him no matter what happens.

Later, the partisan sees the Stranger sometimes helping members of the Resistance, but at other times apparently working against them. The partisan sends appeals for help to the Stranger. Some of these are answered; others apparently ignored. The partisan's friends refuse to believe in the Stranger: 'If that's what you mean by his being on our side, the sooner he goes over to the other side the better.' On the basis of his encounter with the Stranger, however, the partisan refuses to lose faith in him, though that faith is sometimes severely tested.

The parable illustrates the way in which the Christian holds together the certainty of believing and the ambiguities of living. Life is full of contradictions and to some of man's deepest questions replies simultaneously 'Yes' and 'No'. But, says Paul, in one of his glorious asides, even if you think me fickle and changeable, there is no 'ambiguous blend of Yes and No' in Christ. He is God's resounding 'Yes', and on that fact our faith is based.

2 CORINTHIANS 1:23–2:11

'I wanted you rather to know the love, the more than ordinary love, that I have for you' (v. 4, N.E.B.).

What clearly prompted Paul's stern rebuke of the believers at Corinth was his love for them.

In one of his books the Methodist Donald Soper pays tribute to 'my severest critic and the saintliest man I ever knew, my father'. Most of us rarely associate our critics with sanctity. We tend to explain their words in terms of personal animosity, resentment, or little-mindedness. And possibly we are sometimes right. For most speakers of severe words are usually, if unconsciously, more concerned about themselves than the person or persons under review. Paul's rebuke of his friends, however, was obviously motivated by his genuine concern for their welfare. He did not wish to assert himself, or to domineer them. His one aim, as he said, was to add to their joy. And this explains why he spoke out.

Paul's concern for the churches under his care cost him dearly. He agonized over his spiritual children. Caring is costly, sometimes in time, sometimes in money, often in nervous energy. When the Anglican priest, Raymond Raynes, was working in South Africa, his colleagues were frequently disappointed because young people they tried to help let them down. Raymond would say, 'It doesn't matter if your heart is broken, you must never give up and never stop minding.'

2 CORINTHIANS 2:12–17

'Wherever I go, thank God, He makes my life a constant pageant of triumph in Christ' (v. 14, Moffat).

SURRENDERING TO CONQUER. Still recording his recent movements and distress, Paul describes his unhappiness in having to proceed to Macedonia without Titus (who had taken his 'severe letter' to Corinth) and so without news of the situation there. Suddenly he burst into an exclamation of triumph. Despite all the heartache and anguish his journey could still be compared to the victory procession of some Roman general returning from war.

Paul's distress of spirit did not diminish the victory—nor did his conception of spiritual victory exclude the possibility of deep anguish. Strength in weakness and triumph in tribulation were favourite themes with Paul. Contrast Moffatt's translation (above) with that of Ronald Knox: 'I give thanks to God, that He is always exhibiting us as the captives in the triumph of Christ Jesus.' Paul's place in the victory procession was here a very humble one. He was a notable prisoner displayed by a conquering general as proof of his triumphs.

More than a translator's difference of emphasis can be seen here. Spiritual victory follows surrender: those conquered by Christ become invincible.

2 CORINTHIANS 3:1–6

'It is plain that you are a letter from Christ, drawn up by us, and written not with ink but with the Spirit of the living God' (v. 3, Jerusalem Bible).

THE PLUS OF THE SPIRIT. Having refuted the charge of fickleness, and shared with his readers his recent trials, Paul sought to counter any suggestion of mere self-justification. He did not need to write for himself a testimonial letter such as travelling teachers sometimes carried (Acts 18:27). The Corinthians themselves constituted such a letter, since it was through Paul they had received the life-transforming gospel.

The image of the Corinthians as 'living letters', written by Paul and his fellow workers 'with the Spirit of the living God', is a deliberate contrast with the ten commandments, engraved upon stone. The careful reader may well be startled, if not shocked, by the idea of men writing 'with the Spirit of the living God'. Is not this an irreverent reversal of roles?

Of course it is true that God's Spirit uses men for His purposes: we cannot use Him for ours. The truth enshrined in Paul's vivid image is that man is more than a passive instrument in God's hand. There is a place in the Christian life for waiting upon God, for opening our hearts to the Spirit's coming. There must also be times when we act—perhaps conscious only of great weakness—yet confident that the Spirit is working with us. It is well to ponder the saying of Charles Davis that 'we should always see the Spirit as enhancing, not replacing, our activity as men'.

2 CORINTHIANS 3:7–11

'If there is a splendour in the proclamation of our guilt, there must be more splendour yet in the proclamation of our acquittal' (v. 9, Knox).

GREATER GLORY. Paul's contrast between 'living epistles' and the stone tablets of the ten commandments leads him into one of his many exciting digressions. The giving of the ancient law was accompanied by great glory: how much greater, he argues, is the splendour surrounding the proclamation of God's free grace.

Remembering that it was Pharisees and lawyers who were Christ's bitterest enemies, and recognizing the blighting effect of guilt in many lives, we may question how there was any splendour 'in the proclamation of our guilt'. Yet the giving of the law was a necessary stage in the moral education of mankind. That man is responsible before God is part of his glory.

'Two things fill the mind with ever new and increasing wonder and awe,' claimed Immanuel Kant: 'the starry heavens above me and the moral law within me.' It is those last two words—within me—the Christian would emphasize. The gospel completely reverses the relationship between the law and fellowship with God. Under the law men struggled to become righteous so as to earn God's love. The gospel calls guilty sinners into fellowship with

God; what was unattainable by effort of will then becomes a free response to love.

2 CORINTHIANS 3:12–18

'And we, with our unveiled faces reflecting like mirrors the brightness of the Lord, all grow brighter and brighter as we are turned into the image that we reflect' (v. 18, Jerusalem Bible).

A NEW WAY. Transforming human character is the aim of all the great religions and there are few individuals who have not made their own attempts in this direction. Yet how hopeless the task often seems. 'It is quite idle, by force of will, to seek to empty the angry passions out of our life,' urged Henry Drummond. 'Who has not made a thousand resolutions in this direction, only and with unutterable mortification to behold them dashed to pieces with the first temptation?'

Law may modify conduct (sometimes at great cost in terms of inner strain): it can never change character. A character in Boris Pasternak's *Doctor Zhivago* says, 'I think that if the beast who sleeps in man could be held down by threats—any kind of threat, whether of jail or of retribution after death—then the highest emblem of humanity would be the lion tamer in the circus with his whip, not the self-sacrificing preacher.'

Raymond Nelson pertinently observed that 'change of conduct means that you stop doing certain things—you try harder, you compare yourself with others, you become self-conscious; but there is conflict unless and until there is a change of character. That is something you have to accept from God as a gift.'

Paul, who knew all about broken resolutions, found elsewhere the secret of inner transformation. Commitment to, and communion with, Christ accomplished what all his struggles had failed to achieve.

2 CORINTHIANS 4:1–6

'For the same God who said, "Out of darkness let light shine", has caused His light to shine within us, to give the light of revelation—the revelation of the glory of God in the face of Jesus Christ' (v. 6, N.E.B.).

THE CREATIVE COMMAND. To Paul, life in Christ was nothing less than a new creation, as mysterious and astonishing as

God's creative act which brought into being the universe itself. The illumination of the human heart by the light of God's grace was like that first dispersal of darkness by the divine command, 'Let there be light' (Genesis 1:3).

Influenced by Greek philosophy, Christian teachers have stressed the idea that God created the world *ex nihilo*—out of nothing. Commenting on the creation story, the Old Testament scholar Gerhard von Rad has added that it 'moves not so much between the poles of nothingness and creation as between the poles of chaos and cosmos'. Is this not also how the Spirit of God works upon human personality, ordering and harmonizing the primeval material of instinctive drives? Sanctification is not a process of subtraction but of integration.

The light which by divine grace shines in our hearts reveals 'the glory of God in the face of Jesus Christ'. This sublime phrase focuses all the rich majesty of our Christian faith. Since God revealed Himself in a Man the mystery of existence has been illuminated, and the commonplace made holy.

2 CORINTHIANS 4:7–15

'We have this treasure in fragile earthen pots, in order that the surpassing greatness of the power may be seen to be God's and not to come from us' (v. 7, Weymouth).

HOLD ON TO THIS PARADOX. Few writings emphasize as clearly as this letter the strange paradox in the life of the believer, 'the paradox of comfort from suffering, of life from death, of strength from weakness, of wisdom from foolishness'. Paul's eloquent description of the glory of the Christian gospel is instantly followed by this insistence upon the human fragility of the messengers.

Paul's own experience may have been foremost in his mind at this point. His enemies had poured scorn upon his personal appearance (10:1, 10) and his lack of oratory (10:10; 11:6), and he appears to have suffered a recurring physical disability (12:7). A second-century work described the apostle as: 'A man of little stature, thin-haired upon the head, crooked in the legs, of good state of body, with eyebrows joining, and nose somewhat hooked, full of grace.' Paul is also following the Old Testament tradition which never allows us to forget our earthy origin. Long before the theory of evolution was proposed Bible writers saw man as sharing physically a common origin with the brutes in 'the dust of the ground' (Genesis 2:7, 19; Job 34:15).

If we let slip this paradox—God's power manifested in our weakness—all kinds of misunderstandings arise. We expect our faith to exempt us from suffering; we fall prey to grandiose illusions of our own perfection, we forget the bond we share with our fellows. 'Priceless treasure in an earthen vessel'—both are true for the believer, not one without the other.

2 CORINTHIANS 4:16–5:5

'Once this earthly tent-dwelling of ours has come to an end, God, we are sure, has a solid building waiting for us . . . that will last eternally in heaven' (5:1, Knox).

PRESENT EXPERIENCE AND FUTURE HOPE. E. L. Mascall records the story of an army recruit who, when asked for his religion, replied that he was a Methuselahite. To the further inquiry as to the tenets of his sect he replied, 'We believe in living as long as possible.' This resolve, together with an obstinate refusal even to think of death, sums up the philosophy of many people today. This life is real; any other is too questionable to consider.

By contrast Paul views this life as transitory, like dwelling in a tent, and the future life God has prepared as permanent, like living in a solid house. This is because the apostle sees death as the climax of a process in which 'the outer man does indeed suffer wear and tear' (v. 16, J. B. Phillips). James Denney has well said that 'the decay of the outward man in the godless is a melancholy spectacle, for it is the decay of everything; but in the Christian it does not touch the life that is hid with Christ in God.'

Shortly before his mother died Augustine had a memorable conversation in which they spoke of that life which 'never comes to be but is . . . because it is neither past nor future but present only, for it is eternal'. Then, he records, 'As we talked and yearned after it, we touched it for an instant with the whole force of our hearts.' It is this experience of the eternal in the present which assures the Christian that the present is not the sum of all his hopes.

2 CORINTHIANS 5:6–10

'All of us have a scrutiny to undergo before Christ's judgment-seat' (v. 10, Knox).

AN AFFIRMATION AND A CALL. The judgment-seat of Christ: what terror this phrase has sometimes held. Charlotte

Brontë, for instance was sent as a child of eight to a school run by a Mr. Wilson, whose books for young people were 'full of whippings and death-beds, and the wrath of God suddenly and justly visited on children', whose God was a 'swift admonisher and punisher' and who therefore felt he 'had a moral excuse for every stringency and discipline'.

How may 'the judgment-seat of Christ' be set firmly in the context of God's love? Geoffrey Ainger, a Methodist minister, gives us a clue. During the Adolf Eichmann trial, when this mass murderer of thousands of Jews sat impassively through recitals which deeply moved veteran reporters, Ainger found himself picturing a quite different scene. 'The impassive Eichmann now sat on the bench and filled the public galleries. In the dock was a man pleading to be found guilty of his crime, insisting upon being held responsible for what he had done. But in vain. It was not his fault; it was his parents, his glands, his environment, or his undesirable associates. He is treated entirely as a patient; no longer as a man.'

New Testament pictures of judgment affirm and dignify our humanity. The judgment-seat of Christ is not 'a shadow cast on the Christian hope'; it is a symbol of God's loving call to responsible living.

2 CORINTHIANS 5:11–17

'His purpose in dying for all was that men, while still in life, should cease to live for themselves' (v. 15, N.E.B.).

NEW MOTIVATION. The above comment suggested that 'the judgment-seat of Christ' be seen as a loving call to responsible living. In Paul's mind it was not the inhibiting and terrifying image it later became. 'I am controlled by the love of Christ,' he goes on to claim (v. 14, Moffatt). He was love-impelled, not fear-driven.

This was because the Cross of Jesus was at the very heart of the apostle's faith, totally transforming his morality and his relationships. In place of the anguished and hopeless struggle to observe a written code there was now a loving response to One who knew every hidden recess of his personality and yet counted him worth dying for.

This genuinely 'new outlook' revolutionized Paul's attitude to his fellows. 'I estimate no man by what is external,' he writes (v.

16, Moffatt). When men adopt a 'do-it-yourself' morality they cannot help placing others upon a scale of comparative success and failure. Censoriousness always accompanies legalism. The morality whose starting point is, 'I am loved despite my sin', must recognize that others are similarly loved.

As H. H. Farmer has written: 'In the presence of the Cross all men are reduced to a level. A piercing X-ray strikes down from the Cross through all the external wrappings, all those surface qualities to which our feelings so quickly respond, and lays bare the one essential thing—namely, that this man, any man, every man, is just a poor sinner needing desperately, and being offered, the forgiving love of God'.

2 CORINTHIANS 5: 18–21

'He has reconciled us men to Himself through Christ, and He has enlisted us in this service of reconciliation. (v. 18, N.E.B.).

LOVE WITH AN INITIATIVE. The assertion 'God is love' would be empty and meaningless if it denoted merely a passive attitude. Christians believe God's love is constantly active in history and was particularly manifested in Jesus Christ. The Cross allows us to glimpse the costliness of God's reconciling action.

Paul sees himself as an ambassador of Christ, calling men to respond to God's initiative. It is an apt title. An ambassador communicates only the message he receives, not his own opinions: yet he is a man invested with great authority. He needs humility, yet may possess a legitimate pride.

Having been reconciled to God in Christ we become agents of reconciliation. Albert van den Heuvel tells the story of a young pastor in East Germany who was sent to a town where the local communists were very anti-church. He and his wife were subjected to many irritations and annoyances. After some time the local party boss displeased the authorities and was sent away as secretary to a co-operative farm near the Polish border. On holiday in that area, the young pastor looked up his former enemy and went fishing with him for a few days, 'I have enough friends,' he said. 'He hasn't.' The communist remained a communist, and the pastor a Christian. Their relationship, however, was cleansed of all bitterness and misunderstanding. Reconciliation of ideas is not always possible: reconciliation of persons usually is.

2 CORINTHIANS 6:1–13

'We have "nothing to bless ourselves with" yet we bless many others with true riches. We are penniless, and yet in reality we have everything worth having' (v. 10, Phillips).

STOICISM PLUS. Here once again Paul eloquently describes his paradoxical experience of humiliation and glory, an experience all believers share in varying degrees. The trials of his apostleship are enumerated in three groups of three: the first containing trials of a general nature; the second, those inflicted upon him by other men; and the last, hardships the apostle willingly took upon himself for the cause of the gospel. Far from just accepting humiliation with stoic endurance, the apostle saw each trial linked to an enrichment for himself or others. No wonder Simone Weil urged that Christianity's great strength lay in the fact that it did not claim to cure suffering, but it did profess to use it!

It is in this spirit that Paul Hunt, a sufferer from muscular dystrophy, sees his disability. 'If those of us who are disabled live as fully as we can, while being completely conscious of the tragedy of our situation . . . then somehow we can communicate to others an awareness that the value of the human person transcends his social status, attributes and possessions or his lack of them . . . Perhaps we can help prepare others for the almost certain day when they themselves lose, at least in old age, some of the advantages that are so highly valued . . . Those who implicitly believe that a man's worth depends on his good fortune must be building their lives on rather inadequate foundations, and they will perhaps find contact with us a thought-provoking experience.'

This reading concludes with the Apostle asking believers in Corinth to be as frank and open with him as he has been with them. The next comment deals with the reason for the break at this point.

2 CORINTHIANS 6:14–7:1

'Stop trying to run in double harness with unbelievers' (v. 14, Barclay).

IN THE WORLD BUT NOT OF THE WORLD. The introductory notes at the commencement of the first epistle explain briefly the occasion of this passage.

Paul was not urging believers to dissociate themselves from human society (1 Cor. 5:10). This we cannot do. The web of life is spun so closely that we cannot withdraw without hurt to ourselves and without harm to others as well. We are indebted to the dustman, the milkman, the postman, the man next to us on the factory floor, all of whom we see daily, not to mention the multitude whom we do not see—and possibly never shall—but by whose labours we live.

Nevertheless, with Christian compassion we must maintain inviolate our Christian standards. This does not require us to spurn men. Jesus made friends with publicans and sinners, and would doubtless have been equally friendly with the scribes and Pharisees—had they been willing to become His friends. But He never condoned the all too free and easy ways of the one, nor the censorious self-righteousness of the other.

Holiness of heart and life is not born in isolation—whether a physical isolation or an isolation of the spirit. Salt must be mixed with the food it is intended to preserve if corruption is to be prevented. Yet the salt must retain its own inherent savour in order to do its purifying work. This is the twofold Christian task to which believers are called.

2 CORINTHIANS 7:2–11

'The pain God is allowed to guide ends in a saving repentance never to be regretted, whereas the world's pain ends in death' (v. 10, Moffatt).

HOW THE RAREST OF ALL VIRTUES GROWS. Recall for a moment the circumstances behind this letter! Paul's brief visit to deal with a difficult situation at Corinth had made matters worse and resulted in his writing a severe letter from Macedonia. Having dispatched it with Titus, he had so worried about its reception and been impatient for an answer that he had journeyed to meet the returning Titus, ignoring the evangelical opportunity at Troas. The news had been good, far better than the Apostle had dared to hope; these verses indicate something of his joy and relief. He subsequently explained that the sternness of his rebuke had been the measure of his love.

Unless criticism is given and received in a spirit of mutual caring and respect, it is better left unsaid. 'Every leader of God's people', said General Albert Orsborn, 'has to learn how to administer rebuke properly. He has, indeed, often to be a living rebuke. Yet this duty is often mishandled. Some are too careless, praise-loving, gain-seeking, or fearful to rebuke wrongdoers.' In other words, criticism without love encourages resentment, inferiority, self-justification, and hatred. But even unloving and unjustified criticism, if received in the right spirit, can develop the rarest of all the virtues—humility.

2 CORINTHIANS 7:12–16

'My letter was written to you ... in order to let you realize before God how seriously you do care for me' (v. 12, Moffatt).

TOO INHIBITED? What masters some of us become in the art of masking our deeper emotions! Englishmen particularly are notorious for the 'stiff upper lip' approach to life. It is time we recognized this as emotional impoverishment, not commendable self-discipline.

Paul was glad he wrote severely to the Corinthian church because the subsequent crisis brought to the surface the believers' deeper feelings for the apostle. Until then they had not realized how much they cared for this man who founded their church. Shall we try today to be more generous in our expressions of affection, gratitude and appreciation?

Describing his early training as a biologist Karl von Frisch writes, 'Thinking back on those years I am filled with a bitter sense of self-reproach. My father showed the keenest interest in my early efforts at independent research of which he was unashamedly proud. I could not have given him greater pleasure than by letting him share the thoughts that occupied my mind from morning to night, the plan worked out in the evening for the experiments of the following day, the daily triumphs and setbacks—all the excitement and turmoil of my early development. Unfortunately, his eager interest made me feel embarrassed and inhibited, and I always remained reserved and silent in his presence.'

Certainly there is material here for the fruitless regrets we considered above. All of us have missed countless opportunities to express love. Let us rather dismiss our regrets and repent.

2 CORINTHIANS 8:1–9

'Do you remember the generosity of Jesus Christ, the Lord of us all? He was rich beyond our telling, yet He became poor for your sakes so that His poverty might make you rich' (v. 8, Phillips).

THE THEOLOGY OF GIVING. In Jean-Paul Sartre's play *The Flies* Orestes asserts his complete independence of Zeus who created him. 'I, O Zeus, am a man,' he cries, 'and every man must find his own way . . . What have I to do with you or you with me? We shall glide past each other, like ships in a river, without touching . . . Each of us is alone, and our anguish is akin.'

This practical atheism is unthinkable to the Christian because of the Incarnation. God and man do not 'glide past each other' without touching. They meet, in Jesus Christ. The initiative in this meeting is taken by God; the cost is borne by God. Man does not grope his way to the divine; God comes to meet him in the midst of his life. In different ages the wonder of this divine-human encounter is variously expressed: Jesus 'came down' from heaven, He 'emptied Himself' of His divine attributes. All attempts to explain this mystery witness that God's revelation in Christ was at immense cost to Himself and of untold blessing to man.

Surprisingly, this most profound Christian doctrine is linked by Paul with the mundane business of making a collection. Yet is it so surprising? R. V. G. Tasker has commented: 'No one can love to order, and no one can show liberality, which is an expression or love, to order'. Giving which is not a wholehearted response to love degenerates all too easily into 'cold charity'.

2 CORINTHIANS 8:10–15

'Readiness of the will must be completed by deeds, as far as your means allow' (v. 11, Knox).

THE DISTANCE BETWEEN. Writing about his work, the artist Francis Hoyland says, 'I find the best thing to do when my mind refuses to work or, worse still, works in the wrong way (irrelevant thoughts destroying one's concentration) is to make some sort of a mark as soon as possible. It is better to let the act of painting drive the unwanted thoughts out than to wait before one starts to work until one's mind is clear—one could wait for ever!'

This distance between intention and action, between will and deed, is a problem we all have to face. A year before Paul sent this letter, the Corinthians had begun a collection for impoverished Christians at Jerusalem and the apostle placed great importance upon this expression of unity. Much had happened at Corinth, however, to delay the completion of the collection. Now the church was reconciled to the apostle, Paul urges his readers to fulfil their original plan.

How easy it is to leave some worthy project in the realm of intention, failing to carry it through into action. Every delay makes it more likely that the letter will never be written, the reconciliation never achieved, the encouragement never given. The distance between impulse and action lengthens the longer we wait. This kind of failure sometimes requires close self-examination: unconscious resistance may be paralysing our will. At other times we need to take ourselves by the scruff of the neck and, like the artist—get started!

2 CORINTHIANS 8:16–24

'We want to guard against any criticism of our handling of this generous gift; for our aims are entirely honourable, not only in the Lord's eyes, but also in the eyes of men' (vv. 20–21, N.E.B.).

DOWN-TO-EARTH SANCTITY. Knowing that his enemies would be only too ready to accuse him of mis-appropriating church funds, Paul arranged that Titus should be accompanied by two unnamed men—one of them traditionally identified as Luke—when he journeyed to Corinth to arrange for the handing over of the collection for the Christians at Jerusalem. Paul's concern was to live above suspicion, and to this end he made careful plans for the handling of money not his own.

What stands out is this great Christian leader's capacity for practical detail. He was a mystic and an outstanding theologian, yet his painstaking attention to the demands of routine administration belie the charge that heavenly minded people are of no earthly use. Far too many believers have made their preoccupation with the 'spiritual' an excuse for their neglect of the 'material'. They have dreamed of the New Jerusalem and ignored their mundane responsibilities near at hand, thinking of them as either unworthy diversions or time-wasting chores, other people's time, of course!

Their imagined spirituality has been matched only by their zeal to escape the irksomeness of ordinary affairs in daily life. The corrective is seen in Paul's example of down-to-earth sanctity and practical goodness, qualities without which religion becomes an exercise in pious self-indulgence. True saints always make life easier for the harassed and overworked.

2 CORINTHIANS 9:1–6

'Do not forget: thin sowing means thin reaping; the more you sow, the more you reap' (v. 6, Jerusalem Bible).

UNFORCED GENEROSITY. Encouraging the Corinthians to give generously to the collection for Jewish Christians, Paul reminds them of how eagerly they first embraced the project. He had even boasted of their enthusiasm to other churches. Nor should they now imagine their first response was misplaced zeal. Echoing sentiments in the book of Proverbs the apostle assures his readers that generosity is never unrewarded: 'One gives away, and still he grows the richer: another keeps what he should give, and is the poorer. A liberal soul will be enriched, and he who waters will himself be watered' (Proverbs 11:24, 25, Moffatt).

Generosity comes naturally when we are keenly aware of God's boundless mercy and faithful provision. Jack Stoker, early-day Salvation Army officer, had been lifted from the depths of despair by God's grace. His generosity was prodigal. Coming home from an early morning meeting one day, he saw a man in rags. Taking off his jacket he handed it to the tramp, 'Take this, old chap, it will help to keep you warm.' Jack arrived home in shirt sleeves to ask his wife, 'Where's that old tunic of mine? I think I'll wear that today.' 'You told me to give it to a poor man yesterday,' she replied.

As Michel Quoist has written: 'When you stop giving you stop loving. When you stop loving, you stop growing, and unless you grow you will never attain personal fulfilment, you will never open out to receive the life of God.'

2 CORINTHIANS 9:7–15

'Thanks be to God for His unutterable bounty to us' (v. 15, Knox).

ALL HIS GRACE. Money may be far too mundane to have spiritual significance to the sentimentally pious, but Paul viewed it differently. In this passage (explains R. P. C. Hanson) he deliberately uses 'the language of ministration at a religious sacrifice (pagan as well as Jewish) in connection with this charitable work of the collection'. The giving of the Corinthians was to be 'an overflowing tide of thanksgiving to God' (v. 12, Phillips). So firmly does the apostle set this collection in a spiritual context that he is led finally to declare its indissoluble link with the divine self-giving.

What did the apostle mean by God's 'unspeakable gift'? Commentators are divided, some seeing this as the grace of God referred to in the previous verse, others as God's gift of His Son. Perhaps their very uncertainty reminds us that a rigid distinction is unnecessary. In all His giving what God truly gives is Himself. No other giving is really worth while.

'It is all incarnation,' Norman Pittenger has asserted. 'In differing ways, in varying degrees of intensity, God is self-expressed. Something of Him is shown in living matter; still more in the movement of history towards righteousness, justice, beauty, and goodness. Above all, in the personalities of men and in their concrete historical situations, He is at work.'

2 CORINTHIANS 10:1–6

'Human indeed we are, but it is in no human strength that we fight our battles. The weapons we fight with are not human weapons; they are divinely powerful, ready to pull down strongholds' (vv. 3–4, Knox).

HOW TO KEEP CALM IN AN ARGUMENT. Chapters 10 to 13 are so drastically different in tone from the previous nine chapters that many scholars are convinced that they are part of the severe letter to which Paul twice refers in other places (2 Corinthians 2:4; 7:8). Certainly the contrast is vivid and suggests that the two sections were written on entirely different occasions. The opening verses of chapter 10 indicate that Paul was answering a charge of cowardice. He was reputed to be the kind of individual who said nice things to people's faces and then went away to write them letters of abuse. He was further charged with having ulterior motives, an accusation with which he was by now familiar.

The Apostle's defence was given in a spirit of strong gentleness and meekness. The word for 'meekness' is translated by Knox as 'courtesy'; by Barclay as 'sweet reasonableness'; and by Phillips as 'sympathy'. If only all disagreements between Christians were characterized by such qualities! But this spirit of reconciliation did not make Paul soft or weak. He still forthrightly stated his point of view, but without losing his temper, or lamenting that he was not appreciated, or threatening to withdraw his service. The explanation was his complete freedom from personal considerations (his position, reputation, future), a freedom revealing his preoccupation with eternal realities.

2 CORINTHIANS 10:7–11

'You may think that I have boasted unduly of my authority (which the Lord gave me, remember, to build you up not to break you down), but I don't think I have done anything to be ashamed of' (v. 8, Phillips).

FREE ASSENT. In trying to reassert his authority over the rebellious members of the Corinthian church Paul reminds them that his authority is no mere denial of their freedom. It was given him by Christ to 'build them up'. Authority can be either the enemy of free development—in which case it is our Christian duty to expose its pretensions—or it can stimulate growth. How shall we distinguish good authority from bad?

Peter Fletcher, in his book *Emotional Conflict*, provides a useful illustration. He says, 'Your authority is the grip you maintain on the saddle to prevent the bicycle from going too fast or too far before the boy can control its speed and direction. Your discipline is the strength you use to restrict your pupil's freedom of action at a point where he is in danger of losing it; that is, when otherwise he would lose his balance and fall off. But your pupil does not fear your authority, or resent your discipline, because he knows, and he knows you know, that you impose restraints for the purpose of enabling him to do without them.'

Good authority, whether in home, church or society, aims at securing the free assent of others. While it relies upon compelling an unwilling obedience it falls short of its true purpose. Once indifferent to gaining that free assent it is no longer good authority.

2 CORINTHIANS 10:12–18

'All they are doing, of course, is to measure themselves by their own standards or by comparison within their own circle, and that doesn't make for accurate estimation, you may be sure' (v. 12, Phillips).

FOOLISH COMPARISONS. Accused of cowardice by his opponents, Paul replies by making ironic confession that one thing indeed he would not dare—he would not dare join the ranks of those who write their own testimonials, unsupported by evidence. The sheer folly of human comparisons was probably highlighted for Paul by memories of his pharisaic past. H. L. Goudge comments: 'The Pharisees . . . assumed that the divine standard of righteousness was the Mosaic law, as they had come to interpret it. Their spiritual pride was due to the fact that they judged themselves simply by this standard, no Pharisee comparing himself with anybody except other Pharisees'.

How easily we all fall into this trap of comparing ourselves with other people! The habit is both unrealistic and unhelpful. It is unrealistic because we all commence life very differently, some with tremendous handicaps, others with great advantages. Not only our starting points but our goals are in some senses different, for God has a unique purpose in each life. We wouldn't compare two runners participating in two different races which happened to be taking place in the same stadium. No more should we compare our own progress with that of others.

Human comparisons are unhelpful because they invariably lead either to complacency or despair, both of which block spiritual development. Our one helpful standard of comparison is Jesus Christ and then only if we recognize that we become Christlike, not by agonizing effort but by openness to His Spirit.

2 CORINTHIANS 11:1–10

'I am afraid that your thoughts may be corrupted and you may lose your single-hearted devotion to Christ' (v. 3, N.E.B.).

DANGEROUS COMPENSATION FOR SPIRITUAL DEFEAT. To his embarrassment, Paul found himself having to compare his credentials with those of the false teachers within the church at Corinth. These self-appointed 'super apostles' (as Paul called them) were trying to discredit his teaching by smearing his character and ridiculing his ability. The Apostle, though readily agreeing that he was an unpolished speaker, an evidence surely of his humility rather than the truth, insisted that he did nevertheless know what he was talking about.

Paul recognized the danger of lukewarm believers, irritated by the demands of single-hearted devotion to Christ, seeking compensation for their spiritual dissatisfaction by indulging in exciting heresies. This explains why religious sects so often attract the disgruntled members of other churches. Yet self-evidently the answer to such a serious soul condition is not the acceptance of ideas contrary to the mind of Christ, ideas that impress by their promise of 'cheap grace' and spiritual ecstasy. They are as futile as the outlook of some defeated Christians who imagine that the hell of their inner chaos can be made heavenly by the simple expedient of a holiday, a change of circumstances, or a change in somebody's else's attitude, even God's!

Paul, however, knew that 'single-hearted devotion to Christ' defeated every ungodly influence, heresy included. As Archbishop Temple wisely observed: 'To the Church heresy is more destructive than conscious sin; to the individual conscious sin is more destructive than heresy; to both, idolatry—worship of God falsely conceived—is deadlier than either heresy or sin, for it is the prolific source of each.'

2 CORINTHIANS 11:11–15

'Satan himself masquerades as an angel of light' (v. 14, N.E.B.).

STRIP THE MASK. Paul's opponents at Corinth were neither unbelievers nor immoral. That he roundly accuses them of 'doing the devil's work', may seem all the more surprising. The most likely explanation for their conduct is that they had allowed partisan feelings and personal vanity to possess them. They no longer recognized their own true motives. Self-interest and lust for power hid beneath a religious cloak.

Paul's comment that 'Satan himself masquerades as an angel of light' is highly significant in this context. It is unrecognized evil which holds the greatest threat. The result of not 'seeing through' the disguises assumed by our own ulterior motives may well be that we become agents of evil while still thinking we serve the good. For instance, the personal counsellor with unrecognized problems will invariably project these on to the people coming to him for help, so increasing their confusion. The preacher with unrecognized guilt will verbally lash his congregation, inducing unhealthy reactions in young and sensitive people. The social service worker with an unrecognized need to feel superior will unconsciously seek to maintain others in a state of dependence.

It follows from this that only a growing self-awareness can enable us to penetrate the deceptive guises which evil assumes. Strangely enough, once our own mixed motivation is recognized it rarely becomes an instrument of evil, which frequently depends upon deception for its success. No wonder Jesus called the devil 'the father of lies' (John 8:44 N.E.B.)!

2 CORINTHIANS 11:16–27

'More overworked than they, scourged more severely, more often imprisoned, many a time face to face with death' (v. 23, N.E.B.).

THIS BOASTING BUSINESS. Paul had already claimed human comparisons were foolish. Yet we are grateful the apostle begged to be 'in on this business of boasting' (v. 17, Phillips), for the list of his trials proves how incomplete is the record of his life in the Book of Acts. Five floggings from the Jews, two beatings with rods, and three shipwrecks, all occurring before his last visit to Jerusalem, are known to us only from this passage.

We need not take the apostle's ironic references to his 'foolishness' too literally. Much more than personal vindication was at stake here. Paul's opponents were tyrants as well as braggarts (v. 20) and he meant to rescue his converts from their clutches at all cost. His boast, we note, was of his sufferings for Christ.

It is a challenging exercise to allow the apostle's catalogue of trials to remind us of all who suffer for their faith. In 1952 Mgr. Kiung, Catholic bishop of Shanghai, addressed these words to a group of his clergy: 'Fathers, you must no longer entertain any illusory hopes . . . You are condemned. There is no emergency exit for you. Once and for all, you must now look prison and death in the face . . . You have nothing to lose any more. If we deny our faith, we shall disappear, and there will be no resurrection. If we remain faithful, we shall disappear just the same—but there will be a resurrection.'

Is this how we view suffering for Christ?

2 CORINTHIANS 11:28–33

'Who is weak, and I do not feel his weakness? Whose faith is hurt, and I am not aglow with indignation?' (v. 29, Moffatt).

CARING THAT COUNTS. The amazing record of Paul's afflictions culminates in the suffering of his fatherly concern for his converts. Who can say which cost him most: the physical trials of persecution or the spiritual anguish of caring? Certainly no service is redemptive which refuses the price of costly identification.

When the Italian Robert de Nobili went to India as a member of the Portuguese mission in 1605 he found a Christian community living outside the city of Madara. He soon realized this mission was merely an outpost of Portugal, the Indian converts being encouraged to abandon their own culture to become imitation Portuguese Christians. To the horror of his fellow missionaries he left the mission station, dressed as a Brahmin, and became the first European to master the Tamil and Sanscrit languages and the sacred literature of Hinduism. Eventually many learned Brahmins joined him to form a truly Indian Church.

Almost three centuries later, the first Salvationist missionaries on that continent followed their own path of costly identification, renouncing the privileged position of white missionaries and begging their food like Indian holy men.

To what kind of sacrifice does caring lead us? A secular environment may compel us to lay aside dearly-loved expressions of our faith in order to convey the heart of the gospel in a way men understand. We may have to act when we would rather speak, or wrestle to find a new terminology when a 'take-it-or-leave-it' approach is less demanding.

2 CORINTHIANS 12:1–10

'My grace is enough for you: My power is at its best in weakness' (v. 9, Jerusalem Bible).

ALL YOU NEED. George Matheson, the blind poet-preacher of Scotland, once prayed, 'My God, I have never thanked Thee for my thorn. I have thanked Thee a thousand times for my roses, but not once for my thorn. Teach me the glory of my cross: teach me the value of my thorn.'

Just what Paul's 'thorn (or stake) in the flesh' was has been endlessly debated. A recurring physical malady is the most obvious interpretation, and from the apostle's claim that the Galatians would have taken out their own eyes and given them to him it has been assumed that Paul's 'thorn' was some distressing eye complaint (Galatians 4:13–15). Other commentators read the word 'flesh' in its peculiarly Pauline sense as the lower nature which continues to trouble the believer. Chrysostom urged that there were times when God kept the apostle humble by the failure of his preaching.

The value of this passage is in no way lessened by our ignorance of Paul's affliction. Rather the reverse; for innumerable believers, in diverse trials, have appropriated the words of Christ to their own situation, 'My grace is all you need; power comes to its full strength in weakness' (v. 9, N.E.B.). The grammar of the original Greek suggests that this answer of the risen Lord, who Himself had prayed three times to be spared the humiliation of the Cross, was not simply something past, but a recurring assurance 'which continued in its consoling power'.

2 CORINTHIANS 12:11–18

'You had all the miracles that mark an apostle done for you fully and patiently—miracles, wonders, and deeds of power' (v. 12, Moffatt).

PROOF OF SPIRITUAL AUTHORITY. In concluding his defence, which he found distasteful but necessary, Paul came to what was really the basis of his argument.

He said that his apostleship was proved by the effectiveness of his service. Now we must be careful that we give this claim its correct interpretation. Paul was not suggesting that fruitful service was infallibly indicated by, for instance, the number of converts recorded or the amount of money raised. He knew that what sometimes passed for the work of the Holy Spirit was really the result of crafty techniques or outstanding organizing ability.

But he was sure that God's work done in God's way, whatever the human assessment of its success or failure, was characterized by vitality and power. Unfortunately, some zealots think of spiritual effectiveness in only startling or spectacular terms, judging their own service, and particularly other people's, in ways sometimes at variance with the values of God's kingdom. Dr. W. A. Visser 'T Hooft provided a profound corrective when he observed: 'We must make sure that we do not decide to succeed. If we decide to succeed, then we may succeed without succeeding in God's way. But if we go on from day to day, seeking to do His will, then we shall be prepared to receive success from Him if He wills it: and if He does not, then humbly to say: it is God's decision that David shall not build the temple, but He will raise up Solomon.'

2 CORINTHIANS 12:19–21

'All this time you have been thinking that our defence is addressed to you, but it is before God that we, in Christ, are speaking . . .' (v. 19, Jerusalem Bible).

ALIENATION. In a play by N. Richard Nash, Starbuck, an unrealistic visionary, complains to Lizzie that the real world always falls short of his dreams, 'Nothing's as pretty in your hands as it was in your head.' Lizzie, however, assures him that he could learn to love the real world, and real people, if he saw them truly. She describes an exercise she sometimes undertakes looking at 'Pop' while she is washing the dishes. 'At first I'll see an ordinary middle-aged man—not very interesting to look at. And then, minute by minute, I'll see little things I never saw in him before. Good things and bad things—queer little habits I never noticed he had—and ways of talking I never paid any mind to. And suddenly I know who he is—and I love him so much I could cry! And I want to thank God I took the time to see him real.'

If we could take the time to see people 'real', most of our prejudice and dislike would dissolve. Antagonism breeds in isolation. Separated by distance from Paul, the Corinthians had slowly built up a picture of the apostle as a mediocre, crafty schemer. Through their distorted vision they no longer saw the spiritual giant, the valiant soldier of Christ. Misunderstandings had accumulated, wrong motives imputed, past happiness forgotten. How tragic but how human!

2 CORINTHIANS 13:1–4

'It is no weak Christ you have to do with, but a Christ of power . . . and though I am weak as He was weak, you will find that I am alive as He is alive by the power of God' (vv. 3–4, Moffatt).

THE STRENGTH OF CHRISTIAN 'WEAKNESS'. An old Christian of Alexandria was surrounded by people who ridiculed him for his faith. He was subjected to every humiliation, insulted and cursed, and physically maltreated. At length one of his tormentors asked him in mockery what miracles his beloved Christ whom he vaunted so much had performed. The old man replied: 'He wrought this miracle, that I should endure the injuries which you heap upon me without losing my tranquillity of mind, and should be ready to endure even greater injuries for love of Him, if you were to proceed to inflict them.'

Today's reading is a study in the terrifying strength of Christlike 'weakness'. Paul's leniency and patience were interpreted by his critics as timidity and cowardice. They thought of power as self-assertiveness, as the authority to control other people and to bully them if necessary into submission. But the only redemptive power in the world is suffering love, a truth which the Cross of Christ supremely reveals. And it was in this spirit that Paul sought to live. Such apparent weakness is foolishness to the world, and it always involves a cross, but it explains the essential nature of spiritual strength and why it is that, when we are weak, weak with the meekness of Christ, then only are we strong.

2 CORINTHIANS 13:5–10

'We can make no progress against the truth; we can only work for the truth' (v. 8, Phillips).

ULTIMATE REALITY. Paul's suggestion that the Corinthians should change the target of their criticism, and scrutinize their own lives instead of his, is valid for all avid fault-finders. To be hypercritical is always a sign that something is wrong—with us. The apostle is deeply concerned that his readers should discover the truth, even if that results in an unfavourable verdict on him. Lies and distortions provide no basis for spiritual progress. In any case, truth will out sooner or later. Resisting it is the ultimate futility.

In his autobiography, Bertrand Russell claimed that, although he subsequently spent many years unlearning the philosophical approach he was taught at Cambridge, there was one habit of lasting value he acquired there—intellectual honesty. 'I cannot remember any instance,' he writes, 'of a teacher resenting it when one of his pupils showed him to be in error, though I can remember quite a number of occasions on which pupils succeeded in performing this feat. Once during a lecture on hydrostatics, one of the young men interrupted to say: "Have you not forgotten the centrifugal forces on the lid?" The lecturer gasped, and then said: "I have been doing this example that way for twenty years, but you are right."'

2 CORINTHIANS 13:11–14

'Be perfect' (v. 11).

THE APOSTOLIC BENEDICTION. In his final challenge Paul calls to the Corinthian Christians to 'Be perfect', on which Samuel Chadwick commented:

'Christian perfection does not indicate finality, but fitness. To make perfect means to make fit, to put in order, adjust, arrange, and equip, so as to secure effectiveness and efficiency for the result to be achieved. The meaning is the same when applied to Christian life and experience. It is the adjustment, cleansing, and equipment of man's nature for all the purposes of the life in Christ.'

In taking leave of this Church, that had so rent his heart and disturbed his mind, the Apostle gave to the world the 'apostolic benediction'. All are saved by Jesus' grace; all have their part in God's love; all share in the gift of the Holy Spirit. How abundantly are our spiritual needs met in the triune God: Father, Son and Holy Ghost.

J. E. McFadyen observes: 'The benediction sweeps majestically from eternity to eternity. It contemplates the love of God rooted in the infinite past, realized in the historical Jesus, and perpetuating itself through all time by the Spirit.'

THE EPISTLE TO THE GALATIANS

INTRODUCTION

The discussion which still continues as to the precise date of this letter and to which group of churches it was specifically addressed, makes little—if any—difference to the revolutionary assertion of the Apostle Paul that the acceptance by faith of God's forgiving love is the only way of salvation.

Both here, and elsewhere in the New Testament, the apostolic message was that 'by grace ye are saved through faith'. Faith needed no addition. It was not a case of faith *and* circumcision, or grace *and* works. Spiritual life and liberty were found in Jesus alone.

But the Apostle had also to prevent the liberty wherewith the sons of God are set free from degenerating into licence (Gal. 5:13 ff.). The truth is that no way of life is more exacting than the way of love, for love never gives a man either freedom to injure his neighbour or to disobey the Lord of love.

GALATIANS 1:1–5

'Commissioned as Special Messenger not by man but by Jesus Christ and God the Father . . .' (v. 1, Phillips).

MAN WITH A MISSION. The opening sentences in Paul's letters usually yield valuable clues to what will follow. The basic salutation in correspondence at that time—A to B, greeting—was expanded by the apostle to include truths he intended to expound fully in the body of the letter. In this case Paul asserts, in no uncertain manner, his apostolic authority. He did this, not because he sought personal vindication, but in order to claim divine inspiration for his interpretation of the gospel. Both Paul's authority and his message were being called in question by his opponents in Galatia.

Paul claims to be 'an apostle'—that is, 'one who is sent'. He had been commissioned by Christ Himself and was therefore indifferent to human ordination. The title 'apostle' was usually reserved for the first disciples of Jesus and their immediate successors, but it also defined an important aspect of Christian discipleship.

Every Christian is an apostle. The first disciples were chosen by Jesus in order that 'they should be with Him, and that He might send them forth . . .' (Mark 3:14). Often we highly value the privilege of being with Christ—but forget our mission to the world. T. W. Manson described Israel's failure by saying that she thought of herself as a brand plucked from the burning, but her real mission was to be a torch to illuminate the world. Is our presence in 'the world' a witness and even a confirmation of the love of God? In this calling what we are will speak far more eloquently than what we say. Not only to His first-century disciples but to His twentieth century followers as well, the Master says: 'As the Father sent Me, so I send you' (John 20:21, N.E.B.).

GALATIANS 1:6–10

'They want to distort the gospel of Christ' (v. 7, Moffatt).

NO BURDENSOME DEMAND. Paul usually opened his letters with an expanded salutation, followed by a thanksgiving.

Even when he was later to rebuke his readers he began by praising them. His letter to the Galatians is the exception to this rule. In place of praise we have a passionate outburst which is the measure of the apostle's deep anxiety. He saw that the very truth of the gospel was at stake in the churches of Galatia. Paul's opponents were claiming that no Gentile could be a Christian unless he undertook to observe the Mosaic law. In this way the gospel of grace was being replaced by a burdensome demand. Christianity was in danger of becoming only a sightly different version of Judaism.

The Christian gospel is hopelessly distorted when it is presented only as a demand to repent, as a law to be obeyed. First and foremost it is good news of God's love and mercy, an assurance of His gracious acceptance of us. Out of this relationship with God flows the desire and the power to live holy lives.

Thomas Carlyle was sitting by the fireside with his aged mother one day, criticizing the preachers of his time. 'If I had to go to preach', he claimed, 'I would go into the pulpit and say no more than this: "All you people know what you ought to do well, go and do it."' His mother continued silently knitting for a while and then said: 'Aye, Tammas; and will ye tell them how?'

The good news must come first!

GALATIANS 1:11–17

'I received it [the gospel] through a revelation of Jesus Christ' (v. 12, N.E.B.).

VITAL RELATIONSHIP. Throughout this chapter Paul is amplifying the point he made at the beginning, that his apostleship had come to him from none other than Christ. After his conversion, he says, he consulted with none of the leaders of the Church, but went away to Arabia to think out the profound implications of his conversion experience. When he did eventually go to Jerusalem he went not with the intention of seeking instruction, but to make the acquaintance of Peter; he also met James, the brother of Jesus. Later he undertook some missionary preaching, a work to which he had not been commissioned by the Church, but which was obviously approved.

We are not to think, however, that in all this Paul was arrogantly asserting his superiority. We should think of him as stressing with humility his own personal relationship with Christ on which, for him, everything hinged.

It was only when, as he puts it, God 'chose to reveal His Son to me, and through me' (v. 16, Barclay) that Paul came to a knowledge of the truth, for truth is not simply something we accept; it is something we experience. Truth is knowing Christ. Paul was ready and glad to bear witness to his personal encounter with truth; he was a 'man in Christ'; his religion was a relationship. And, if it is to be significant and satisfying, our own faith must also be expressed in a similar loving relationship. As Helmut Thielicke has written: 'The pinnacle of promise is not what Christ gives, but what He Himself is to me.'

GALATIANS 1:18–24

'They only heard it said, "Our former persecutor is preaching the good news of the faith which once he tried to destroy"' (v. 23, N.E.B.).

INNER CONFLICT CAUSES INTOLERANCE. Paul asserts his spiritual independence of the other apostles in order to prove that both his message and his commission to preach it came from God alone. After his dramatic encounter with the risen Christ on the Damascus road it was three years before he met Peter and James. Paul was still unknown by sight to the Judean Christians; they simply rejoiced that the former persecutor had turned evangelist. The apostle never ceased to feel remorse for his former persecution of the Church or to wonder that he, of all men, should experience God's mercy.

Paul's early hatred of the Church reflected his own inner disharmony. Before he found Christ he experienced a prolonged and painful tension between the demands of the law and the desires of his own nature (Romans 7:19). Nothing is more natural than for a man in such a state to project his inner conflicts on to the outside world and to become intolerant of his fellows. As A. Graham Ikin has reminded us, 'It is so much easier to spend our energies fighting evils outside ourselves, to save ourselves from facing the enemy within.' Following his conversion Paul became an increasingly integrated person. He lost none of his former zeal but he was freed from fanaticism. Finding peace within the love of God his attitude to his fellows became wholly creative and positive.

GALATIANS 2:1–5

'The liberty which we enjoy in Christ Jesus' (v. 4, Knox).

FREEDOM OR BONDAGE. The slaves of Jamaica prepared for the day of their liberation by ascending the highest peak they could find. All through the night they climbed until the mountain top was crowded with negroes awaiting the dawn. Eagerly they watched the east until the first rays of the sun broke the horizon. Then laughing, singing and shouting they embraced each other and cried, 'Free! Free! Free!'

Paul's release from bondage into the liberty of Christ was no less ecstatic. No wonder he calls the ultra-conservative believers, who insisted on Gentiles obeying the Mosaic law, sham-Christians (v. 4, N.E.B.). Describing a visit he made to Jerusalem with the Gentile Titus, Paul recalls the demand of some Jewish Christians that Titus should show submission to the Mosaic law (by circumcision).

Two totally opposed views of religion were at stake in this issue. The Jews—and those Christians who insisted on Gentile submission to the Mosaic law—saw obedience as an attempt to win God's favour. Paul had travelled that road long enough to know that it ended in either hypocritical self-righteousness or grim despair. Conversion for Paul meant that obedience became not an attempt to earn God's love, but a response to His love. Grace not law was primary. Reverse this order and the gospel ceases to be good news and the very springs of religious life are poisoned. We must ourselves see whether our religion is a prideful attempt to earn God's love, or a glad response to a love which we know does not depend on our worthiness.

GALATIANS 2: 6–10

'James, Cephas, and John, accepted Barnabas and myself as partners, and shook hands upon it' (v. 9, N.E.B.).

WHEN GOOD MEN DIFFER. Continuing his passionate defence of his right to preach that gentile Christians are not bound by the Law of Moses, Paul goes on to record a second visit he paid to Jerusalem fourteen years after either his conversion or his first visit—it is not clear which. His intention was to explain his preaching to the leaders of the Church. Not that he had any doubts as to the rightness of what he was saying; not that he felt he was required to explain himself; but because he was a man of generous spirit, and it was not in his nature to ignore the officially recognized leadership of the Church and cause a rift in what should be a wholesome, truly Christian relationship.

The question of differences of opinion among good men cannot be ignored. That there are times when such situations arise is obvious. In *Soldier Saint*, his biography of George Scott Railton, an early Salvationist leader, Bernard Watson does not play down the differences of opinion that arose between the subject of his book and his leader, William Booth. But the story shows that their differences of opinion, serious though they were, were not stronger than their love for each other which was rooted in their love for God.

We cannot expect to agree with our fellow Christians in every matter; but we can differ and still love; be unyielding in our own convictions and yet be sympathetic to the views of others. Only when love goes out does sin come in.

GALATIANS 2:11–14

'When Peter came to Antioch I had to oppose him publicly, for he was then plainly in the wrong' (v. 11, Phillips).

INSIGHT AND ACTION. This disagreement between Peter and Paul is puzzling only if we fail to appreciate the centuries-old prejudice which Peter had to fight, or hold an unrealistic view of how God works in our hearts.

Jews were prohibited from eating with Gentiles, but at Antioch, where Gentile Christians probably outnumbered Jewish believers, this barrier had been transcended. Peter happily accepted this Spirit-inspired unity. The arrival of Jewish Christians from Jerusalem, however, reminded him of the practical problems involved in overcoming this ancient segregation, and he withdrew from table fellowship with his Gentile brethren. Paul was surely right in rebuking his fellow apostle but we do Peter an injustice if we underestimate his dilemma.

Peter faltered in his loyalty to a truth he had already accepted: he was unwilling to face the consequences of his own deepest insights. This time-lag between insight and action is not unusual. God works slowly, patiently, and almost imperceptibly in our personalities—the New Testament is honest enough to recognize this fact even in one of its greatest characters. We are undisturbed by Peter's failures before Pentecost but we want him to be infallible after. We want instantaneously bestowed perfection rather than the steady, painful response to each new insight which makes for spiritual growth. We also wrongly assume that God only uses perfect people, but as B. D. Hendy has reminded us, 'Effective disinterested work can be done by that part of us which is already redeemed, while redemptive work is going on in other departments of the personality.'

GALATIANS 2:15–21

'With Christ I hang upon the cross, and yet I am alive; or rather, not I; it is Christ that lives in me' (v. 20, Knox).

TRUSTFUL ABANDONMENT. These moving words of personal experience describe how Paul cast off his burdensome subjection to the law, through which 'no man is ever justified', and discovered true life in Christ. His bold claim to share Christ's crucifixion raises an urgent question, for it suggests the most rigorous self-denial. We may well ask: in what sense is the Christian life a liberation if it merely replaces bondage to the law with stringent asceticism? Is this not a case of 'out of the frying pan into the fire'?

Paul repeatedly contrasts two types of religion. One seeks to earn God's favour by meticulous observance of the law: the other enjoys loving communion with God based on simple trust and abandonment. Abraham was the greatest Old Testament instance of a man who 'committed himself to an uncharted journey' in simple trust. But even the example of the patriarch pales beside the figure of One upon a Cross whose trustful obedience led to untold suffering but who never ceased to call God Father.

When Paul encountered the risen Christ he gave up bargaining with God and ceased his futile attempts at self-improvement. He saw that the heart of religion was trustful abandonment to a loving God—even in suffering, even from a Cross. Being crucified with Christ meant, not a programme of harsh ascetism, but sharing Christ's undeviating trust and obedience. It meant saying 'yes' to God at all times and in all places. Only in fellowship with Christ was such a life possible. Simone Weil has truly said that 'he whose soul remains ever turned in the direction of God while the nail pierces it, finds himself nailed on the very centre of the universe.'

GALATIANS 3:1–6

'You stupid Galatians! You must have been bewitched—you before whose eyes Jesus Christ was openly displayed upon His Cross!' (v. 1, N.E.B.).

WHEN THE CROSS IS FORGOTTEN. Without necessarily implying that he believed in magical arts Paul accuses the Galatians of acting like men under an evil spell. Christian life had begun for them when Jesus Christ the crucified was 'placarded' (Moffatt) before their eyes. If only they had kept their eyes fastened on that early vision all would have been well. When the Cross, which speaks of God's freely bestowed grace and unconditional love, is kept central you don't start trying to run up a credit account with God. Religion then means a loving relationship not a legal transaction.

The Cross of Jesus embodies a fundamental law of Christian life. We do not outgrow this principle after conversion. This exactly was the perverse error of the Galatians. Beginning with grace, they then embraced the law, as though the love relationship which the Cross established was inadequate for further spiritual development.

The Cross of Jesus invites our free and ever-deepening response. A Russian writer has observed: 'The mystery of Golgotha is the mystery of liberty. . . . Every time in history that man has tried to turn crucified truth into coercive truth he has betrayed the fundamental principle of Christ.' Just because God refuses any compulsion save that of love it is always possible for us to commit the error of the Galatians—and forget the Cross.

GALATIANS 3:7–12

'It is the men of faith who are Abraham's sons' (v. 7, N.E.B.).

TRUE DESCENDANTS. The Apostle was not short of illustrations to drive home his viewpoint.

Firstly, he used the experience of Abraham. The patriarch had undeniably received God's blessing and promise; and the reason, argued Paul, was obvious. It could not have been his observance of the Law, for that was not given until more than four hundred years later. Therefore, self-evidently, it must have been his faith and obedience, his implicit trust and unconditional surrender. Paul developed that argument in a way that must have startled the Jews. They believed that physical descent from Abraham made them inheritors of the promise. Not so, insisted Paul. His true descendants were men of every race who exhibited the same faith and obedience; the promise was made to them (vv. 8, 9, 14).

Secondly, he used the experience of the Law. Paul took the conflict right into his opponents' camp. The man who lives by the Law, he insisted, is bound to fail and consequently, on the authority of Scripture itself, is 'cursed' (v. 10). Then why this hankering after the way of enslavement and death?

Thirdly, he used the experience of conversion. 'Christ hath redeemed us from the curse of the Law,' he cried, 'being made a curse for us' (v. 13 A.V.). Had the Galatians forgotten the cost of their salvation? If the Law were sufficient, then why the Cross? Whatever our anxiety, we must follow Paul's example and make central to our thinking the suffering of Christ, its nature and purpose.

GALATIANS 3:13–18

'From this curse invoked by the law Christ has ransomed us, by Himself becoming, for our sakes, an accursed thing . . .' (v. 13, Knox).

LIBERTY—AT A PRICE. By His costly identification with humanity Christ is able to make men spiritually free. This truth is powerfully expressed in the word 'ransom', a reference which would have been easily grasped by Paul's first readers who lived in a society based on slavery. The apostle claims that to break the bondage of the law, Christ had Himself to suffer the law's curse by dying on the Cross. This principle—salvation by identification—has a wider significance which embraces every human condition.

Before he painted 'A Snowstorm at Sea' the artist Turner had himself lashed to the mast for four hours in a storm, in order to learn what a storm looked like from within. This provides an imperfect analogy of God's identification with the human condition in His Son Jesus Christ.

Take, as but one example, the pain of loneliness. W. E. Sangster shows how Christ's oneness with us can set us free even in this experience. 'It has been the comfort of martyrs at all times that somewhere in the world there were those who sympathized with them, and understood the cause for which they died. Even this was denied Jesus. His sacrifice mystified the people who loved Him most. It mattered to all the world that He died for love, but no single soul in the world understood that He was doing it. . . . No one understood Him. No one on earth approved. He was lonely with the awful loneliness of God. Can it be doubted that He can succour the lonely still?'

GALATIANS 3:19–29

'Gone is the distinction between Jew and Greek, slave and free man, male and female—you are all one in Christ Jesus!' (v. 28, Phillips).

ONE IN CHRIST. In view of all Paul had been saying, the question: What purpose had the Law, then, in the purpose of God for man? was bound to arise and demand an answer (see v. 19). Paul saw the Law as having but a secondary and temporary purpose—to keep men 'in ward', as it were, until freedom should come in Christ, the freedom of full-grown sons no longer requiring a 'tutor' (verses 23–26 should be read in a modern translation).

This sonship in Christ is available to all who, as Paul expresses it, 'put on Christ'. And with sonship comes equality, for there are no distinctions of race, class or sex in Him. This is a truth we are slow to learn, but what a difference it will make to the world when we do! This can only be when the universal Fatherhood of God is acknowledged and men discover they are truly brothers in Christ.

Wrote Dr. Trevor J. Davies: 'When we pray "Our Father . . ." we are praying also "Our family". Social and international problems loom large on our horizon but the roots of the matter run down to the homes and hearts of the people. Statesmen cannot make peace in a world where nations, groups, individuals, are selfish in their attitude and greedy in their conduct, or else simply indifferent to the existence of other individuals about them. Our new-found proximity has made a sense of community essential.' What kind of a contribution are we making to the brotherhood of men?

GALATIANS 4:1–5

'Then God sent out His Son on a mission to us' (v. 4, Knox).

ROOTED IN ETERNITY. 'God sent His own Son.' This basic Christian assertion puzzles many modern people, seeming to imply a pre-scientific view of the universe and to suggest that a God 'up there' sent His Son on an errand to us 'down here'. The same truth can be expressed differently, however. The life of Jesus fits into the broad canvas of history and is related to every other part of that canvas, as is every historic event and each individual life. But this does not explain the significance of Christ's life. He transcends history.

Martin Buber, the Jewish philosopher, seemed to tremble on the verge of Christian faith when he wrote, 'From my youth onwards I have found in Jesus my great Brother. That Christianity has regarded and does regard Him as God and Saviour has always appeared to me a fact of the highest importance which, for His sake and my own, I must endeavour to understand. . . . My own fraternally open relationship to Him has grown ever stronger and clearer, and today I see Him more strongly and clearly than ever before. I am more than ever certain that a great place belongs to Him in Israel's history of faith and that this place cannot be described by any of the usual categories.'

Why are the usual categories which we use to describe greatness all inadequate? Why is it that the life of Jesus cannot be understood simply in its historic setting? Christians believe this is because the origin of this life was not in time but in eternity. God, who is everywhere active, was uniquely active in Christ.

GALATIANS 4:6–11

'God has sent into our hearts the Spirit of His Son, crying "Abba! Father!"' (v. 6, N.E.B.).

RETREAT INTO SLAVERY. Do you want to be sons or slaves? This is the question with which Paul faced the Galatians. Their experience of adoption was real enough. They knew the joyful recognition of God as Father which came when the Spirit of His Son entered their hearts. What puzzled Paul was that, having been adopted into the family of God, the Galatians were now reverting to the position of slaves.

These verses echo the parable of the Prodigal Son. His request, 'Make me as one of thy hired servants', was an evasion of the full position and responsibility of a loving relationship. The master-servant relationship is far more manageable than the deeply personal relationship of the family. Responsibility between master and servant can be neatly calculated—we know where it begins and ends. And, if you have failed badly in a personal relationship, you do tend to opt for something more manageable, something less all-embracing than the relationship of love. Religion based upon law is just this kind of evasion.

Paul asserted that the Galatians' observance of special days and seasons was little better than their former pagan subjection to the cosmic powers and agencies in which the ancients believed. Jewish formalism and pagan mythology had this in common: both subjected man to rigid impersonal forces. They were thus the very antithesis of that deeply personal and trustful relationship with God into which Christ leads His followers.

John Baillie well reminded us that 'it was the conviction of Jesus, and it is a great part of the distinctive message of Christianity, that the highest of our human values are the values found and developed in the life of the family'.

GALATIANS 4:12–16

'And have I now made myself your enemy by being honest with you?' (v. 16, N.E.B.).

BEING HONEST—WITH LOVE. Remembering his earlier relationship with the Galatian Christians Paul recalls their warm affection for him. Despite an illness which apparently could have caused some revulsion, Paul was welcomed as if he were 'an angel from God'. Did the apostle suffer from an eye affliction or are his words—'you would have torn out your very eyes, and given them to me'—merely a way of saying that their love for him would have shirked no sacrifice? We cannot be sure. What is clear however is that their early affection was now endangered by Paul's honest but loving rebuke.

Showing people the truth about themselves in a helpful way requires compassion. This means more than the cynical comment of one ancient writer that 'it requires as much caution to tell the truth as to conceal it'. It means, as Florence Allshorn wrote in a letter, 'You still have to learn how to give the truth. If you depress a person with it, you have given it without Christ's love constraining you, and without His patience, and you won't lift.'

Receiving the truth about ourselves requires great courage. This is so even when, as with Paul's rebuke of the Galatians, it is given in love. Yet, if self-knowledge and self-acceptance are the way to maturity we should value every honest criticism. Even our unfriendly critics may do us a service if we are brave enough honestly to accept their rebuke.

GALATIANS 4:17–20

'I feel the pangs of childbirth all over again till Christ be formed within you' (v. 19, Phillips).

HOW TO HELP STRUGGLING SOULS. The depth of Paul's affection for his Galatian converts is nowhere more evident than in these verses. The apostle likened his intense anxiety to the pain of childbirth: acute but potentially creative. Elsewhere, in a moving description of his sufferings, he catalogues his outward trials: shipwreck, imprisonment, stoning, beatings, hunger and thirst. But equally exhausting was the inner burden he carried, his 'anxious care' for the Churches. Sometimes we too have the chance to travail over another soul. Parents, teachers, youth leaders, officers and social workers cannot escape this role, but the privilege is not theirs alone.

What qualities do we need to share creatively in the struggles and development of others? We must know ourselves well enough to avoid the temptation to manipulate people, even for their supposed good. We must help the seeker to achieve his own insights rather than supply him with ready-made answers. We need to recognize that each person has his own rate of growth and his development must accord with his own nature. Although the grand objective is that Christ should be formed within every disciple this does not mean a monotonous uniformity. Each truly developed personality will reflect Christ in different ways. Above all, if we are genuinely to help others, we must care deeply about them and must offer them the acceptance which we have found in God. Good advice may at times be helpful, but love is more important.

GALATIANS 4:21–5:1

'Stand, then, as free men, and do not allow yourselves to become slaves again' (5:1, T.E.V.).

IMPULSE OF LOVE. Reading today's rather strange passage we might wish that Paul had illustrated his argument in a more convincing manner. But he was a trained rabbi, and here employs the rabbinic custom of allegorizing an Old Testament story to illustrate God's purposes with men. The rabbis of Paul's day would not have quarrelled with the apostle's method, but would have strongly disagreed with the conclusions he reached. The interpretation he gives to the story of Abraham and his wives is the exact reverse of its obvious meaning for a Jew. Hagar, Abraham's slave-wife, represents the Law given at Sinai, says Paul, and the Jews, still in bondage to the Law, are her true descendants. Sarah, Abraham's free-born wife, represents the covenant inaugurated by Christ, and all men of faith, whether Jews or Gentiles, are her true descendants.

This may all seem strange to us, but the heart of the matter is plain enough. It is summed up in the words, 'So my brothers, we are the children, not of the slave girl, but of the free-born wife . . . Stand firm, therefore, and do not submit again to the yoke of slavery' (5:1, Jerusalem Bible).

This freedom, which Paul sees as a vital element in the gospel means that a believer can do what he pleases, but only in the sense of Augustine's well-known phrase, 'Love God and do what you will.' The crucial words are love God. Having Him at the centre of our lives means that we do always the things that please Him.

GALATIANS 5:2–12

'Once a man becomes a Christian, whether or not he is circumcised is meaningless. What matters is faith working in love' (v. 6, Barclay).

FAITH ACTIVE IN LOVE. One of the outward signs marking Jews off from gentiles was the rite of circumcision, and the great issue here was: Should the Galatians be circumcised? Paul saw that if they accepted that they should, they were repudiating the claim that Christ alone is essential to salvation. They could not say that they were utterly dependent on Christ and at the same time give way to the appeals of the Judaistic teachers. They must choose either Christ or the Law as the source of their salvation. Thus once again Paul stresses that Christianity is Christ. More than Christ is unnecessary; less than Christ inadequate.

The important words in this reading are those of our text. Paul wanted to stress that loving, self-giving, in Christ is the important thing, the only thing that really matters. In comparison questions of ritual, forms of worship and church order are simply trivial.

Commenting on this verse, John A. Allan says, 'This is one of the great New Testament statements of the essence of true religion ... a deprecating of the formal or ritual elements in religion, and a confronting of the soul with the great, simple realities of faith and love and the redeeming work of Christ. It would be well if we had the courage to bring all our ecclesiastical and theological differences into the searching light of this verse. If "circumcision" is to be regarded as in effect covering everything in religion that is not directly associated with faith and love, it covers very many things that we make a great pother about in Church circles.'

GALATIANS 5:13–15

'Do not make your freedom an incentive to your lower nature; but serve one another in love' (v. 13, Weymouth).

FREEDOM IS NOT LICENCE. Throughout his missionary career Paul had to fight on two fronts, generally at the same time. Against those who wanted to enforce the Jewish law on all Gentiles he protested that Christ set men free from this ancient bondage. But on the other hand some converts made their Christian 'freedom' an excuse for irresponsible and immoral behaviour. In this letter Paul passionately pleads for freedom but he also guards against this opposite danger. The way he does this is highly significant.

The alternative to licence is not bondage to the law but service motivated by love. Paul's insight here is amply confirmed by modern psychology. A child can learn to control and direct his unruly desires only within a loving relationship. Merely to threaten punishment will make him repress his rebellion and this creates a divided personality which may well persist into adult life. But in a truly loving relationship he can accept the rebellious tendencies within himself and gradually learn to direct them. This is the way to integration and inner harmony. For his children in Christ Paul desired neither enforced obedience, nor irresponsible licence, but the freedom of love-motivated living.

Paul pointedly contrasts 'the whole law'—its endless and burdensome complexities—with the 'single commandment' to love our neighbour. The Christian programme for moral living is not only effective but basically simple.

GALATIANS 5:16–21

'Let your lives be guided by the Spirit, and then you will not fulfil the cravings of your lower nature' (v. 16, Weymouth).

THE WAY OF VICTORY. Two misunderstandings of the Christian life may arise from a casual reading of today's passage. We may wrongly suppose that the believer can hope for nothing more satisfying than a state of inner civil war, with both spirit and flesh locked in mortal struggle. Certainly some tension and conflict is an inevitable part of the Christian life, indeed of human existence. One writer pointed out that throughout history being good has seemed like going uphill whilst being selfish has seemed like going downhill. The moral struggle is not to be shirked: we would probably be weaklings without it.

Yet it remains true that the believer should not be a man divided against himself. Paul clearly asserts that the Spirit-guided life sets a man free from the dictates of his lower nature. He should not be a beleaguered, hard-pressed defender of the citadel of virtue: he should be a conqueror on the field. He achieves this not by battling with his lower desires (though when they assert themselves they must be checked) but by obeying the desires of his spiritual nature. Thomas Aquinas says, 'No man can live without pleasure, therefore a man deprived of pleasures of the Spirit surrenders to the pleasures of the flesh.'

The other error we are likely to make from casually reading this passage, especially in the Authorized Version, is that the desires of 'the flesh' means only sensuality, laziness, gluttony and other evils linked with the body. Paul means by the flesh every aspect of human nature which is naturally opposed to God and this includes selfishness, hatred and the other sins of the spirit.

GALATIANS 5:22–25

'The harvest of the Spirit is love, joy, peace . . .' (v. 22, N.E.B).

HIS WORK IN US. The perceptive reader of church history, and the watchful observer of present-day developments, is delighted by the wide diversity of the Holy Spirit's operations. The impressive beauty of great liturgy, the gay abandonment of evangelical revival, the imposing edifice of theological systems, the penetrating insights of prophets and poets: all these may bear the unmistakable imprint of the Spirit. No one church, no one interpretation of the faith, can claim a monopoly of the Spirit, who sometimes seems to delight in ignoring the qualities we think are important. Yet though His operations are as diverse as life itself, and though within the Church He bestows varying gifts, in the heart of the individual His work is consistent and easily recognizable. There is a family likeness among the saints. Wherever the Spirit is given free access in the personality the same kind of harvest appears.

In Paul's time pagan philosophers often compiled catalogues of vices and virtues. Similar lists appear in the Apostle's letters. But for Paul, Christian virtue is not man's achievement though man's co-operation is required. The harvest of the Spirit is not a catalogue of virtues but the vivid description of an experience. As Evelyn Underhill wrote, 'The spiritual life consists of His action within us—His supernatural love and life more and more invading, growing up in us; His sap rising quietly and secretly in the soul, bringing forth, not merely nice devotional flowers—but fruits.'

GALATIANS 5:26–6:2

'Help one another to carry these heavy loads, and in this way you will fulfil the law of Christ' (v. 2, N.E.B.).

SHOULDERING OTHERS' BURDENS. 'The first moment of genuine religious feeling I can remember with any vividness', wrote W. B. J. Martin, 'is a feeling of concern and guardianship for two friends in my class at school. I felt that I had a responsibility for them, and when Noel started swearing or Len began to frequent the billiard saloon, it seemed to me that I was being challenged. . . . It may sound priggish . . . but I believe that God was within and behind the sense of responsibility which I felt.'

Such a sense of responsibility for others is an essential part of Christian discipleship. A caring community provides the best expression of the Christian faith. Discussing what part Christian symbols may play in the task of communication, F. W. Dillistone has suggested that when the television screen can show a body of Christ's people caring, then the world sees again the life which was manifested fully in Christ.

Loving concern for others, which is the law of Christ, is 'the overflow of gratitude by those who have got far past the cautious morality of "doing as you would be done by", and are now exploring the infinite ranges of that new world which is open to those who "do as they have been done by", being constrained by the love of Christ'.

GALATIANS 6:3–6

'Each of us, then, will have his own load to carry' (v. 5, Knox).

OUR OWN CONTRIBUTION. Self-examination, which Paul advises here (v. 4), does not mean an endless morbid turning over in the mind of one's sins, which would be a denial of the grace of God to forgive. He is here thinking of conduct and Christian service and saying, in connection with his exhortation to support the faulty brother (vv. 1, 2), that it would be a sure safeguard against any feeling of superiority to make an honest estimation of oneself. But such an examination will be authentic only when comparison is made, not with what others have attained, but with the requirements of the law of Christ, the essence of which is love.

Another point: at first sight it might appear that verses 2 and 4 (in the A.V.), contradict each other. In fact two different words in the original are both translated by the one English word 'burden'. The earlier appeal (as has been noted) is to support each other in need. The second (v. 5) is an exhortation to each Christian not to shirk his share of responsibility for God's work. 'Every man shall "shoulder his own pack"' is J. B. Phillips's translation.

The next verse is a blunt reminder of the Galatians' duty to support those who teach them in the word; who give their whole time to this arduous and necessary duty. And we, in our own day, have no right to expect to enjoy the ministry and fellowship of the Christian Church unless we put something into it. We must regularly check up on what we do and give, keeping in mind our time, talents and financial resources.

GALATIANS 6:7–10

'Don't delude yourself into thinking God can be cheated: where a man sows, there he reaps' (v. 7, Jerusalem Bible).

SOLEMN REMINDER. The word Paul uses for 'mocked' is a colourful word meaning, literally, 'turning up the nose'. One commentator says that 'the idea suggested is that of a bargainer in a market who has cheated his customer, and who thereupon reflects upon his own cleverness and the purchaser's simplicity with a grin of self-complacency'. But we can't 'take God in' like that, though men try sometimes, even religious men.

When we substitute outward acts of religion for worship from the heart motivated by love to God, or for loving deeds towards our fellows motivated by love to men, we may possibly deceive ourselves into thinking we are doing what is required, or even, on a lower level, be trying with open eyes to get by in our religion with as little inconvenience as possible. But (in Phillips's translation) 'you cannot make a fool of God'.

These stern words underline an inexorable law of life. The universe works only one way—God's. When a man goes counter to that he does not so much break the law as he is broken on it. When we repent God forgives us and restores the relationship with Him that sin severed; this is the wonder of the gospel. But the consequences of that sin may remain. We may learn, by God's help, to bear them with cheerfulness, though we may have to bear them for the rest of our life. This is not an imposed punishment of an offended God, but the outworking of the inviolable law of a dependable God.

GALATIANS 6:11–18

'God forbid that I should glory in anything except in the Cross of our Lord Jesus Christ . . .' (v. 14, Weymouth).

WHERE LIGHT SHINES. In his novel, *The Blood of the Lamb*, Peter de Vries tells the story of eleven-year-old Carol, dying slowly and painfully from leukaemia. During an 'intermission', when a new drug had temporarily stayed the disease, Carol went to the movies and later told her father about an old-fashioned comedy she saw in which the characters had thrown custard pies at each other. 'The man who throws the first pie makes no effort to defend himself,' she said, 'he just stands there and takes it.'

Months later Carol died in hospital. Her father had been on his way to the hospital with an iced cake for his daughter's birthday. Later, outside a church, he noticed a large crucifix. His bitter anger against the universe exploded and he hurled the cake so that it landed squarely on the face of the figure, just beneath the crown of thorns. Then he remembered Carol's description of the man in the film who 'just stands there and takes it'.

The great burden of undeserved suffering which lays upon humanity baffles the mind and at times tempts us to ask rebellious questions. Yet if light shines anywhere upon this problem it shines from Calvary. There we see, not a remote impassive God, but a God who bears our sin and carries our sorrows on His heart. We may well agree with Paul that all boasting is out—except boasting in the Cross.

THE EPISTLE TO THE EPHESIANS

INTRODUCTION

In a brief introductory note there is space only for the things most surely believed about this letter.

The first is that it was written by Paul when in prison near the close of his life of missionary service (3:1, 4:1, 6:20).

The second is that it seems to have been a circular letter addressed to Christian churches in Asia—including Ephesus, of course, though scholars point out that the words 'in Ephesus' (1:1) are missing from a number of early manuscripts.

The third is that the theme is the unity which God purposes to accomplish in Christ. Every aspect of life is included in the divine desire. Acceptance of Jesus as Saviour and Lord will restore a man to fellowship with his Maker (2:6), and with his neighbour, no matter of what race (2:14, 3:4). A man will also be at peace with himself (4:17–24); love will reign in his home (5:22–6:4) and goodwill in his daily employment (6:5–9). To live in this exemplary way on earth believers can be made strong in the Lord (6:10 ff.).

The company of the Church, of which Christ is the Head, is the instrument which God plans to use so that His will may be done on earth as in Heaven (1:22, 23).

EPHESIANS 1:1–10

'He has made known to us His hidden purpose . . . that the universe, all in heaven and on earth, might be brought into a unity in Christ' (vv. 9 and 10, N.E.B.).

DISTANT GOAL AND PRESENT MEANING. After the usual opening salutations this letter produces an outburst of exalted praise rarely equalled in Scripture. Paul is all but overwhelmed by the staggering immensity of God's offer in Christ, and verses 3 to 14 would be better sung as a rhapsody of thanksgiving than analysed into doctrinal statements.

The central theme of the book—God's purpose to unite all things in Christ—is introduced at verse 10. The Greek word translated 'to sum up' literally means 'bringing to a head'. In arithmetic this referred to the process of adding a column of figures and placing the total at the top of the column, not at the bottom as we do today. The word was then applied in oratory to the summarizing of important points in an argument at the end of a speech. This, and much more, is implied in Paul's assertion that God's purpose is 'to sum up all things in Christ'.

It was Bertrand Russell's claim that ultimately, when the universe ran down, the whole temple of man's achievements would be buried in the debris of a ruined universe. Despite this utter indifference of the cosmos, Lord Russell pleaded for kindness and tolerance. The Christian, however, in seeking love and unity, does not feel he is working against the grain of the universe. Christ is both the meaning of his present life and the distant goal towards which everything moves.

EPHESIANS 1:11–14

'And you too, when you had heard the message of the truth, the good news of your salvation, and had believed it, became incorporate in Christ . . .' (v. 13, N.E.B.).

IN CHRIST. The great Pauline phrase 'in Christ', or one of its equivalents, recurs eleven times in the first fourteen verses of this letter. Those with a touch of mysticism in their nature, who sometimes experience in prayer a keen sense of Christ's presence, find this description of Christian living very precious. For the same reason, it disturbs those for whom discipleship means mainly obedience and brotherly love; whose prayer life is rarely, if ever, emotionally exalted.

While mystical experience played an important part in Paul's life, it is important to realize this was not the central meaning of being 'in Christ'.

We best understand the phrase by remembering Paul was a Jew. Even to this day a pious Jew, in the liturgy of the Passover festival, relives the experience of his people. In every generation, says a Jewish writer, each one of us should regard himself as though he himself had gone forth from Egypt. Similarly, W. D. Davies suggests, the true American 'is one who has, in his own experience, crossed the Atlantic with the Pilgrim Fathers, wrestled with the wilderness of early America, fought the war of Independence and the civil war'.

To Paul, being 'in Christ' meant sharing in Christ's death and resurrection so that these crucial events increasingly become personal experience. The reality of this is proved, not by mystical exaltation but by Christlikeness in daily life.

EPHESIANS 1:15–23

'What surpassing virtue there is in His dealings with us, who believe. Measure it by that mighty exercise of power which He shewed when He raised Christ from the dead' (vv. 19 and 20, Knox).

HOW DO WE MEASURE? Paul's mood of exaltation leads on from praise to prayer. Great dynamic words follow each other in rapid succession, making analysis difficult but lifting the heart to share the apostle's sublime confidence.

Paul first prays that his readers may possess that spiritual wisdom which leads to knowing God. This knowledge is first experimental. In *The Journal of a Soul* the future Pope John XXIII, then preparing for ordination, wrote, 'God preserve me from under-estimating study, but I must beware of attaching to it an exaggerated and absolute value. Study is one eye, the left eye; if the right one is missing, what is the use of a single eye, of study by itself? ... In future I shall study with more enthusiasm than before, but ... I shall be studying not so much for the examinations as for life itself, so that what I learn will become an integral part of me.' Theological students are not unique in being tempted to mistake knowledge about God for the knowledge of God.

While knowledge of God must be experimental we should not limit God to what we have experienced. So Paul insists that his readers measure the vast resources available in terms of Christ's resurrection. Is this how we think? Do we reckon God's power in human life by our own mixed experience of victory and failure? Do we more wisely measure it by the lives of the saints? Or have we the audacity, with Paul to see it in terms of the miracle of Easter?

EPHESIANS 2:1–10

'It is, remember, by grace and not by achievement that you are saved' (v. 5, Phillips).

PARADOX OF GRACE. The heart of this passage is also Paul's gospel in a nutshell—'By His grace you are saved, through trusting Him.' More than most, Paul was equipped to preach salvation through trust in God's love, for his efforts to attain righteousness had been long, arduous and fruitless. What has been described as a 'hardening of the oughteries' was familiar experience to this Pharisee long before modern medicine linked mental strain and physical illness.

We are not saved by faith, as is sometimes asserted. We are saved by grace, that is, by God's unmerited love and mercy. We receive this by abandoning all trust in our own goodness, by recognizing that God loves us because of who He is, not for what we are. As Paul Tournier once wrote: 'The elite of the gospel is not made up of the "advanced", but of poor devils who accept God's grace.'

The paradox of Christian experience is that trust in God's grace does not lead to moral laziness and indifference. Resting in God's unqualified love we become active in genuine goodness, which is quite different from the phoney 'good works' of those striving to keep on the right side of a God they do not love. 'What a strenuous man was Paul,' remarked W. B. J. Martin. 'His writings abound in such active verbs as "strive", "fight", "run" and "do". He can even talk of "winning" Christ (Philippians 3:8). Perhaps only the man who knows that the whole of life is a gift can muster the necessary energy to go in and possess it.'

EPHESIANS 2:11–16

'He is our peace, He who has made both of us a unity and destroyed the barrier which kept us apart' (v. 14, Moffatt).

CONTEMPT ON ALL MY PRIDE. Separating the Court of the Gentiles from the inner court of the temple in Jerusalem was a stone balustrade bearing the inscription: 'No man of another nation to enter within the fence and enclosure round the temple. And whosoever is caught will have himself to blame that his death ensues.' This 'wall of partition' symbolized the spiritual apartheid of the ancient world.

Historically, the establishment of a church where Jew and Gentile had equal rights might be considered Paul's supreme achievement. Often against bitter opposition, this 'apostle of the Gentiles' fought for the universal application of the gospel. Yet he would strenuously have denied that this spiritual partnership between Jew and Gentile was his accomplishment. Division had been overcome through the Cross: the achievement was Christ's.

The Cross abolished the ancient barrier between Jew and Gentile by exposing their equality in sin and revealing God's universal mercy. Jewish religion, as well as Gentile government, put Christ to death. More than all else it is pride that divides men. Before the perfect love revealed at Calvary no man or nation has anything to be conceited about, though they have everything to be glad about. To receive this mercy a man needs no status or qualification—Jew, Gentile, White, Black—only his membership of the human race. Should he seem some additional security to lift him a little above his fellows he will find the security of God's love seems that much less real.

EPHESIANS 2:17–22

'You belong now to the household of God' (v. 19, Phillips).

THE CHRISTIAN IN SOCIETY. God's purpose to unite all things in Christ, which is the theme of this letter, is accomplished first in the Church. Belonging to the Christian community is here described in three vivid metaphors: citizenship of a commonwealth, members of a household, stones in a sacred temple. If the transition from citizenship to parts of a building seems incongruous to us we must remember that ancient temples, unlike modern churches, were regarded as the actual abodes of the deity. In Christianity the belief that God dwelt in a visible sanctuary was replaced by the view that His people constituted His temple.

The church as 'the household of God' has a particular modern ring because the Greek word, *oikos*, is now used in academic circles to describe the various communities in which men are organized. Philip Potter points out that we speak of business houses, royal houses, houses of assembly or parliament. Schools are divided into houses. A Greek work meaning 'the management of the house' is behind our word 'economics'—national housekeeping.

Membership of God's household means infinitely more than belonging to just one more community. For this reason it must not involve taking our membership in business house, trade union, school or society less seriously. Withdrawal from these other social structures (as far as we can achieve this) is precisely what makes the Church 'just another club'. If God's purpose is to unite all humanity in Christ we must so live in society that it is increasingly penetrated by the spirit of love.

EPHESIANS 3:1–6

'It was by a revelation that His secret was made known to me' (v. 3, N.E.B.).

WHAT GOD REVEALS. Paul's prayer is certainly subject to interruption! Beginning at 1:17 it breaks off three verses later in a description of God's work in Christ. The prayer is about to be resumed at the beginning of chapter 3 when Paul digresses again. He begins his prayer for the third time at 3:14. This apparent disjointedness is further evidence of the apostle's exalted mood. It is not so much that prayer is broken off as that everything is lifted to the level of vision and communion.

Paul claims that God's purpose to unite all things in Christ was made known to him by revelation (v. 3). Perhaps he was thinking of his Damascus road experience or of other 'visions and revelations granted by the Lord' (2 Corinthians 12:1).

Revelation is often described as though God imparted particular items of knowledge to receptive men. But revelation is not the communication of information: it is the unveiling of a Person. What God reveals is Himself. Paul was not merely informed that

Jew and Gentile were to be joint heirs of divine grace, as though this were some additional fact to be placed alongside other revealed truths. Rather, seeing the infinite love of God in Christ, he knew without doubt that this love embraced all. Basic Christian beliefs are always of this kind. What is truly fundamental in our faith and what is peripheral can be distinguished by asking: Is this belief an inevitable consequence of the character of God seen in Jesus Christ?

EPHESIANS 3:7–13

'The principalities and powers of heaven are to see, now, made manifest in the Church, the subtlety of God's wisdom' (v. 10, Knox).

POWERS MADE POWERLESS. The heavenly rulers, powers and authorities referred to in this letter (1:21; 2:2; 3;10; 6:12) played a prominent role in the thoughts of first-century man. The stars and planets were associated with demonic beings who exercised a mostly evil influence in the affairs of men. We could hardly take this view seriously today. If demonic rulers did indeed control the heavenly bodies we would have to regard them 'as models of propriety in their meticulous obedience'—not as usurping rebels.

It is not clear to what extent Paul accepted a literal belief in these spiritual rulers. He was utterly certain that all rebellious powers had been rendered ineffective by Christ's triumph. A believer need fear them no longer, either in their literal form or as symbols of the power of evil.

In Jean Cocteau's version of *Antigone* King Creon is incensed to find that Antigone has buried her brother's body against his orders. How did she have the audacity to disobey his decree? he asks. 'It was not made by Jupiter,' is her simple reply. Appealing to the unwritten divine laws which nothing can efface she adds, 'Ought I, then, for fear of man's opinion, to disobey my gods?'

Men cease to tremble before hostile powers when a higher power is perceived. This was how the Early Church banished the fear of demons. God's love and Christ's victory rendered them ineffective. We too can know that God's loving purpose is stronger than everything opposing it.

EPHESIANS 3:14–21

'I pray that Christ may make His home in your hearts through your faith' (v. 17, Weymouth).

KINDLY GUEST. Jews usually stood to pray. When they knelt they did so with body bent forward and head touching the ground, as the Moslem does today. In the New Testament kneeling is usually associated with deep feeling or a sense of urgency. When Paul says, 'I kneel in prayer to the Father,' we may be sure he shares with us his deepest concern.

The heart of Paul's prayer is that his readers may be made strong through Christ's indwelling. What does this mean? Dr. Martyn Lloyd Jones quotes an article in a religious journal describing a Christian as:

> A mind through which Christ thinks,
> A voice through which Christ speaks,
> A heart through which Christ loves,
> A hand through which Christ helps.

This, says Lloyd Jones, is a travesty of Christian teaching, suggesting 'that the Christian is a man whose personality has gone out of existence, while Christ is using his various powers and faculties'.

The Christian is neither on his own, struggling unaided to produce the fruits of the Spirit, nor is he annihilated in favour of a divine presence which 'takes over'. Rather, his personality is reinforced, enriched and refined by the indwelling Christ. No kindlier guest can we invite into our hearts than Christ, nor one who values more what is of worth in us. This is why saints are more truly themselves than sinners, yet also bear the family likeness of those 'in Christ'.

EPHESIANS 4:1–6

'Accept life with humility and patience, making allowances for each other because you love each other' (v. 2, Phillips).

LIVING IN UNITY The first half of this letter has dealt mainly with Christian doctrine. This reading marks the shift to questions of Christian conduct. That the two are inseparably linked is emphasized in the Authorized Version by the word, 'therefore'. It is because God's boundless mercy has been made real to us in Christ that we see our everyday relationships in a particular way.

As Roger Schutz has written: 'All communication with God leads towards one's neighbour. The authentic sign of ... all relationship with Jesus Christ is the discovery of one's neighbour. If our neighbour disappears from our dialogue with Christ, our love for God is founded upon a mythical divinity having no relationship with our humanity, rather than upon the Christ of the gospel.'

The link between belief and conduct is particularly clear in this passage. God's unifying purpose was the theme of the opening chapters: now Paul calls for virtues which alone maintain true community—humility, patience, love.

When Florence Allshorn founded the St. Julian's Community to provide a centre of renewal for missionaries and Christian workers, she and her companions discovered just how difficult it is to live in unity. 'We had many words about fellowship,' she later wrote, 'but we had yet to put words into deeds, and we little knew what that would entail ... When people talk about starting communities we look at each other. They seem to us like people starting for the North Pole without even knowing that they need a warm coat.' Despite the difficulties, however, Florence and her helpers discovered the way to harmony, bringing their frustrations and resentments to the light so they could see them from the other's point of view, refusing to leave their relationships on any level except that of Christian love.

EPHESIANS 4:7–13

'So shall we all at last attain ... to mature manhood, measured by nothing less than the full stature of Christ' (v. 13, N.E.B.).

CHRISTIAN MATURITY. No beliefs are more important to education, claims one psychologist, than those we hold about man's possibilities. When our ideas about human capacity change, the goals of teaching change too. The same can be said of our attitude to our personal development. Looking at the advertisements which bombard us from hoardings, newspaper pages and television, William Peek said, 'If I'm the sort of being the man who designed those advertisements thinks I am, then I'm not the sort of being the gospel thinks I am.'

In the light of God's resources Paul urged his readers to measure their capacity, and the goal of their development, by Jesus Christ. To be mature is to be Christlike. The varied gifts granted to the Church were for the purpose of creating unity and maturity (vv. 11 and 12).

Jesus Christ is not only the believer's standard of maturity—He makes development possible. In a play by the playwright James Baldwin one character says to another, 'I think there's a lot of love in you, Juanita. If you'll let me help you, we can give it to the world. You can't give it to the world until you can find a person who can help you—love the world.' Maturity means the ability genuinely to love; it is also true that we cannot give love until we have received it. So the believer finds in the love of his Lord both his example and the One who nourishes growth.

EPHESIANS 4:14–16

'We are not meant to remain as children at the mercy of every chance wind of teaching' (v. 14, Phillips).

IMMATURE DEVICES. What has immaturity to do with being swept away by heretical teachings? Paul obviously sees a close link, and to make this connection does not mean overlooking that a close relationship can exist between immaturity and rigid orthodoxy.

The immature person tends to seek outside of himself for solutions to his problems. Eagerly grasping at each new fashion of thought he hopes that here at last is his salvation. He fails to see that maturity comes only by increasing self-awareness and integration. Genuine Christian experience facilitates this because in the unconditional love of God a man can face his own depths without despair.

Some immature people are a prey to every passing 'wind of doctrine' because they live almost entirely in the realm of ideas. Their emotions, being essentially unmanageable, are shut out of consciousness. They are often poor in relationships for these too can be unpredictable. Ideas are safer than emotions or relationships. These people give to the intellect an exalted value it does not warrant.

The immature Christian sometimes embraces each new heresy because to agree with his fellow-Christians would make him too ordinary and uninteresting. This is what makes the compulsive rebel, as distinct from the genuine prophet whose nonconformity derives from a vision of truth he dare not disobey.

EPHESIANS 4:17–24

'You must be made new in mind and spirit, and put on the new nature of God's creating, which shows itself in the just and devout life called for by the truth' (vv. 23 and 24, N.E.B.).

MAN'S EFFORT AND GOD'S GRACE. Perhaps the stark contrasts between pagan life and Christian discipleship can be appreciated only by those converted from one to the other. Paul wanted his readers to continue seeing the difference in black-and-white terms so that they would eschew every compromise.

The transformation of personality requires passive and active attitudes of mind. Paul writes of 'being made new'; this is God's work in the believer. Yet he also urges his readers, 'Put on the new nature of God's creating'—this demands the Christian's active effort. In Christian experience 'man's effort and God's grace rise and fall together'. So the believer never feels God is doing it all for him, but neither need he fear that he must accomplish his own transformation.

The Christian is to 'put on the new nature' as a man might don a coat or a woman a dress. New clothes do not really feel 'us' when we first put them on, and this is certainly true of some Christian virtues. William James' advice about exchanging new attitudes for old is helpful at this stage of conscious effort: 'In the acquisition of a new habit, or the leaving off of an old one, we must take care to launch ourselves with as strong and decided initiative as possible ... Seize the very first possible opportunity to act on every resolution you make, and on every emotional prompting you may experience in the direction of the habits you aspire to gain ... Keep the faculty of effort alive in you by a little gratuitous exercise every day.'

EPHESIANS 4:25–32

'Never go to bed angry—don't give the devil that sort of foothold' (v. 26, Phillips).

ANGER AND THE BODY. Having reminded his readers that in Christ they entered upon a new moral life, Paul now proceeds to illustrate how this manifests itself in various situations. One of these concerns the Christian when he is angry. Human relationships have been analysed into a threefold movement: towards people, away from people, against people. As may be seen from the life of Jesus there are occasions when each one of these movements is right. Predominantly He moved towards people in love, sometimes He withdrew from them for prayer and solitude, occasionally He moved against them in righteous anger (though this was never a loveless antagonism).

Some ancient moralists urged that all quarrels be composed before sunset. Paul gives similar advice. Even in 'civilized' man anger creates the bodily conditions for a fight. Blood pressure rises, the heart beats more strongly, muscles become tense and the blood supply is redirected from the digestive processes to the skin and muscles. Taking our anger to bed, it is more likely to become a chronic condition, keeping our bodies in a harmful state of perpetual mobilization.

Sometimes we become angry simply to create this internal situation—when we are tired, run-down or overworked. 'Crises were the order of the day,' writes Elizabeth Salter of Edith Sitwell the poet. 'But she needed her crises as she needed her pests.' The aging poet's 'pests' were the people who annoyed her and her anger helped to revive her failing energies. Yet, as her biographer pointed out, this unnatural stimulation 'took its inevitable toll'.

EPHESIANS 5:1–5

'As children copy their fathers you, as God's children, are to copy Him' (v. 1, Phillips.)

PROTEST AND COMPASSION. The word 'imitation' has unpleasant associations, yet children learn a great deal by this method. 'Imitation is not a bad thing if (a) it is an imitation of a good model, and (b) it does not try to pass itself off as the original article'. Imitation is a means to an end in discipleship; the goal is spontaneous goodness.

Paul's protest against sexual immorality has relevance today when we suffer similar confusion in this area of life. Significantly, the apostle linked sexual vice with greed for material gain. Both are dangerous substitutes for the true life of love.

We need to combine an awareness of the dangers of sexual immorality with a deep compassion for its victims. Arguing that modern society is far too permissive of corrupting influences, Pamela Hansford Johnson records that during the Nazi occupation of Poland the bookstalls were deliberately flooded with pornography. This was done believing that 'if you permit all things for self-gratification, you are likely to encourage withdrawal from any sort of corporate responsibility'.

On the other hand, we must remember that people who break the sexual code are nearly always basically unhappy people who have failed to achieve truly satisfying relationships. The idea that they enjoy pleasures denied to the more moral is an illusion soon dispelled by acquaintance with them.

EPHESIANS 5:6–14

'Live like men who are at home in daylight' (v. 8, N.E.B.).

THE LIFE OF OPENNESS. Light is one of the great primary symbols shared by many different religions. The name Buddha simply means 'the enlightened one': light and darkness were constant themes in the religions of ancient Persia and Greece: one of the Dead Sea scrolls deals with 'The War of the Sons of Light with the Sons of Darkness'. We know how frequently this symbol appears in the Bible.

Religious symbols sometimes grow old, failing to speak with their former persuasiveness. This, claims John Macquarrie, has happened with the symbol of light. To ancient man light was utterly mysterious, to us it 'has become just another physical phenomenon'.

Searching for a modern equivalent to the biblical symbol of light, Macquarrie suggests the word 'openness'. In the deep forest it is where the wood has been opened up that light comes in. To live in the light, as Paul exhorts in this passage, is to live open to others, to life and to the future. God is light because He is not shut in on Himself. As Calvary proves, He is utterly open to His creation, exposing Himself to man's hatred and anger. Christ is the light of the world because in Him the openness of God to man, and the openness of man to God, are united. Does this help us to see what it means for us today to live in the light?

EPHESIANS 5:15–21

'Make the very most of your time' (v. 16, Moffatt).

ENTHUSIASTIC GOODNESS. Paul seemed to have two kinds of conduct in mind here: indifferent piety and enthusiastic perverseness. The former is certainly no match for the latter. Drunkenness, perhaps associated with pagan worship, could not be dealt with by prohibition. It needed replacing by the fruitful stimulus of the Spirit's indwelling. Christians working among young people 'living for kicks' know that only full-blooded discipleship can attract those addicted to artificial stimulations.

Passionate goodness seeks to make the most of time. It is claimed you have a better chance of getting something done by a busy man than by an idle one, for the busy man has learnt the secret of economizing his time. On the other hand, we can be too busy for those who need us. Raymond Raynes, Anglican missionary, was sometimes late for appointments simply because with him people came first. 'He seemed to have learnt the right use of time,' said one of his fellow-workers, 'and when it was your turn he would give it to you. I never heard him say how busy he was, nor did he make excuses for being late.'

Michel Quoist has reminded us that we should make the most of every opportunity 'to take a new hold on yourself, and to welcome God into your life: while waiting for the bus, or for your motor to warm up, or for the milk to boil, or for the coffee to cool off, or for the traffic lights to change . . . Don't kill time, no matter how short it is; it can be a moment of grace. The Lord is there, and He is inviting you to reflection and decision so that you can become a man in the fullest sense of the word.'

EPHESIANS 5:22–33

'Husbands, love your wives as Christ also loved the church and gave Himself up for it' (v. 25, N.E.B.).

EQUAL BUT DIFFERENT. Does Paul here endorse the idea of male superiority, so widely held in the ancient world and by no means abandoned today? Since the apostle elsewhere stresses the equality of men and women in Christ it is only fair to interpret his words as pointing to the natural difference of roles. A reversal of roles in the marriage relationship creates unhappiness and tension in both partners, and confusion in their children. If the lordly male is to us a stupid anachronism the 'henpecked' husband is even more pathetic.

The apostle urges that the wife should recognize a certain leadership in her husband: the man is to love his wife 'as Christ also loved the Church'. Here is a further illustration of that 'living in the light' which was recently interpreted as complete openness to others.

Paul Tournier describes how a medical colleague proudly showed him a newly purchased ophthalmoscope. 'We had each looked into one end of the apparatus,' he writes, 'and we had each been able to see right to the bottom of the other's eye, taking in all its detail. Then his wife came into the room and I felt his sudden withdrawing within himself. I looked at the ophthalmoscope on the desk and I thought of what relaxing of tensions might take place if only each of them could look into the depths of the other's soul.'

EPHESIANS 6:1–4

'Fathers, don't over-correct your children or make it difficult for them to obey the commandment' (v. 4, Phillips).

HUMAN EMBODIMENT. A closely knit family life has long been one of the strengths of the Jewish people. Consequently, Jesus was more concerned about the dangers of exclusive, self-contained family affection than about family breakdown (Matthew 10:37). Pagan society, however, presented a different picture and Paul regarded disrespect for parents as a symptom of social disintegration (Romans 1:30; 2 Timothy 3:2). He wanted Christian families to check the disruptive elements in their environment by their wholesome stability. If this placed an obligation upon the children it also required loving wisdom from the parents.

The over-strict, authoritarian parent is less common today. Perhaps modern parents are more prone to inconsistency: they are strict when the mood takes them, or when driven by their own insecurity, and lax as a general rule. As children formulate their picture of God upon their family experience both these failures have serious consequences. There is little to choose between a tyrant god and a capricious god. If overstrictness is responsible for the first image, inconsistency forms the second.

Even outside the parent-child relationship the love of God often awaits human embodiment. 'I do not see this person of whom you speak,' said a distressed man to Chad Varah, founder of the Samaritans, after being told that God loved him. 'My senses tell me that you are the only person here with me,' he continued. 'Do you love me?'

EPHESIANS 6:5–9

'You masters . . . give up using threats; remember you both have the same Master in heaven, and He has no favourites' (v. 9, N.E.B.).

TYRANNY AND SLOTH. Paul's charter for slaves and masters was revolutionary, for in the ancient world slaves had no rights. In the light of the gospel, says the apostle, both slaves and masters have responsibilities to each other. Translated into modern terms this passage suggests that no true Christian can be either a tyrannical boss or a lazy worker.

'The trouble with the tyrant,' claims Earl Kelly, 'is basically that he does not have any faith in anyone except himself . . . he believes nothing worthwhile will happen unless he forces it to happen.' Of course, deep down, the tyrant does not greatly believe in himself either. This means, strangely enough, that the hatred he earns himself only makes him more oppressive, whereas someone with the ability to help the tyrant believe in himself, and so in others, will often make him more amenable.

Workers are not tempted to tyranny, but sometimes to laziness, especially if the work is uninteresting. Many have proved that even routine drudgery can be offered to God. Writing to a friend from China, Teilhard de Chardin said, 'It seems to me that in a sense the true substance to be consecrated each day is the world's development during that day—the bread symbolizing appropriately what creation succeeds in producing, the wine (blood) what creation causes to be lost in exhaustion and suffering in the course of its effort.'

EPHESIANS 6:10–13

'Draw your strength from the Lord, from that mastery which His power supplies' (v. 10, Knox).

THE FACT OF CHRIST. We have seen that behind the reference in this letter to heavenly rulers, powers and principalities there lies a whole world of first-century mythology. 'Spiritual wickedness in high places' (v. 12 A.V.) originally meant not corruption among political or religious leaders but those malign powers associated with the stars and planets.

In different periods man portrays the evil threatening him in various ways. The Christian response, howevei, remains essentially the same: God in Christ has faced and overcome this evil—in His strength the believer is likewise victorious. Contrast two Christian writers, one from the fourth century the other present day.

Sharing the same world-view reflected in Ephesians, Athanasius argued that it was fitting that Christ should die on the Cross, for he who dies by crucifixion 'dies in the air'. The atmosphere was the abode of demons, rulers, heavenly powers. 'Thus being lifted up,' claimed Athanasius, 'He cleared the air of the malignity both of the devil and of demons of all kinds.'

Today we see some evil arising from the depths of man's unconscious. Dr. Frank Lake encourages Christians who are suffering from depression and anxiety to see Christ treading the same path in Gethsemane and Calvary. He too felt abandoned and isolated. Christ's next appointment with us may be 'in the depths from which flight is no longer necessary'. Contrasting these two writers we see that, whatever our particular view of evil, it is the fact of Christ sharing our conflict that saves.

EPHESIANS 6:14–17

'Take up the great shield of faith, with which you will be able to quench all the flaming arrows of the evil one' (v. 16, N.E.B.).

SHARING CHRIST'S VICTORY. Whether our conflict is with external powers of evil, or with rebel emotions and irrational fears, Christ offers us adequate equipment. Paul's description of the Christian's armoury may well owe something to the uniform of the Roman soldier who guarded him.

The shield of faith envisaged here was a large body shield, not the small circular shield used by the Greeks. 'Faith' carries a variety of meanings in the New Testament, sometimes indicating simple trust, at other times the body of Christian doctrine, or the ability to perceive unseen spiritual realities. Here 'faith' means the capacity of the believer to unite himself with Christ, and so with His victory. This may result in a resounding triumph or simply the endurance to keep on fighting when it would be easy to capitulate.

Antony, the hermit monk who died at the age of one hundred and five in A.D. 356, went into the desert to wage spiritual war on the evil powers believed to dwell there. Under one assault of evil he replied, 'So many demons to one poor monk! If you had any power one of you would be sufficient. But Christ has hamstrung you and so you try to frighten me with your numbers.' Though the spiritual struggle is conceived differently today Antony's words form the classic Christian attitude. The victory over evil has been won. Faith links us to Christ, enabling us to share His triumph.

EPHESIANS 6:18–24

'Pray on every occasion in the power of the Spirit' (v. 18, N.E.B.).

WIDE-RANGING PRAYER. Paul's description of himself as 'an ambassador—in chains' is a delightful touch. An ambassador is rarely, if ever, imprisoned for he can claim diplomatic immunity. Despite the apostle's worldly status he did not relinquish his exalted view of his vocation.

Continuing his account of the Christian warrior in spiritual conflict, Paul drops descriptive metaphors and makes a straightforward plea for prayer. It is in prayer we receive and use the spiritual armoury God supplies. Praying 'in the Spirit' is not necessarily ecstatic prayer. It is to pray as Jesus prayed. Remembering this we may have to revise our whole concept of spiritual victory. 'Nothing could seem less like power than the agonized figure in Gethsemane, whose sweat was, as it were, great drops of blood; and yet this living, undeterred obedience is the might which overthrows principalities and powers (wrote John Huxtable). Into this weakness of God which is stronger than men the Spirit initiates us when He enables us to pray'.

Prayer modelled upon Christ's, and inspired by His Spirit, will be free from narrow, constricted concerns. What breadth of interest, and deepening of sympathy, is introduced into the life of anyone who intercedes 'for all God's people' (v. 18), including those far removed in the ecclesiastical spectrum. Picasso, who has influenced modern art so much, hated travelling, and said, 'I can do all the travelling I want in my head.' Should we do a little more 'travelling' in our prayers?

THE EPISTLE TO THE PHILIPPIANS

INTRODUCTION

This is another letter from prison, written by Paul either when his trial had been adjourned or before the main judicial proceedings had begun (1:7). But this makes no difference to the Apostle's feelings for his friends in Philippi. Always he thinks of them with joy (1:4).

Even the fact that some Christian workers acted as if they were his rivals, not his comrades, in the preaching of the gospel (1:15) did not dismay him. For ever he kept the example of his beloved Lord in view (2:6 ff.) and nothing would deflect him from the goal which God had set before him (3:14).

The generosity of believers in Philippi was ever the sweetest of memories, and his faith was that God would continue to supply their every need as well as his own (4:19).

PHILIPPIANS 1:1–6

'Paul and Timothy, servants of Jesus Christ' (v. 1, R.S.V.).

COMMITTED AND COMMISSIONED. The word servants which Paul here applies to Timothy and himself means, literally, slaves. According to Deissmann (says Ralph P. Martin) the title can be traced to the Hellenistic custom, 'in which the slave was set free by a money payment and thereby became a devotee of the deity'. The word in its Hebrew form goes back to the Old Testament and is used of Moses and the prophets to signify their authority as messengers of God. It is in this form a title of dignity, denoting a high calling. In the Christian context both meanings of the word are valid. Paul was a slave of Christ, an utterly devoted follower, but also a man with a commission to preach the gospel.

Christian experience begins when a man commits himself to God in Christ and so becomes a 'new creation'. Even the best scheme for a better world will fail unless it is recognized that only renewed men, men committed to Christ, can renew society.

Then the committed man becomes a commissioned man with responsibility for helping spread the news that there is a God, that He is not dead, and that He is like Jesus, loving and forgiving. It is estimated that today two-thirds of the population of the world do not know of the love of Christ. What should we do about that? First of all, we ought to look around our own neighbourhood where there are many who have not heard the gospel, and many who do not seem able to hear. The urgent question is: What are we going to do about them?

PHILIPPIANS 1:7–11

'And this is my prayer, that your love may grow ever richer and richer in knowledge and insight of every kind, and may this bring you the gift of true discrimination' (vv. 9–10, N.E.B.).

LEARNING TO LOVE AWKWARD PEOPLE. Christian discipleship, infers the Apostle Paul, is an adventure in loving, in caring with sensitive understanding. Love that is blind causes a mother to pamper her child, and a married partner to be dominated for the sake of peace and quiet.

Indeed, love that is not enlightened poisons its every relationship. It exploits the beloved to satisfy its own self-centredness and thereby further blunts its perception. Paul surely had such a possibility in mind when he told his friends at Philippi to be 'sincere and without offence', for even sincerity does not always exclude calculating and critical goodness.

Few individuals do greater disservice to the cause of Christ than fervent believers whose love is devoid of insight and whose moral crusading lacks gentleness. But how can love acquire understanding, the quality that transforms sincere intentions into creative caring? One answer, as today's verses indicate, is by sharpening love's insight on the anvil of prayer.

This involves more than merely asking to be made loving; the saints unanimously affirm that it also necessitates unhurried gazing into the steady eyes of Christ, notably at the foot of His Cross, and seeking complete identification with the circumstances of the persons beloved in fact or desire. As Florence Allshorn advised a woman concerned about an awkward friend: 'You will have to get where she is and take her on from there, and that takes time. It is the danger of all us single-minded fanatics because that is what we do become if we can't get where the other person is.'

PHILIPPIANS 1:12–18

'ALL THINGS WORK TOGETHER FOR GOOD.' Some years earlier, in a period of comparative peace, Paul had written to the Roman Christians: 'And we know that all things work together for good to them that love God, to them who are the called according to His purpose' (Romans 8:28). Now in prison, in the Rome to which he wrote those words, he can say, 'the things which happened unto mc have fallen out rather unto the furtherance of the gospel'.

Doubtless the Apostle's many friends had looked upon his imprisonment as sheer disaster, as the inevitable silencing of a very necessary voice. But their fears had been unfounded. What looked like disaster proved to be an opportunity such as Paul could have had in no other way. He makes two points. Firstly, the gospel was now known throughout the imperial regiments from which his guards were chosen. Perhaps some of the soldiers chained to Paul were unwilling listeners, but who can doubt that many came to welcome—and then spread—the truth. Secondly, the Apostle's courageous bearing had put iron into many a timid Christian so that the witness of others had been made the more effective.

We can face each day in the confidence that no adverse circumstances need be detrimental to our religious life or our service for Christ.

> I want Thy constant presence, Lord,
> Then e'en a dark adversity
> Will be a blessing in disguise;
> Live Thou Thy life in me.

PHILIPPIANS 1:19–26

'I very much want to leave this life and be with Christ, which is a far better thing: but it is much more important, for your sakes, that I remain alive' (vv. 23, 24, T.E.V.).

CONSPIRACY OF SILENCE. There seems to be a conspiracy of silence on the subject of death, though it is the one certainty there is. With the help of good food and a welfare service, we may postpone its coming, but we cannot abolish it. Paul did not share the reluctance most of us feel to talk about death (especially our own!) though his apparent indifference to his fate did not mean he was anxious to escape from the responsibilities of life. John Keats might write, 'I have been half in love with easeful death', but not the Apostle. He was not the victim of any death wish, but neither was life everything to him. Only in Christ—in life or in death—was there meaning for him.

A realistic appreciation of the fact of death affects our approach to life: for one thing it teaches us the limitations of the material world. There are values in life apart from material values—love, honour and beauty. Every generation produces those who are willing to die for a cause, an ideal, a person. Not all of us call them fools, though we do not always see their full merit: rather do we acknowledge with them that there is more to life than just living.

Another point: There is no need to fear that coming to terms with the transitory nature of life will make us less concerned about human need here and now. Who lived a fuller, more adventurous, more purposeful life than Paul? If, like him, we face the fact of death, like him we may go on to live completely and joyfully in Christ.

PHILIPPIANS 1:27–30

'You are given, in this battle, the privilege not merely of believing in Christ, but also of suffering for His sake' (v. 29, Phillips).

THE PRIVILEGE OF SUFFERING. In a moving personal story, *Appeals From Russia*, a Russian woman writes of her husband, imprisoned for his faith. 'Glory be to the Lord that He has given us also a little chip of His Cross to bear . . . My children now wait for their father to come home . . . he put his life at stake for Christ, to suffer for the faith once for all delivered to the saints.' Powerful opposition to the Christian faith is not a thing of the past only. Paul's references to 'enemies' and to 'suffering for His sake' are not unrelated to the contemporary scene. He writes here, however, not merely of the stoic acceptance of suffering for Christ, but of the privilege of doing so. Have his words any point for Christians living in a society where the Faith is at least politely tolerated?

Persecution in our setting may not be physical or organized, and we should hesitate to equate our little inconveniences with the sufferings of those in less favoured lands. Nevertheless, there are those who today know the hardness of social ostracism, or the hurt of misunderstanding because of their faith. Here is a teenage girl trying to live as the one committed Christian in a home where the interests of the other members of the family do not extend beyond bingo and the television set, and where real religion is something of a joke. There is no attempt by any member of the family to understand her. It is hard to live in that kind of tension. People like that girl deserve our prayers and our encouragement. Perhaps we know nothing of hardness ourselves. It might be salutary to ask why.

PHILIPPIANS 2:1–4

'And look out for each other's interests, not just for your own' (v. 4, T.E.V.).

CARING FOR OTHERS. Paul's exhortation to 'look out for each other's interests' provides us with a rule of life. Some commentators, making an allowable alternative translation of the original, interpret Paul's meaning here as: look on the good qualities of other people, certainly good advice. Nothing will keep us humble as to our own moral attainment like appreciatively; nothing the good points of others. However, we ought to notice what there is to learn from the more usual interpretation that we should not neglect the needs of others.

One of the sad results of the urbanization of our society is the diminishing sense of community and neighbourliness. People are becoming more and more wrapped up in their own concerns and less conscious of the existence, let alone the needs, of those who live around them. The obvious result is the rapid increase of loneliness. It is estimated that there are 4,000,000 lonely people in Britain, not all of them old people (though this age group undoubtedly suffers) but young people also.

Armand Georgés has made a study of the problem, and in his book *Loneliness* quotes a letter written by a young person to his parish priest, 'I came to London, sure I would find here all the opportunities I needed to be recognized for what I am. Alas, nobody wants to know where I am or even who I am . . . *Everybody is so taken up with his or her own affairs, they have no time to give so much as a thought to me.*' The italicized words are an indictment of a self-centred society. The problem exists where we live. As Christians, what is our personal duty in this matter?

PHILIPPIANS 2:5–11

'For the divine nature was His from the first; yet He . . . made Himself nothing' (vv. 6, 7, N.E.B.).

EMPTIED HIMSELF. It has been suggested that the Moravian Zinzendorf was the first to formulate the truth embodied in his friend Charles Wesley's lines: 'Emptied Himself of all but love'. Since then many scholars have used this thought to link the eternal Son, one with the Father, with the historic Jesus of Nazareth.

This is a mystery into which man, as well as angels, would enquire, and it could be that the significance of a truth of this description is better expressed in poetry than in prose. This lends colour to the suggestion that this passage is really an early Christian hymn to the praise of Jesus, known to Paul and incorporated by him into this Epistle.

Philippians 2:7 is linked with Isaiah 53:12, and more than one phrase from this servant song is found in the New Testament passage. Another link with the Old Testament is that, in contrast with the first Adam who yielded to the temptation: 'Ye shall be as gods' (Genesis 3:5), the second Adam did not 'cling to His rights as God', but for our salvation 'laid aside His mighty power and glory'. The Apostle turned this major theological fact into a practical guide for believers. They are (in William Barclay's words) to 'try always to have the same attitude to life as Jesus.'

PHILIPPIANS 2:12–18

'Do all you have to do without grumbling or arguing, so that you may be God's children, blameless, sincere and wholesome, living in a warped and diseased world, and shining there like lights in a dark place' (vv. 14–15, Phillips).

SELF-HATE KILLS CHARITY. In a passage as rich as this, we should not overlook one of the principal lessons. It is centred around the word translated grumbling by Phillips, and rendered murmuring in the Authorized Version. As a rule, the grumbler is also the man most likely to pull a friend's character to pieces!

This was clearly in the mind of Ronald Knox when he wrote: 'Murmuring is a sin against God because it betrays a want of detachment. There are very few of God's gifts which we use so lavishly, with so little regard to mortification, as the gift of speech. So much unnecessary talk; we surely ought to start cutting it down somewhere; and . . . what more obvious place to begin at than our uncharitable conversations? Yet we don't seem to do it. How odd and how humiliating, that the one self-indulgence we find it impossible to deny ourselves should be this clatter-clatter of tongues over the shortcomings of other people.'

Some of the most conscientious workers for God have also been the worst murmurers. They grumble and grouse, criticize and gossip with a relish born of unconscious self-disapproval. Some individuals hate themselves too much to be charitable!

PHILIPPIANS 2:91–24

'I hope, if the Lord wills it, to send Timothy to you soon' (v. 91, Barclay).

WHAT THE LORD WILLS. The Apostle's plans to send Timothy on a visit to the Philippians and to visit them himself are both conditional, he says, on what the Lord wills. He was a man so closely identified with Christ that he could think of no future action without relating it to the will of the Lord. Is not this the ideal to which every Christian should aspire?

The words 'Thy will be done' often deter us. We misunderstand the term, associating it with the tragedies and irksome duties of life, instead of seeing it as something God wants for our good, or something He wants us to go out and do joyfully. William Temple once said we have turned 'what was meant to be a battle cry into a wailing litany'. To equate the will of God only with tragedy and loss is blasphemy. True, sometimes in the immediate His will may lead through a 'glen of gloom', but only that we may emerge eventually into the full sunshine of His grace.

It may be, of course, that sometimes we know more about the will of God for us than we care to admit. The trouble then is not discovering it, but being willing and courageous enough to comply with it. We want the Kingdom of God—but on our own terms. The misconception of the phrase 'Thy will be done' and our reluctance to do what we know should be done are linked. If we can believe that God's will is only for our good, then we shall do it whatever it is, and do it gladly.

PHILIPPIANS 2:25–30

Epaphroditus 'is my brother and comrade both in labour and in arms, and is your messenger who has ministered to my needs' (v. 25, Weymouth).

'GAMBLERS' FOR CHRIST. Hearing of Paul's imprisonment, the Christians at Philippi sent a gift to him by the hand of Epaphroditus whom they also commissioned to remain in Rome as the Apostle's personal servant. This assignment demanded rare courage, for association with a prisoner on trial for his life was full of dangerous possibilities. When the messenger–servant fell ill and almost died, Paul decided that he (Epaphroditus) should return home, but this return left him open to charges of coward and quitter. So the Apostle gave him a testimonial, calling him his brother, his fellow worker, and his fellow soldier; he also described him as 'your messenger to meet my wants' and finally said of him that he lived as one 'not regarding his life'. In other words he had 'gambled with his life' to be of service to Paul.

Later there were Christian brotherhoods whose members, because of the risks they took in the service of the plague-stricken and fever-ridden, became known as 'the Gamblers'. The best of Christians, while shunning mere foolhardiness, have shown a responsible indifference to personal comfort and safety.

'I am God's gambler', said Kagawa, 'I have staked my life on Him.'

Studdert Kennedy's lines about Jesus portray a way of life for His followers.

> 'He was a gambler too, my Christ,
> He took His life and threw
> It for a world redeemed.
> And ere His agony was done,
> Before the westering sun was down,
> Crowning that day with its crimson crown,
> He knew that He had won.'

PHILIPPIANS 3:1–7

'Finally, my brethren, rejoice in the Lord. To write the same thing to you is not irksome to me, and is safe for you' (v. 1, R.S.V.).

KEEP ON REJOICING. There has been a good deal of discussion among scholars as to what Paul meant by 'the same thing', in today's text. It may have referred to previous warnings about disunity in the Church or to the exhortation to rejoice in the preceding sentence. The translations by Moffatt and J. B. Phillips and the recent Living New Testament translation support the latter view.

Two points emerge. The first emphasizes the necessity for us to be constantly recalling those fundamentals of Christian faith and practice that we have received. In this case it was a reminder to continue to rejoice, but it applies equally to other truths we so easily forget. 'It is not sufficiently considered', wrote Dr. Johnson, 'that men more frequently require to be reminded than informed.' Our quest for new truth is not only valid but necessary; nothing is more tragic than a Christian with a closed mind. Nevertheless, to follow unquestioningly every fashion of thought as it appears is certainly unwise and might be destructive. Prayerful reference to God's word will help keep a right balance.

Secondly, we have a duty not only to rejoice in the Lord but also to spread the radiance of our faith. Though not unaware of the sorrows of life—he is not himself immune from them—the Christian has a joy that nothing can take away. Paul's repeated exhortation to rejoice should be taken to heart by all of us.

PHILIPPIANS 3:8–11

'I would know Him in the power of His resurrection and the fellowship of His sufferings' (v. 10, Moffatt).

APPROPRIATING SPIRITUAL POWER. Paul's constant aim was to know Christ with deepening intimacy. To this end, he related his experience of Christ's power to his sharing of Christ's suffering. Some believers pray for power simply for the sake of feeling powerful, of having adequate spiritual resources in case of emergency.

God, however, never bestows His power for unspecified causes. He provides grace, not in anticipation, but only as it is needed; the believer steps forward in faith to meet a challenging situation, often despite his feelings, and knows the power of God by using it. He suffers for Christ and thereby experiences the dynamic of divine energy. This was one reason why Paul gloried in tribulation. He did not enjoy pain and sacrifice, if only because he recognized the difference between being a martyr and having a martyr complex. But he realized that the obedience behind his suffering and sacrifice, as distinct from the suffering and sacrifice themselves, released God's power in his soul. And the more he shared Christ's trials the more he appropriated Christ's triumph.

Perhaps the best way to experience the power of the resurrection is to attempt for God something which we know to be beyond our own native powers. Then in our weakness we experience His power.

PHILIPPIANS 3:12–16

'I have not yet reached perfection, but I press on, hoping to take hold of that for which Christ once took hold of me' (v. 12, N.E.B.).

LIVING WITH MONOTONY. Paul wanted to be perfect, a word meaning full-grown mature, complete. A thing was reckoned to be 'perfect' when it completely fulfilled the purpose for which it was made; and the Apostle wanted this kind of perfection for himself. He knew that on the Damascus road Christ had taken hold of his life for a purpose, and it was this divine dream and ambition that Paul wanted to come true. To this end he made two practical decisions.

First, he determined to turn his back upon the defeats of the past. How some of us need to cultivate the same wisdom! We allow morbidity and guilt to haunt us. Having confessed our sins and reminded ourselves of God's willingness to put them behind His back to be remembered no more, we then creep behind His back, bring them out and start the procedure all over again. Paul, on the other hand, refused to embalm his regrets in his memory. He cast them once and for all into the sea of God's forgetfulness and pressed on, a fact leading to his second decision.

The Apostle determined to turn his face towards the promise of the future. He did this, not by becoming other-worldly, piously indifferent to his daily responsibilities, but by keeping his eyes on his glorious destination in Christ that the sometimes drab and tedious obligations of his daily journey might shine with their real significance and purpose. Such an outlook is not beyond any of us.

PHILIPPIANS 3:17–21

'But we are a colony of Heaven, and we wait for the Saviour who comes from Heaven, the Lord Jesus Christ' (v. 20, Moffatt).

OUR TRUE CITIZENSHIP. Very few preachers can say, 'Do as I do'; most of them have to say, 'Do as I say.' But the Apostle Paul could write without arrogance: 'Agree together, my friends, to follow my example' (v. 17, N.E.B.), a verse which J. B. Lightfoot renders: 'Vie with each other in imitating me.' A concrete example of Christian discipleship was particularly necessary at this time in the Philippian church. Certain believers were surrendering to the cravings of the flesh without shame, explaining that what happened to the body was unimportant; all that mattered was the spirit, which the body could not affect!

The Apostle countered this teaching by pointing to the way in which he buffeted his own body to keep it in subjection; and also by reminding the true believers that they were a 'colony of Heaven'. 'We are citizens of Heaven,' he told them. Now Philippi was one of numerous Roman colonies, which were at strategic centres throughout the empire and reflections in organization, dress, language and virtually every particular of Rome itself. Whatever their geographical setting, these centres were uncompromisingly Roman. Paul's argument was that similarly every Christian fellowship was, or should be, a little bit of Heaven, an illustration of what the world would be like if it accepted Christ as Lord! There could be no higher ideal of Christian brotherhood and we have a personal responsibility to make it come true.

PHILIPPIANS 4:1–7

'Euodias and Syntyche, I beg you by name to make up your differences as Christians should! And you, my true, fellow worker, I ask you to help these women' (vv. 2, 3, Phillips).

HARMONIOUS RELATIONSHIPS. The only thing we know about these two women, each of them probably leaders in the Church at Philippi, is that they quarrelled and refused to be reconciled.

Few developments are more damaging to the cause of Christ than squabbling Christians. It was with such a truth in mind that someone observed: 'One proud believer does greater harm to the Kingdom of God than ten atheists.' Of course, even saints, being finite and fallible, do not see 'eye to eye' in all things; they have their own deeply held points of view. But this does not make them discourteous in their disagreements. Their strength is always gentle, their truthfulness never rude, and they know the difference between conviction and obstinacy, and principle and opinion. Equally important, they invariably take the initiative when apologies are necessary, but never as an insincere means to a desirable end. From their hearts, they forgive and seek forgiveness, thereby making possible the restoration of broken relationships.

The two women at Philippi were apparently not prepared for such a step. They harboured their resentment, which poisoned the secret springs of their whole beings and blurred the essential vision to which we referred yesterday. So Paul asked the fellowship to which they belonged to help them sort out their differences. He knew that quarrelling Christians, apart from bringing discredit upon their Lord, shut out God and destroy their own inner peace. Hence his plea that the entire body of believers should accept responsibility for the securing of perfect harmony, which meant that any estranged Christians among them should be the immediate focal point, not of condemnation and despair, but of united caring and prayer.

PHILIPPIANS 4:8

'Whatever is excellent and admirable—fill all your thoughts with these things' (N.E.B.).

GOODNESS WITHOUT GRACE? The virtues itemized in this verse have been described as 'pagan' virtues. They are virtues none the less, and should be acknowledged as such. One translation reads: 'Wherever virtue and merit are found, you must take them into account'.

If God is the source of all goodness—as He is, then wherever goodness is to be seen we must acknowledge His presence. Our faith does not require us to attribute the decency of the ordinary man to some evil agency. Even a drunkard, in his own way, can be fond of his ten-year-old daughter. We might well say that he would be able to care for her better were he to master his personal weakness. But we cannot deny his affection, even if we regret its self-imposed limitations.

The virtues of life are to be seen in men of various views—religious, often irreligious, or political. Human courage is none the less courage when displayed by a Marxist. A willingness to suffer for one's convictions is to be respected at whatever end of the religious spectrum it may be seen. Our task is not to decry the worth of another man's motives but ourselves, as God shall help us, consistently to reflect the spirit of the highest example ever given to men—that of Jesus Himself. To follow the Christian way does call for Christian grace.

PHILIPPIANS 4:9–14

'He who fills me with His dynamic power has made me able to cope with any situation' (v. 13, Barclay).

ABLE TO COPE. Paul's claim to be 'able to cope with any situation' (how arresting is William Barclay's rendering here!) would be palpably absurd were it not for the acknowledgment that this was possible only in Christ. The difference between the humanist view of human nature and the frank recognition of the New Testament is just here. In face of all the evidence to the contrary, the humanist says that man is sufficient of himself to achieve full development and find complete happiness. The Christian, on the other hand, cannot ignore the fatal flaw in man and his need for help.

This is not to say there is no good in man. An impressive record of human achievement, kindness, wisdom and sacrifice shows there is. And, of course, man cannot be wholly bad when he recognizes and strains after goodness. There is a 'problem' of good as well as a problem of evil. Dr. John Baillie puts the truth this way: 'Human nature is not a bad thing, but a good thing gone wrong'. There are tremendous and exciting potentialities in man if he is humble enough to acknowledge his need of God.

No man had a more purposeful, radiant life than Paul—and he lived for Christ. This is the secret of success both in being and doing. We need not plod in the marshlands of inadequacy and defeat, but climb the mountain of victory. Let our prayer be that we might experience in increasing measure all Christ has to impart.

PHILIPPIANS 4:15–23

'I have all I need, now that Epaphroditus has brought me all your gifts. These are like a sweet-smelling offering to God, a sacrifice which is acceptable and pleasing' (v. 18, T.E.V.).

SERVING GOD IN MAN. In the closing words of the letter Paul was concerned to thank the Philippians for the gifts they had sent to make his imprisonment more tolerable. His words to them were generous, like their gifts to him. His gratitude was heartfelt. It revealed something about Paul, for the common courtesies of life are always more symptomatic of character than the spectacular deeds we are usually more eager to perform. A gifted and persuasive preacher was known to be unkind almost to the point of cruelty to his wife in their home. His preaching, despite its eloquence, was ineffective. The man was judged by his lack of love.

Paul's generous words were such as we might expect from him. But something else he said regarding the Philippians' gifts was not so predictable. He said that the Philippians' generosity to him was pleasing and acceptable to God. Here is underlined the truth Jesus taught that the strength and reality of our relationship to God is measured by the quality of our relationship to others. What we do to help, encourage and, so far as we are able, supply the needs of others, God accepts as an offering to Himself. 'Whenever you did this (exercise practical care) for one of the least important of these brothers of mine,' said Jesus, 'you did it for me!' By our giving in love we share in the love God feels for the world. But Jesus also said that the converse is true: our neglect of others is a denial of our love for God.

THE EPISTLE TO THE COLOSSIANS

INTRODUCTION

Here is another letter written by Paul when in prison (4:3, 18), although he did not know personally any of those belonging to the church in Colossae. He was sufficiently interested in their welfare, however, to warn them against influences which, if unchecked, might undermine their faith in the supremacy (1:15) and adequacy (2:3) of Jesus.

Believers were not to trouble themselves, nor be troubled by, speculation about the power of the stars, or of spirits, or of demons (2:8), nor pay attention to the call to angel worship (2:18), nor to the demand to observe certain ritual practices (2:16), nor to give way to any personal misconduct (3:5).

Their lives were to be hid with Christ in God (3:3), and the richness of their spiritual experience would be seen in the quality of their daily behaviour (3:18–4:1).

COLOSSIANS 1:1–6

'We have heard of the faith you hold in Christ Jesus, and the love you bear towards all God's people. Both spring from the hope stored up for you in heaven . . .' (vv. 4 and 5, N.E.B.).

GOOD NEWS NOT GOOD ADVICE. Following the usual pattern in Greek correspondence Paul opens his letter to the Colossians with a salutation, followed by a thanksgiving for the welfare of the persons addressed. The Apostle expresses gratitude for the faith, love and hope of the Colossian Christians.

Greek ethical writers were fond of compiling lists of virtues—and vices. Paul himself followed this practice on occasions, but more frequently we find him describing the Christian character as a blend of three principal virtues—faith, hope and love (1 Thess. 1:3; 5:8; Gal. 5:5 and 6; 1 Cor. 13). Yet these virtues cannot be sought separately, as though one could first become competent in the exercise of faith, then undertake to develop hope and so on. Rather are they different aspects of one unified character. The faith and the love 'spring from the hope'.

Paul goes on to assert that this hope became possible upon hearing the gospel. In other words, Christian character is the response of the whole person to the good news of Jesus Christ. W. B. J. Martin suggests that Christianity has been regarded in three ways: (i) as bad news for sinners—if you continue in sin you will be severely punished; (ii) as good advice—this is how you ought to live; (iii) as good news—this is how much God loves you and this is what He has done for you. It is this understanding of Christianity as good news about God which produces Christian character.

COLOSSIANS 1:7–10

'We pray that you may bear fruit in active goodness of every kind, and grow in the knowledge of God' (v. 10, N.E.B.).

A CRUCIAL TEST. The first century was an age of great religious uncertainty. In the absence of any one recognized faith the field was wide open for all kinds of speculation and fanaticism.

Under the influence of Greek philosophy the main quest was for religious knowledge, yet this was often unrelated to the conduct of everyday life.

In this mental climate Christian teachers were sometimes tempted to present their own faith simply as superior knowledge. After all, the heart of the Christian religion is a new revelation of God in Christ. The apostolic writers spent much time pointing out that genuine knowledge of God must make a difference to the way a person lives. Knowledge that could be assimilated by the mind without any impact upon the character was not knowledge of God. 'Active goodness' was the crucial test.

An anonymous writer in *The British Weekly* once described the sixty-year ministry of his father at a factory gate. During the midday break this fine Christian, who was also a lay preacher and Sunday School teacher, would make his witness. 'Then, when his meeting was over, he'd walk right through those gates to live out what he'd been witnessing to his workmates about.'

Like the first-century Christians we also live in an age of intellectual confusion when 'knowing the answers' can appear the supreme goal. We too need the reminder that Christian faith is essentially something lived out in everyday life. It must express itself in 'active goodness'.

COLOSSIANS 1:11–14

'May He strengthen you, in His glorious might, with ample power to meet whatever comes with fortitude, patience, and joy' (v. 11, N.E.B.).

THE HIGHEST ART. Paul's prayers for his readers give as much insight into the nature of the Christian life as his more direct descriptions. In today's passage, for instance, the word 'strengthen' translates a tense which indicates a continuous experience. Christian living does not depend upon a tremendous initial impetus, with gradually diminishing effects: it is a life of constant renewal.

This inward strengthening, claims the apostle, enables the believer 'to meet whatever comes' with joyful endurance. We could dismiss this claim as armchair extravagance were it not from the pen of a man who was closely acquainted with suffering and persecution. As it is, Paul fully practised what he preached, turning every trial to some spiritual gain. 'Arrest the man (wrote

H. R. MacDonald) and put him in jail; he holds a prayer meeting and converts the jailer. Bring him into court to be questioned by the king; he turns the courtroom into a church and preaches Christ to king and commoner. Lock him in a dungeon to get him out of the way; he spends his years writing New Testament scriptures'.

To be able to wrest spiritual gain from suffering and frustration is perhaps the highest art of all. We can begin to learn it only as we embrace the cause of Christ, which transcends our own narrow interests, and as we recognize that the most painful experience can contribute something to future usefulness, if not in this life then in that higher service to which God will one day call us.

COLOSSIANS 1:15–20

'Christ is the visible expression of the invisible God' (v. 15, Phillips).

A LANGUAGE WE CAN UNDERSTAND. False teaching was gaining ground at Colossae. This suggests that Christ was but one of many spiritual beings who stood between God and man, all of whom needed to be reckoned with. Following the customary greeting, thanksgiving and prayer, Paul plunges straight into a refutation of this error. He does not argue with the false teachers; he simply affirms, in all its splendour, the Christian view of Jesus.

Jesus Christ is unique. Paul claims that the relationship of Jesus to God and to the visible and invisible worlds is without parallel. Jesus is supreme because He alone fully shows us the nature of God, who must be largely mysterious to our human minds. A God perfectly understood is no God. But Jesus 'has translated God into a language you and I can understand' wrote Raymond Raynes.

Because Jesus is the perfect 'image of the invisible God' (N.E.B.) we are assured that God is love. Christ healing the sick, caring for the outcast and the disreputable, loving His enemies from the Cross reveals the vast compassion of the Father. This is why the Protestant theologian, James Denney, said that he envied the Catholic priest his crucifix because he too would like to go around holding aloft this representation of the death of Jesus and saying: 'God loves like that!'

COLOSSIANS 1:21–23

'God has reconciled you to Himself, so that He may present you before Himself as dedicated men, without blemish and innocent in His sight' (v. 22, N.E.B.).

POSITIVE GOODNESS. Cecil Alexander's well-known lines —'He died that we might be forgiven, He died to make us good'— repeat the same truth which Paul declares here. The purpose of the Cross is fulfilled in holy lives. In this respect the New English Bible's use of the phrase 'dedicated men' is highly significant. Holiness has too often been regarded negatively as an absence of evil. Nothing could be further from the truth. Professor J. G. McKenzie tells the story of a woman who, in great distress over her failure to attain to a good life, said, 'I do try so hard to be good.' He comments that actually she did nothing of the kind, she exhausted her strength trying not to do wrong. We cannot become good merely by trying to avoid evil.

Dedicated people are those whose lives are knit together by one absorbing purpose. Even apart from religious motives such purpose often has a purifying effect—it becomes 'the expulsive power of a new affection' which saves a man from unworthy aims. So we find John Wain, in his autobiography, claiming: 'I am in possession of the one gift that makes the longest life seem short. It is a gift which the artist shares with the man of science, the priest, the scholar: a sense of purpose in life, an over-riding object which he finds worthy of his last drop of blood. To me, the struggle to write well is a sufficient task for a lifetime; whatever misfortunes come to me, there can never be any of the dreaded ennui, the feeling of living on mechanically from day to day, that makes so many lives into stuffy little purgatories.'

The struggle to write well is a worthy objective but it is still a limited one. We have been reconciled to God in order that we may know the total and joyous commitment to seeking first God's Kingdom. No part of our lives is left uninfluenced by such an ambition.

COLOSSIANS 1:24–27

'The secret is this: Christ in you, the hope of a glory to come' (v. 27, N.E.B.).

AN OPEN SECRET. The pagan religions of Paul's day placed great emphasis upon mysteries which were made known only to the initiated. Probably the false teachers in the church at Colossae were also claiming to possess secret knowledge which could be shared only by a gifted minority. Such claims seem reasonable enough at first glance. People with advanced mathematical training find a deeply satisfying beauty in complex mathematical formulae—most of us are just mystified. Musicians who, over many years, have developed an acute sensitivity to harmony will gain pleasures from a piece of music which the majority miss. So with art and many other spheres of human endeavour. The richest enjoyment and understanding become ours only by the right initiation and training.

Is the same true of the Christian religion? Paul answers this question by agreeing that certainly there is a secret, a mystery—but it is an open secret. In other words, it can be understood only by those who have a certain experience, but the experience is open to all. No special intellectual ability is required, as is essential for the would-be mathematician; no innate gift, as we find in many musicians. No, the humblest person of any age, living in any circumstances, can understand first-hand this experience.

'The secret is this: Christ in you. . . .' Part of the wonder of this to Paul is that Christ should indwell the Gentiles—this was a revolutionary idea to a Jew. But the permanent wonder, then as now, is that God should indwell human personality. The conditions? No initiation rite, but a sincere and simple openness to Christ. An invitation made to Him on the basis of His promise, 'If anyone hears My voice and opens the door, I will come in and sit down to supper with him and he with Me' (Revelation 3:20, N.E.B.).

O live in us this day.
O clothe Thyself, Thy purpose yet again
In human clay:
Work through our feebleness Thy strength,
Work through our meanness Thy nobility,
Work through our helpless poverty of soul
Thy grace, Thy glory and Thy love.

COLOSSIANS 1:28–2:5

'In Him [Christ] lie hidden all God's treasures of wisdom and knowledge' (v. 3, N.E.B.).

THE ALL-SUFFICIENT CHRIST. Similar questions to those raised at Colossae appear whenever Christianity moves into a new environment—or into a new age. The Indian acknowledges the good which Christian influences have achieved in Europe but questions whether the gospel is adequate for him with his vastly different culture. The modern teenager will say 'Christianity meant everything to my parents but what has Jesus to say to the new space age?'

Paul's message to this first-century Church—that Christ was fully adequate in their complex society—is highly relevant to our day. Revolutionary changes are taking place and many will find that the adjustments they must make will be difficult and painful. But just as Christianity outlived the Roman Empire and later the feudal society of the middle ages, and was found to have a message for the new circumstances which emerged after them, so Christ will be God's Word for the new age which is coming to birth.

Christian biography bears testimony to the way in which men and women in all lands and different centuries have found that Christ meets the deepest needs of the human heart. Jesus will always be relevant because He shows us that the meaning of life is to be found in loving God and loving our neighbour, He reveals what a truly human existence should be, as well as showing us the nature of God.

In an age of change we must take to heart the words with which Herbert Butterfield concluded his book, *Christianity and History*: 'I have nothing to say at the finish except that if one wants a permanent rock in life and goes deep enough for it, it is difficult for historical events to shake it. There are times when we can never meet the future with sufficient elasticity of mind, especially if we are locked in the contemporary systems of thought. We can do worse than remember a principle which both gives us a firm Rock and leaves us the maximum elasticity for our minds: the principle: Hold to Christ, and for the rest be totally uncommitted.'

COLOSSIANS 2:6–15

'Just as you received Christ Jesus the Lord, so go on living in Him . . . Grow out of Him as a plant grows out of the soil it is planted in' (vv. 6 and 7. Phillips).

GIVE HIM OUR ATTENTION. That the Christian lives his life in Christ is a theme which recurs throughout all the Pauline letters. Here the apostle purposely mixes his metaphors—'Be rooted in Him; be built in Him' (N.E.B.)—in order to bring out two distinct ideas. Rooted refers to something completed in the past, something fixed once and for all: built, however, speaks of the present steady growth of Christian character. The Colossians were tempted to engage in all kinds of wild speculations, and to seek salvation by trying to come to terms with many spiritual agencies. The apostle insists that nothing more is required for Christian growth than an increasingly close union with Christ.

W. E. Sangster asked how it is possible for us to live in Christ, and Christ in us. He concluded that first we must believe in its possibility, then we must want it ardently, and finally we must deliberately open our minds to Christ's incoming. 'All our school days,' he wrote, 'our teachers urged us to "give our minds" to things. There is nothing mysterious here. It is all summarized in the word "attention". We give our mind to Christ when we attend to Him; think of him; talk to Him; work with Him; rest with Him; walk with Him . . . and the more we give Him our minds, the more He gives us His.' Experience will teach us that 'as our Lord grows within us, we begin to see things as He sees them and, after a while, we begin to see Jesus in the things we are looking at.'

COLOSSIANS 2:16–23

'All these things have at most only a symbolical value: the solid fact is Christ' (v. 17, Phillips).

FALSE PRIORITIES. False teachers at Colossae were claiming that only by observing detailed prohibitions and many man-made rules could the spiritual life be properly lived. The emphasis had become a negative one and Paul saw the danger that such teaching would lead to despair on the one hand and pride on the other. Moreover, such an emphasis displaced what is the central objective of Christian living—love to God and man.

Søren Kierkegaard invited his fellow Christians to measure the value of all religious practices—creeds, ceremonies, rules of behaviour—by considering how far they help us towards the goal of loving God and our fellows. All too often such practices become goals in themselves. As the parable of the Good Samaritan shows they can even become an evasion of the prime duty of love.

Religious practices may be regarded as maps, suggests one writer. There are good maps and poor maps. Similarly some beliefs are inadequately stated, some ceremonies tend to obscure the truth and some prohibitions are unnecessarily burdensome. On the other hand there are many religious practices which have been proved of tremendous value. But what counts is not the map, but making the jouney. Am I loving God and my fellows better because of the religious practices I have embraced? This is the question we must constantly ask ourselves.

COLOSSIANS 3:1–4

'Since then you have been raised with Christ, aim at what is above, where Christ is, seated at the right hand of God' (v. 1, Moffatt).

THE ETERNAL DIMENSION. In few passages of Scripture is the Christian life so clearly defined as in these thrilling verses which provide one of the Easter Day readings in thousands of churches. The believer is 'raised with Christ' and shares the very resurrection life of His Lord. Yet this does not result in an effortless perfection, he still has to 'aim at what is above'. Moreover, Christian conduct to which Paul turns at this point in his letter, is the outcome of the gospel, the theme of the first two chapters. Christian faith must issue in Christian living.

When Paul urges the Colossians to 'aim at what is above' he means that their ambitions should transcend physical and material well-being, they should live even now in a spiritual dimension. They are to seek first the Kingdom of God—the values which are embodied in the risen and enthroned Christ. How easily we lose the vision of the eternal dimension, and become superficial in our living. Thomas Chalmers preached for years a formal, lifeless religion until a transforming experience changed his life. Looking back on his earlier days he wrote: 'Mathematician as I was, I had forgotten two magnitudes—the shortness of time and the vastness of eternity.'

Living in the eternal dimension will not be possible, however, by an act of will, nor by frequent reminders that such a dimension exists. It becomes a reality in as far as we are linked in fellowship with Christ.

COLOSSIANS 3:5–11

'You have discarded the old nature with its deeds and have put on the new nature, which is being constantly renewed in the image of its Creator and brought to know God' (vv. 9 and 10, N.E.B.).

GOD'S PART—AND OURS. In the pagan mystery religions of Paul's day a candidate for initiation was dressed in a sacred robe to indicate the new condition he was supposed to enter. Possibly a similar custom prevailed at Christian baptism. Paul frequently speaks of the Christian life as a change of garment (Romans 13:14; Galatians 3:27; 1 Thessalonians 5:8).

This passage is a timely reminder that Christian living means co-operation between God and the believer. We must strive to discard 'the old nature with its deeds'—moral apathy can find no place in the life of a disciple of Christ. Yet a mere struggle for self-reformation is quite useless, as many of us know to our cost. It is God's part constantly to renew the new nature 'in the image of its creator'. When Kagawa of Japan first committed himself to Christ his prayer to God was: 'O God, I want to be like Christ! O God, make me like Christ!' This recognition, that only God can produce Christlikeness in us, is just as important as our determination to do what he can to leave behind the old self-centred way of life.

Speaking of the great artists John Ruskin said that their power is not so much 'in them, but through them'. The same is true of every Christian. Being open to God and living in fellowship with Christ is the only way in which daily renewal can be ours.

COLOSSIANS 3:12–17

'Forgive as freely as the Lord has forgiven you' (v. 13, Phillips).

CAN WE FORGIVE? 'There is no revenge like the revenge of a saint,' wrote W. E. Sangster, illustrating this comment by describing an encounter witnessed by his father between some early Salvationists and 'the Skeleton Army'. 'Outside the Eagle Tavern in the City Road, London, a Salvationist was offering Christ to the people one day when a half-drunk man came out of the public house and, with one savage blow, knocked the preacher from his box. As he fell, the soldier of Christ struck his head against the curb with such force that everyone thought he was dead. Then he came round, staggered to his feet, and saw, through his swimming eyes, the brute who had done it—almost sobered now with fright. Raising his hand in love, he said: "God bless you" as he resumed his address.'

Among the qualities the believer is to don in place of the rags of the old nature, Paul includes that of kindly forgiveness. While recognizing the heroic forgiveness displayed in this story we have to admit that it is in less dramatic situations, involving people with whom we are closely linked as friends, colleagues and relatives, that forgiveness is most difficult. Significantly, Paul links our ability to forgive others with our own experience of God's free pardon. The self-righteous always find it intolerably hard to forgive: the pardoned sinner living in keen awareness of God's grace would find it hard not to forgive.

COLOSSIANS 3:18–4:1

'Husbands, love your wives and treat them with gentleness' (v. 19, Jerusalem Bible).

RIGHTS AND OBLIGATIONS. 'Christianity has in no way effected a deeper change in the world's life than by placing the family on a new basis.' So writes E. F. Scott, commenting on this passage. It is just because the Christian ethic has so greatly influenced society that we fail to recognize how revolutionary was Paul's teaching. The duty of wives to husbands, children to parents, slaves to masters: these were everywhere acknowledged. But that these responsibilities should be reciprocal, this was 'the great Christian innovation'.

It is in marriage that we experience the deepest antagonism and the highest communion because it is life at close quarters. Family life establishes a pattern which we tend to carry with us into the wider world of human relationships. In particular, our experience of the family as children moulds expectations and fears which accompany us throughout life, most of all when we are unaware of them.

It was surely in the spirit of Paul's claim that all members of the family have rights and obligations that one Christian psychologist established in his own family a ten minute period each day when parents and children could express their complaints and feelings of irritation. He knew the danger of buried resentments, a danger to which families are particularly prone when too much value is placed upon an atmosphere of unruffled calm.

COLOSSIANS 4:2–6

'Pray for us, that God may give us an opening for preaching, to tell the secret of Christ. . . . Pray that I may make the secret plain (vv. 3-4, N.E.B.).

WASTING LIFE. There are few more revealing pictures of the great heart of Paul than this one provided by today's verses. Writing from prison, where he was awaiting trial for his life, he urges the Colossians to pray with perseverance, with watchfulness (keeping wide awake), and with thanksgiving. There is nothing unusual about this. But look at the Apostle's next request.

He asked them to pray not for himself, but for his work (vv. 3–4). Here is the measure of the man's self-forgetfulness. He wanted first not release from adversity and crippling circumstances, but the vision and faith to make the most of his present opportunities. Paul obviously knew the danger of wasting the present in wistful hopes for the future, of waiting for a more favourable situation, a bigger opportunity. He was determined to serve the Kingdom of God just where he was at the moment. Hence his longing for power to overcome his difficulties rather than for a chance to escape from them.

He thought more of his work than he thought of himself. This spirit alone enables the Christian to be content to render service unnoticed and even disregarded. If others are preferred before him, he remains unsoured because his primary concern is God's work, not himself. Always his prayer is for strength and wisdom to make the best for God of his present circumstances.

COLOSSIANS 4:7–11

'And with him I send our dear and trusty brother Onesimus, who is one of yourselves' (v. 9, Weymouth).

A TRUSTY BROTHER. Here is an apparently commonplace verse which hides a whole world of romance. There are many such in the Bible. The letter to the church at Colossae is to be carried by Tychicus and with him will journey Onesimus, a onetime slave of Philemon who had run away after robbing his master. The fugitive found refuge in Rome and it was there he met Paul, became a Christian and remained for a while as the Apostle's personal attendant. Much as Paul would have liked to retain Onesimus he felt it was now right to return him to his master. The letter to Philemon is a gracious appeal, on behalf of the runaway slave, for his master's pardon.

In this passage Paul asks the congregation at Colossae to receive Onesimus as a 'trusty brother'. Although, in terms of first-century society, Onesimus had defrauded his master by running away, that was all in the past. He was now a fellow believer and was to be gladly welcomed as such. Paul expects the church at Colossae to do more than believe in the forgiveness of sins—they are to act upon their belief. Are we willing to do the same, or do we continue to take account of offences which God has pardoned?

It is also noteworthy that social distinctions are graciously but firmly abolished in these verses. Paul describes the runaway slave in the same way as he does the highly honoured Epaphras who founded the Colossian Church—the slave also is 'one of yourselves' (verses 9 and 12). To our modern ears these words have lost their revolutionary ring but they contain within them the dynamite which was eventually to destroy slavery in the ancient world. Nor should we imagine that the application of Christian principles is less disturbing to the *status quo* today.

COLOSSIANS 4:12–18

'He [Epaphras] works hard for you even here, for he prays constantly and earnestly for you . . .' (v. 12, Phillips).

THE LABOUR OF INTERCESSION. Epaphras, who founded the church at Colossae, was probably converted during Paul's mission at Ephesus. It was he who had brought news of the Colossians to the Apostle, and Paul here witnesses to the faithfulness and passion of their leader's prayers for them.

Even prayer can become self-centred, concerned only with the welfare of ourselves and our family. The extent to which our prayers range beyond the circle of our personal interests infallibly indicates how much the love of God dwells in our hearts. In these days of religious questioning doubts are raised about the effectiveness of prayer. Some of these objections are met very wisely by John B. Magee in his '*Reality and Prayer*'. He suggests that the biggest obstacle to a life of intercession is the idea that we are separated from our fellows in much the same way that planets are separated from each other. Yet, in fact, the social sciences, research into telepathy and other modern advances suggest that we are intimately linked with each other. 'The problem of intercession', says Magee, 'is not to make some connection with the person for whom we would pray, but to hallow and use the channels already there.'

The praying of Epaphras was hard work! If we have tried to intercede we know this also. For our encouragement the saints all unite in assuring us that the value of a prayer does not depend upon its ease or its emotional content. The laborious prayer, persisted in against distraction and weariness, is of even greater worth.

THE FIRST AND SECOND EPISTLES TO THE THESSALONIANS

INTRODUCTION

As with the epistles to the Corinthians, these two letters to believers in Thessalonica can be taken together.

Paul's visit to this city is recounted in Acts 17;1–9, but his departure was so hurried that, as soon as possible after leaving, he sent Timothy back to find out how these new converts were faring (I Thess. 3:1–6). The news was encouraging, however, and the Apostle's mind was set at rest (3:7, Barclay).

So far, so good—but some of these recent believers knew so little about their father in God that the Apostle found himself rebutting charges that he was concerned about his own reputation and actually used flattery to get his own way. The truth was that he earned his own living to avoid being a charge on the church (1 Thess. 2:4–9).

Paul's chief concern had to do with misunderstandings which had arisen over the Second Coming. This was expected immediately, and for this reason some believers had stopped working and were just hanging around waiting for Jesus to return. Others were saying that this had already taken place. So the Apostle had to remind them that there was no better way to demonstrate the worth of one's faith than by diligently attending to the business of the day (2 Thess. 3:12). The work-shy man (3:11, Barclay) was no recommendation for Christianity.

1 THESSALONIANS 1:1–5

'We call to mind, before our God and Father, how your faith has shown itself in action, your love in labour, and your hope of our Lord Jesus Christ in fortitude' (v. 3, N.E.B.).

VIRTUE WHICH MAKES A DIFFERENCE. Real beauty of character is not easily analysed into a list of abstract qualities, though ethical teachers in the ancient world often compiled such lists. In his letters Paul sometimes follows their practice, but more often than not Christian character is described in terms of the Christian triad—faith, hope and love. This is so at the beginning of Paul's letter to the church at Thessalonica. What is particularly noteworthy here is the apostle's insistence that these are active virtues: faith is expressed in works, love in labour, hope in endurance. Each of these virtues can easily be mistaken for mere emotional states. Do we not all feel trustful, affectionate and optimistic at times? But Christian virtue is not an emotional spasm, it is a moral dynamic. 'It is not faith and works; it is not faith or works; it is faith that works'.

We can never remind ourselves sufficiently often that the Christian virtues are a response to the Christian gospel. In his novel, *The Keys of the Kingdom*, A. J. Cronin describes a doctor working in China. Although an agnostic, he spent himself unsparingly for others. Finally he caught the plague and was dying. 'I can't believe in God,' he murmured to his friend, a priest. 'Does it matter now?' replied the priest, 'God believes in you.' This is where faith, love and hope first root and then begin to grow.

Spurgeon used to say that 'faith goes up the stairs that love has made, and looks out of the windows which hope has opened'.

1 THESSALONIANS 1:6–10

'As for you, you took us and the Lord as your example . . . (and) you became an example to all in Macedonia and Achaea' (vv. 6, 7, Barclay).

LIVING THE GOSPEL. This passage bears striking witness to the way Christianity spreads. Paul said that he and his companions went to Thessalonica as followers of Christ; the Thessalonians themselves copied their example and other people in other places followed theirs. And so the gospel was passed from heart to heart. How effective for the Kingdom of God is that Christian who really lives out his faith in everyday life!

In *Miracle on the River Kwai*, Ernest Gordon tells how he entered a Japanese prisoner-of-war camp in the Second World War an unbeliever, and emerged after three-and-a-half terror-filled years a convinced Christian. He began to be aware of the reality of God, he says, by observing two fellow prisoners who were Christians—Dusty, a Methodist, and Dinty, a Roman Catholic. 'In each it was his faith that lent a special grace to his personality; through them both faith expressed a power, a presence, greater than themselves,' he writes. 'I was beginning to see that life was infinitely more complex, and at the same time more wonderful, than I had ever imagined. True, there was hatred. But there was also love. There was death. But there was also life. God had not left us. He was with us, calling us to live in the divine fellowship. I was beginning to be aware of the miracle that God was working in the Death Camp by the River Kwai.'

A Hindu friend suggested to C. F. Andrews that he should write a life of Christ for the Indian people 'for you have lived like Him these thirty years in India'. After the death of Andrews some friends went through his papers hoping to find a few chapters written, but without success. 'He did not write his life of Christ', said one of them. 'He lived it'.

1 THESSALONIANS 2:1–7

'We do not curry favour with men; we seek only the favour of God, who is continuallv testing our hearts' (v. 4, N.E.B.).

THE RIGHT KIND OF INDEPENDENCE The truth noted above—that Christlike lives are the very best recommendation for the gospel—can lead to a dangerous misunderstanding. We can become so obsessed with having a good influence, of making the right impression (even for Christ), that we lose the freedom to be ourselves. Some Christians have become unnatural because they are always acting a role—the role of the good Christian. But virtue, to be real, must be spontaneous, not artificially produced in order to make an impression.

This means we must seek to live by deep and abiding principles—then we can leave the question of our influence to take care of itself. We see this truth illustrated in today's passage where Paul is answering some of the charges made against him by Jewish opponents of the Church. These suggested that the apostle was merely a religious charlatan out to feather his own nest. Yet, as Paul reminds his readers, his witness at Philippi, the previous stage of his missionary journey, had cost him imprisonment and suffering. The experience could well have been repeated at Thessalonica.

Paul claims that he and his companions made it their dominant ambition to please God, to live by the light of the gospel they preached and in the strength of the grace which fellowship with Christ imparted. Therefore they had achieved the right kind of independence from men. They were free to be themselves by making their own peculiar and unique response to the love of God.

1 THESSALONIANS 2:8–12

'We chose to impart to you not only the gospel of God but our very selves' (v. 8, N.E.B.).

SELF GIVING. This sentence suggests that the depth of our Christian commitment is measured not by how ready we are to give time, talents and energy, but by how willing we are to give ourselves. It applies to our relationship with Christ, though most of us appear more willing to serve than to surrender. The latter, however, must come before the former—it doesn't work in the reverse order.

Dr. Sangster once told a story to illustrate the point. It concerned a little boy who one day did something unkind to his sister, and their mother noticed it. She was distressed, and the boy saw the hurt look in her eyes. He tried to put things right. 'Can I run any errands, Mummy?' he asked. 'Do you want anything from upstairs?' But nothing could take away the look of hurt in his mother's face. This went on all day and towards bedtime the boy could stand it no longer. He ran to his mother, flung his arms around her and cried, 'I'm sorry, Mummy.' When she was sure he was, she allowed him to do those things he had wanted to do before, and they were both happy. Dr. Sangster added, 'God says, "First My arms, then My errands"'.

And what counts in human relationships also is not an easy handing out of charity, but the giving of ourselves. It is the glory of the gospel that God in Jesus gives Himself to us, and while our giving can never be anything but a pale reflection of His, it should nevertheless be as complete and self-forgetting as we by His grace can make it. True love gives, and goes on giving with no thought of self, and willingly runs the risk of getting hurt.

1 THESSALONIANS 2:13–20

'This is why we give thanks to God unceasingly that, when we delivered the divine message to you, you recognized it for what it is, God's message, not man's' (v. 13, Knox).

HOW CAN WE DISCERN GOD'S WORD? Paul's keen delight in the spiritual progress of the Thessalonians shows that he had the heart of the true pastor. Particularly he was grateful that the Thessalonians recognized the word of God conveyed in the words of the apostles. Since God's word to us is often transmitted in human utterance how can we learn to discern it?

Not every religious word, not every word spoken with authority, is God's word. Early in his career Billy Graham was persuaded to become president of Northwestern Schools, much against his better judgment and against the advice of his wife. The previous president, William Riley, eighty-six and obviously soon to die, had called Graham to his bedside. A thunderstorm added drama to the occasion. Pointing at Graham, Riley said, 'Billy, you are the man to succeed me. . . . You will be disobeying God if you don't.' People who are dogmatically certain that they know God's law easily make their words sound like the word of God.

God's word can be discerned in the words of men only by patient seeking, sifting and testing, and by a frank recognition that we may at times be mistaken. Luther suggested one useful test when he wrote: 'As often as God's word is preached, it makes the conscience joyful in face of God, it enlarges it and gives it certainty. For it is a word of grace, a good and beneficial word. But as often as man's words are proclaimed, they make the conscience sad, narrow and fearful in itself.' No word which does not reflect God's love is from Him.

1 THESSALONIANS 3:1–5

'Troubles are our lot; you know that well' (v. 3, Moffatt).

ALL THAT ARE GODLY WILL SUFFER. This has been true in every age. The Old Testament thought that prosperity was the reward of godliness—a dubious proposition with which the writer of the book of Job wrestled—has no place in the New. 'Followers of Him who wore a crown of thorns cannot expect a bed of roses.'

The wife of the Salvation Army officer appointed in 1937 to Königsberg (now Kaliningrad) was Mrs. Adjutant Seils. This was the largest Salvation Army corps in the predominantly Protestant part of East Prussia. Her husband was conscripted for service in the imperial army at the outbreak of the Second World War and Mrs. Seils took over his place in the corps and community.

In the autumn of 1944 the city was devastated by two successive air raids, and on Aril 9th, 1945, Mrs. Seils was arrested. Two days later the Army hall, which had survived the bombing, was deliberately fired. Liberated after a fortnight, Mrs. Seils earned her keep as a cleaner and washerwoman to the families of Russian officers. She could not communicate with her husband neither did she hear from him. But when asked for her testimony she said: 'Alone, yet not alone. The darker the night, the brighter shine the stars of God's promises.'

1 THESSALONIANS 3:6–13

'May the Lord give you the same increasing and overflowing love for each other and towards all men as we have towards you' (v. 12, Phillips).

LOVE IS ALL. Verses 11–13 constitute a prayer of the apostle for his Thessalonian converts, in which he touches the heart of the Christian religion—love, God's love for men and men's love for each other. The Thessalonians would, he trusted, learn to love each other and learn to love all men.

The Christian community is built on love; it is the very essence of its being; without it, it is not Christian at all. And it is sad indeed to witness lack of real love among those who name the name of Christ. Denominational barriers are being slowly broken down, but the movement towards a true ecumenism can proceed only in the spirit of genuine Christian love. Likewise, the local congregation of any church can be effective in its mission to bring honour to God and to bring men to Christ only as it is a congregation with love at its heart. 'The cement of the Christian fellowship is love' wrote H. Rolston, and Jesus said, 'This is My commandment: love one another, as I have loved you' (John 15:12, N.E.B.)

But the love of Christians is not a self-centred love; it is outgoing, and becomes the effective point of communication with others. What else will do this successfully? Commented Norman Pittenger in *Goodness Distorted*, 'Talk about first cause, unmoved mover, necessary being, logical explanation, and dictator of moral principles, seem to mean little or nothing in a time impatient of metaphysical discussion and doubtful about moral ultimates in the form of codes or laws But talk about love strikes home, for all men —everyone, everywhere—yearn for and need love. Love . . . is what the world is seeking.'

1 THESSALONIANS 4:1–8

'Every one of you should learn to control his body . . . treating it with respect. . . . You cannot break this rule without in some way cheating your fellow men' (vv. 4–6, Phillips).

MAN AND HIS INSTINCTS. 'What a lot of trouble is caused by turning adjectives into nouns!' wrote W. B. J. Martin. 'People talk about "sex" as if it were something separate and independent of a man. There is no such thing as sex in the abstract, but only a person striving to establish relations with another person.' Paul makes the same emphasis in this passage. Disregard of sexual moral standards, widespread in the pagan culture of Paul's day and also prevalent today, always debases personal relationships. Such disregard is corrupting, not because there is something unclean in our sexual desires, but because we are always corrupted when we 'use' other people as things. For that matter the exploitation by some elderly parents of their unmarried daughters can be sadly corrupting.

In a time of moral confusion the Christian must stand his ground on two fronts. We must refuse to panic or revert to a 'Victorian' suspicion of the body. Man and woman are God's creation and not only marriage but the whole of life is enriched by the contribution each makes to the other. Sexual desires are not sinful: it is what we do with them that counts.

Equally, the Christian will refuse to be influenced by suggestions that our instincts must always have the last word. One psychiatrist claims that, although we can admit with Freud that intense repression of the sexual instinct may result in neurotic symptoms, the near deification of this, or any other instinct, is equally or even more harmful. 'What happens,' he asks, 'to the individual who has made a god of his instincts when these begin to wane?' In J. B. Phillips' arresting phrase, Christians will 'avoid sexual looseness like the plague' (1 Cor. 6:18).

1 THESSALONIANS 4:9–12

'Let it be your ambition to keep calm and look after your own business, and to work with your hands . . . so that you may command the respect of those outside your own number' (vv. 11, 12, N.E.B.).

HOW THE GOSPEL IS COMMENDED. The Thessalonians had accepted, and were practising, the principle of Christian love, and Paul commends them for it, going on to exhort them to 'do better still' (v. 11, N.E.B.). They were to live quietly, to look after their own business and to work with their hands. These simple and perhaps surprising attitudes and activities should, he suggests, be the consequence of the love of God shed abroad in their hearts. And we, too, must never fail to understand that God's love in us must be expressed in the events and duties of the everyday. The apostle says that this is the way the gospel will be commended to those outside the Church.

One warm afternoon in 1882, in a Salvation Army hall in Hampstead, London, 'a spruce, black-haired young infidel, bespectacled and bearded' heard a servant girl give a simple testimony: 'My missus says she believes I am saved because I sweep beneath the mats, and I didn't before!' This quaint witness 'let fly a shaft of truth that immediately wrought havoc among (Richard Slater's) carefully acquired theories', and the eventual outcome was his own conversion to Christ. He became an outstanding Salvationist leader and, a brilliant musician, laid the foundations of Salvation Army music which has been so signally used by God.

The truth is, as William Barclay wrote, 'When we Christians prove that our Christianity makes us better workmen, truer friends, kinder men and women, then and only then are we really preaching. The important thing is not words but deeds, not oratory but life.'

1 THESSALONIANS 4:13–18

'We shall stay with the Lord for ever. With such thoughts as these you should comfort one another' (v. 18, Jerusalem Bible).

IN CHRIST FOR EVER. In the face of death there was only despair for the pagans of the ancient world. 'I was not; I became; I am not' was the kind of inscription carved on their tombstones. Consequently the Thessalonians, only recently won from paganism, were troubled by the question: what will happen to those believers who die before Christ's return? an event on which they had received some instruction and which they expected soon. It was to answer this question that the apostle wrote this passage. Those who had died and those who remained alive until Christ returned, he told them, would alike share in the glory of that event.

The gospel does strike a hope-filled note on the mystery of death. It still remains a fact as well as a mystery, but for the Christian it is no longer an all-powerful enemy—it has been vanquished by Christ, the Lord of Life. While the New Testament does not furnish details of our future existence, it does assure us that our trust in God is safe and true and that in death, as in life, believers are in the presence of their loving Lord.

It is not necessary to take today's somewhat obscure passage literally. It is the truth it conveys—that death is but the passport to a fuller more glorious life—that is important. When he was in his final illness Dwight L. Moody said, 'Soon you will read in the newspapers that Moody is dead. Don't you believe it, for I shall be more alive than I am now.'

1 THESSALONIANS 5:1–5

'But you, my friends, are not in the dark, that the day should overtake you like a thief' (v. 5, N.E.B.).

READY WHEN THE CRISIS COMES. The term 'the Day of the Lord' is frequently found in the Old Testament. The prophets spoke about it as a day of terror in which God would come upon men suddenly and unexpectedly. There would be an upheaval on a cosmic scale and God would appear in judgment to inaugurate His everlasting kingdom. (See Amos 5:18–20; Isaiah 13:9–13; 22:5; Joel 2:31).

Now many of the associations of that Day became attached to the Christian idea of the Second Coming of Christ about which, despite Christ's clear word that even He had no knowledge of the day or hour (Mark 13:32), men insisted on speculating. The Thessalonians appear to have been anxious about the matter, and the apostle had to remind them that they did not need more information as to when Christ should return. He would certainly come 'like a thief in the night' but because, as he points out, they are 'children of light', there was no reason why they should be unprepared. If their great concern was to be ready for Him all the time they need not fear they would be found wanting.

Here is a word for us all, not only in preparation for the day of the Lord's return (however we interpret that event) but also for any other eventuality that might make demands upon us. It is always too late to begin to prepare when the crisis has come, but if every moment of every day is lived in the light of His love and grace, no demand will catch us unawares.

1 THESSALONIANS 5:6–11

'God has not destined us to the terrors of judgment, but to the full attainment of salvation through our Lord Jesus Christ' (v. 9, N.E.B.).

A HEARTENING WORD This reading is a continuation of the above exhortation to preparedness in view of the unexpected coming of Christ and also—in our legitimate extension of the meaning—of any eventuality life might bring. Here is now a word of encouragement.

The Day of the Lord as understood in Old Testament times would be a day of judgment and therefore, as commonly understood, a day of terror. But Paul writes to allay these fears of the Thessalonians. Judgment there will be, but for those who are in Christ this will not mean terror. Since Christ died for us He proved the measure of His love and gave the assurance of His perpetual presence with those who believe in Him. Even the stern fact of judgment, therefore, need not rob us of hope and joy. Note again, though, and note well: there is here no denial of judgment, for this is a fact to which the Bible consistently points; there is, however, a denial that judgment holds terror for the believer.

Aware of the real and eternal love of God shown in Jesus, the Christian is full of hope and radiant with joy now, in this present life, and in anticipation of the hereafter. He has, indeed, the best of both worlds. The intimate relationship in which he stands with Christ is never-ending. As Paul says, 'Awake or asleep (we) live in company with Him' (v. 10, N.E.B.). No wonder he can write about our heartening and fortifying one another. With a faith like this how could we do otherwise? The despondency in which, to our shame, we so frequently indulge is all so unnecessary!

1 THESSALONIANS 5:12–18

'Be always joyful; pray continually; give thanks whatever happens; for this is what God in Christ wills for you' (vv. 16–18, N.E.B.).

LIVING IN THE PRESENCE. In his biography of Billy Graham, John Pollock asserts that the evangelist 'spends less time on his knees than in those early Florida days but he prays more, consciously or subconsciously'. This is the goal towards which Paul urges his readers when he writes, 'Pray without ceasing.' The apostle's own life was that of a busy missionary. We can therefore take his advice more seriously than some of the devotional manuals which have been issued over the years. Paul's whole life became a prayer in that all his activity was offered to God, every blessing he accepted with thanksgiving, and he sought God's will in everything.

Continual awareness of God's presence is not an easy attainment. Brother Lawrence, even in the favourable circumstances of a monastery, arrived at this goal only after ten years of patient discipline and perseverance. Those who have travelled far along the path of prayer also warn us against abandoning set periods of prayer. Wrote John Magee, 'When, many years ago, I discovered this technique of praying without interruption to the ordinary course of activities, I thought of it as a fine way to save the time and trouble of special prayer periods. This presumptuous experiment in continual prayer collapsed as soon as it began. The practice of the Presence cannot be employed as a device for reducing prayer to a secondary activity which no longer interferes with other "more important" things.'

Deliberate encounter with God, in private prayer and public worship, should enable us to perceive the religious dimension in the whole of life. We shall thus begin to know what it means to live in the secret of His presence and in the hiding of His power.

1 THESSALONIANS 5:19–28

'Never despise what is spoken in the name of the Lord. By all means use your judgment, and hold on to whatever is really good' (vv. 20 and 21, Phillips).

CRITICAL BUT RECEPTIVE. In his play, *Curtmantle*, Christopher Fry introduces a discussion between Henry II and Becket, who is to be made archbishop. The king asserts that the truth 'is unalterable, the truth being one'. But Becket reminds the king that from different viewpoints the truth appears quite differently.

The truth, like everything else, being of three dimension,
And men so placed, they can stake their lives on the shape of it
Until by a shift of their position, the shape of truth has changed.

The cynic might argue that this is why man can never find the truth. We should see it rather as a challenge to remain open to every insight offered by those who see truth from different vantage points to our own.

Within the Church this means, in Paul's words, that we should 'never despise what is spoken in the Name of the Lord'. God is greater than the vision of any one saint, the truth is vaster than any one person's apprehension of it. From quite unexpected sources we may catch a new glimpse of truth if we are humble enough to remain open and attentive.

Yet this does not require of us an uncritical acceptance of every statement claiming to be inspired. Some believers are too credulous. As Gerhard Ebeling has written: 'Nowhere is there so much sinning in words, and so much sinning against words, as where empty, cheap, worthless words are used to speak of God and to God'. Open receptiveness allied to critical discrimination are the tools of the seeker after truth.

2 THESSALONIANS 1:1–4

'Your faith is growing so wonderfully and the love that you have for one another never stops increasing' (v. 3, Jerusalem Bible).

FAITH, LOVE AND ENDURANCE. This second letter, written very shortly after the first and prompted by reactions to it, opens with thanksgiving, for the apostle finds very good reasons to praise his Thessalonian converts.

In the first place their faith was growing 'so wonderfully'. This might well be linked with his reference to the way they had withstood persecutions and afflictions (another reason to praise, see v. 4), for not only could these be a test of faith but also its effective buttress. The man who is learning of Christ does more than simply endure hardship; he takes hold of it and finds with wonder that it may help faith to grow.

Then, the Thessalonians' love for each other was increasing. The novelist, Iris Murdoch, who makes no claim to be a Christian, has written, 'Love is the perception of individuals. Love is the extremely difficult realization that something other than oneself is real'—words with which no believer could possibly disagree. The inability to love others (which may simply be a refusal to do so) is a sign of our basic self-centredness. No doubt we all readily agree with the words of the popular song that 'what the world needs now is love, sweet love', but what we do not so readily see is that this means our love and not simply somebody else's. It was Evelyn Underhill who once said that we obey Christ's second great commandment (to love our neighbour) only by concentrating upon the first (wholehearted love for God).

2 THESSALONIANS 1:5–12

'For God in His justice is bound to square the account by sending trouble to those who trouble you, and by sending relief to you who are now going through troubles' (vv. 6, 7, Barclay).

JUDGMENT AND PROMISE. Judgment is a constantly recurring theme of the Bible. The prophets of the Old Testament spoke about it, and so did Jesus in the New. We meet it again in this passage where Paul speaks of 'the justice of God's judgment' and points out that 'those who will not obey the gospel ... will suffer the punishment of eternal ruin' (N.E.B.). He uses the language of the Old Testament, but the truth he emphasizes is eternal.

Yet we must not fail to notice the mingling here of promise with judgment, for they always go together in God's dealing with men. Hope is promised to those who believe, but inevitable loss comes to those who wilfully disobey.

Colin Morris has pointed out that they are false prophets who speak a simple word of Promise or Judgment. True prophets speak a paradoxical word of Promise and Judgment. 'So the truly prophetic word has moral depth. It is never flippant or casually simple because it is addressed to Man, who oscillates between extremes of pride and humility, misery and grandeur. And this word speaks of Promise and Judgment because Man needs both to be jolted into a sense of dignity when he is grovelling in the dust and knocked off his perch when he gets cocky and forgets he is human.'

Morris makes the point that all Jesus' promises embodied judgment, and yet His harshest judgments offered men promise. This, he says, 'is the essence of true prophecy—a word of judgment which leads men to repentance and yet embodies promise, the assurance that forgiveness is possible'. This is both a challenge and a comfort to us—as it is meant to be.

2 THESSALONIANS 2:1–4

'Do not suddenly lose your heads ... That day cannot come before the final rebellion against God, when wickedness will be revealed in human form' (vv. 2 and 3, N.E.B.).

THE REALITY OF EVIL. We now come to one of the most difficult parts of these two letters, and it is as well to admit that there are references here we cannot fully understand.

In the first place the apostle was anxious to correct any false notions that the return of Christ was imminent. Believers may have misunderstood his references to this subject in the first letter, so he now points out that he had not taught that the Second Coming 'is already here', nor must they be deceived by anyone else in this regard. Before Christ's return, he says, certain things must happen, one of these being the revealing of the 'man doomed to perdition', the 'Enemy'. Who or what Paul meant here we cannot say with certainty, but it is sufficient to recognize the heart of the matter: there is an evil force in the world which cannot be denied.

Douglas Webster has observed that 'the concept of "the enemy" at work in history is not prominent in contemporary theological writing, but it is remarkably to the fore in fiction, poetry, and drama, all of which are grappling with the problem of evil and of sin more honestly and more passionately than some of our theologians'.

We make a sad mistake if we underestimate the strength of evil but, as we consider below, we need not despair; a greater power is available. As Paul writes elsewhere, 'in spite of all, overwhelming victory is ours through Him who loved us' (Romans 8:37, N.E.B.).

2 THESSALONIANS 2:5–12

'When that happens the Lawless Man will be plainly seen—though the truth of the Lord Jesus spells his doom, and the radiance of the coming of the Lord Jesus will be his utter destruction' (v. 8, Phillips).

MORE THAN A REMOTE POSSIBILITY. This passage is one of the most difficult in the New Testament. Part of the reason is that Paul assumes what he had already said to the Thessalonians in person. Various attempts have been made to identify the 'restraining power' which the apostle says is inhibiting the full emergence of 'the Man of Sin'. In the end we must confess with Augustine, 'we, who do not know what they knew, desire and yet are unable even with all our efforts to get at what the apostle meant'.

Yet, if some things are obscure, others are luminously clear. This passage reminds us that the conflict between Christ and the powers of evil grows in intensity as the gospel wins its way in men's hearts. Best of all, Jesus is here presented as the Lord of history. Only that which is in harmony with His Spirit can finally endure.

Gibson Winter has said that Christian judgment about contemporary issues must be formed by reflecting upon two moments in history: 'The past moment in history that came to its fulfilment in Jesus and the future moment or goal of history to which the event of Jesus points.' Christ's return is not merely something which might happen in four minutes' time or four thousand years, and which therefore tends to be ignored in day-to-day action. Every decision of life is influenced by our faith that the Jesus of whom we read in the Gospels is also the Lord to whom eventually every knee shall bow (Philippians 2:10).

2 THESSALONIANS 2:13–17

'May our Lord Jesus Christ Himself and God our Father, who . . . in His grace has given us such unfailing encouragement and such bright hopes, still encourage and fortify you . . .' (v. 16, 17, N.E.B.).

A LIVELY HOPE. When Pasteur lay ill with a stroke, the Government stopped construction of a laboratory it was building for him. Hearing of this, he declined rapidly. After his friends had appealed to Napoleon III, building operations were recommenced. Pasteur immediately began to recover and lived to make many important discoveries.

One of the greatest losses we can suffer is the loss of hope. Seemingly superhuman efforts are made by men in whom hope is vibrantly alive. No wonder Paul speaks so eloquently of the 'bright hopes' which inspire the Christian. These hopes would remain the cherished possession of the Thessalonians even though they had to readjust their thinking about Christ's return. The how and the when of Christ's victory belong to the outer garments of Christian faith; the hope itself is its very essence. Some Christians attempt, from a close study of the Scriptures, to construct a timetable of last things. They must not be impatient with their brethren who are content just to rest in the hope which God has given, leaving the manner and time of its fulfilment to God Himself.

Let us rejoice that the hope which Christ inspires in us redeems the mundane from pointlessness, invests the routine of life with significance, and can turn even our trials into blessings.

2 THESSALONIANS 3:1–5

'The Lord keeps faith with us; He will strengthen you, and keep you from all harm' (v. 3, Knox).

GOD IS DEPENDABLE. Once again, as in the first letter, Paul appeals for the prayers of his people. How conscious was this great man of his need of God's grace and of the prayers of his followers—even spiritual babes like the Thessalonians. The trouble with some of us is not so much that we feel independent of divine aid, but our reluctance to acknowledge that we may benefit from the prayers and counsel of other men, especially those we might consider (God forgive us!) our inferiors.

Bishop Leslie Brown once told of an old woman who lived in Portsmouth when he was a curate there. She was bed-ridden, poor and could neither read nor write. But all the curates in the parish used to visit her when they were depressed. The educated young clergymen were humble enough to acknowledge that, her illiteracy notwithstanding, that old woman could enrich them in the deep things of life, so great was her experience of Christ. Paul had this kind of humility.

The apostle goes on to speak about the dependability of God. Phillips translates verse 3: 'The Lord is utterly to be depended upon . . . and He will give you stability and protection.' This truth has been the comfort of God's people through the ages. Paul had proved it already and was to prove it especially towards the end of his life. From prison he wrote to Timothy about one of his disciples, Demas, forsaking him; about a man called Alexander doing him harm; and he told how, when he was brought before his accusers, no one was there to support him. 'But,' he added, 'the Lord stood by me and lent me strength' (2 Timothy 4:vv. 14, 15). And upon this same Lord we with equal confidence may also depend.

2 THESSALONIANS 3:6–12

'Even during our stay with you we laid down the rule: the man who will not work shall not eat' (v. 10, N.E.B.).

CONCERNING IDLENESS. We may well think that Paul in dictating this letter was bringing it to a conclusion with the benedictory prayer at verse five: 'May the Lord direct your hearts toward God's love and the steadfastness of Christ.' He then wonders whether he has been sufficiently decisive in condemning the idleness of a section of the Church. So he reminds his readers of his own industry when he was with them, and of his rule that nobody should be allowed to live off the common funds of the Church, unless by their own labour they contributed to those funds.

In *The Lord's Prayer in Today's World*, Gerhard Ebeling reminds us that 'there is profound truth in the insight that man is at bottom a beggar'. He recalls that the last words Luther wrote on a scrap of paper before his death were, 'We are beggars, that is true.' But Ebeling goes on to show that both our daily bread, and the work we must do to obtain it, are signs of our dependence upon each other. Eating is an 'act of fellowship', as those know who are compelled always to eat alone. And work too is one of the chief areas of human co-operation.

The command, 'if any will not work, neither shall he eat', is more than a basic principle of human life. It is a reminder that we are perpetually dependent upon others, but also perpetually responsible to others. It is one way of asserting that life exists for the purpose of creating fellowship.

2 THESSALONIANS 3:13–18

'May the Lord of peace grant you peace everywhere and at all times; the Lord be with you all' (v. 16, Knox).

PRESENT AND FUTURE. It is significant that this letter which has much to say about what is sometimes called 'the second coming of Christ', concludes with an assurance of Christ's continual presence. The New Testament never speaks about a 'second coming'. It uses a word which originally meant 'presence' or 'arrival'. It was sometimes used of the visit of a king. This word came to mean the presence, coming, arrival of the glorified Christ.

J. E. Fison has reminded us of the danger of emphasizing either the 'presence' or the 'coming' of Christ to the exclusion of the other. The Church has continually fallen into this error. So some Christian teachers have rejoiced in the experience of the companionship of Jesus but have little to say of Christ as the Lord of history, and of that fulfilment towards which everything moves. Others have fallen into the opposite error. They have focused their attention exclusively upon last things and apparently know little of the way in which everyday life can be sanctified in His presence.

We must always remind ourselves that He who will come is He who is our constant companion. When Sundar Singh of India was first converted to Christ his father demanded what Christianity had to offer more than his own ancient faith. Sundar answered, 'Christ alive and at my side today, loving and leading me.'

THE FIRST AND SECOND EPISTLES TO TIMOTHY

INTRODUCTION

These letters, together with that addressed to Titus, have much to say about the character and duties of those who held office in the early Christian Church, and also about the behaviour required of church members themselves. Some of these instructions are given to meet a specific situation at a specific stage in the development of society. What is said about the place of women must be read in this light.

But certain passages are addressed to Timothy personally, and speak of the close relationship which existed between Paul and his son in the faith. We hear the Apostle's own voice in these words of testimony and encouragement. He faced the future unafraid and would have Timothy do the same.

1 TIMOTHY 1:1–11

'The ultimate aim of the Christian ministry, after all, is to produce the love which springs from a pure heart, a good conscience and a genuine faith' (v. 5, Phillips).

WHEN DEBATE WEAKENS DEVOTION. F. D. Maurice was professor of divinity at King's College, London, until deprived of his post in 1853 for alleged heresy. When this happened, Charles Kingsley wrote to him: 'Well, dearest master, I shall not condole with you. You are above that. You know what I feel for you. But your cause is mine. We stand or fall henceforth together. I am the mouse helping the lion.' Kingsley—and he was one of a host of young men grateful for their old professor's influence—knew instinctively that charges of heresy were ridiculous in the light of F. D. Maurice's rare sanctity. And so it proved, for later the professor was completely vindicated.

In this first letter to Timothy, Paul strongly makes the point that Christian teaching is only valid and significant to the extent it makes the believer like Christ. He spurns wordy speculations and arguments about doctrine, and condemns people who put debate before devotion. For his primary concern was the relation of religious belief and personal sanctity. Our beliefs are vital and necessary only if they make us more Christlike and easier to live with. Dante claimed that a step of the greatest significance was taken by the soul that ceases to say 'mine' and learns to say 'ours'.

1 TIMOTHY 1:12–17

'Here are words you may trust, words that merit full acceptance: "Christ Jesus came into the world to save sinners"' (v. 15, N.E.B.).

LOVING INITIATIVE. In this passage we meet for the first time the formula, 'This is a faithful saying', which recurs five times in the Pastoral Epistles. These 'sure words' appear to be quotations, in rhythmical form, from well-known Christian sources, perhaps early hymns or liturgy. The one quoted here asserts the divine initiative; it 'breathes the very soul of the gospel'. Of this truth Paul sees himself a striking example: the implacable persecutor of Christ's Church on whom God nevertheless showers mercy.

That God takes the first step in His love for us, without waiting for us to become worthy, is true not only of conversion. Leslie Weatherhead records a conversation he had with Hugh Redwood in which the Christian journalist described a period of stress during which he stayed at a friend's house prior to addressing a big meeting. The friend thoughtfully provided a quiet room for Mr. Redwood to rest in. Before a brightly burning fire an easy chair was drawn up. On a table beside it lay a Bible, open at Psalm 59. Where the Authorized Version reads 'The God of my mercy shall prevent me' someone had pencilled in their own interpretation, 'My God in His loving kindness shall meet me at every corner'. Those words, claimed Mr. Redwood, came to him as a light from the very heart of God.

What is true of the God who sought us remains true of Him who keeps us in His love.

1 TIMOTHY 1:18–20

'So fight gallantly, armed with faith and a good conscience' (v. 19, N.E.B.).

THE SPIRIT BEHIND DISCIPLINE. The two essentials for victorious living here mentioned are faith and a clear conscience. The former means more than right belief, though this is included; it represents the spiritual discipline and devotion demanded by Christian discipleship as a whole. The latter essential—a good conscience—is self-explanatory, though we need to be on our guard against allowing conscience to become a tyrant.

There is all the difference in the world between a good conscience and a fussy preoccupation with the unimportant. Some people are so negatively conscientious that their lives become an obsession with what is not permissible. But the swing to the other extreme is equally devastating, as Paul's reference to Hymenaeus and Alexander illustrates. They had allowed their consciences to become so blunted that finally their faith was totally shipwrecked. Their subsequent deliverance 'unto Satan' probably refers to their exclusion from the Church; but notice that the purpose of this drastic step was intended to be redemptive, not vindictive. The Apostle clearly hoped that this discipline would bring the two men to their senses and lead them back to the fold.

Unless this spirit is behind any discipline we have to apply, we are probably expressing more our hurt pride than our loving concern for the offender, making him the less disposed genuinely to repent.

1 TIMOTHY 2:1–7

'There is only one God, and only one intermediary between God and men, the Man Jesus Christ' (v. 5, Phillips).

THE MEDIATOR. Paul's charge to Timothy gives first priority to the Church's prayers. This leads naturally to the basic statement of Christian belief in one God and Jesus Christ as Mediator. A mediator must be representative and therefore the humanity of Christ, the Man Christ Jesus, is emphasized. This may have been a deliberate contrast to heathen cults in which the agent of redemption was always a 'divine' being who had no real part in this 'inferior, evil world'.

From earliest infancy truth is mediated or made real to us by visible things. A psychologist who has made a special study of early infancy suggests that the very first symbol for human beings is the teddy bear, or similar toy, that represents for the small baby the mother who gave it to him. This enables the child to grasp the reality of mother's love even when he cannot see her. In later years, however sophisticated we become, abstract truth needs concrete manifestation to elicit our response; ideals require to be incorporated in living personalities, affection demands expression, the truth that 'we are accepted' cannot heal apart from a flesh and blood accepting person. Only in a very few branches of human activity, like pure mathematics, does truth appear to exist in wholly abstract form.

'God' can be the most abstract concept of all unless He is made real for us in human terms. For Christians, this happens in Jesus Christ, the Mediator. He represents God to us and He represents us to God.

1 TIMOTHY 2:8–15

'A woman must be a learner, listening quietly and with due submission. I do not permit a woman to be a teacher, nor must woman domineer over man; she should be quiet' (vv. 11–12, N.E.B.).

THE PLACE OF WOMEN IN THE CHURCH. Having said that prayer should be offered with holy hands (we must live as we pray); with holy hearts (we must think as we pray); and with holy faith (we must believe as we pray), Paul goes on to write about the place of women in the Church. Now his seemingly harsh words must be understood in the light of their historical context.

In the ancient world, women generally were held in low esteem. They were considered to be more things than persons, and a part of their fathers' or husbands' property. To have ignored these social conventions within the Church would have scandalized 'outsiders' and resulted in charges of immodesty and probably of indecency. But Paul's guidance about the participation of women in Church affairs does not represent his teaching about their new standing before God. This was concisely stated in his letter to the Galatians: 'There is no such thing as Jew and Greek, slave and freeman, male and female; for you are all one person in Christ Jesus' (3:28, N.E.B.). The Apostle allowed no racial discrimination, and no sex or class distinction within the early Christian community; and this, not his awareness of social customs, reveals his true outlook.

This passage, then, provides an illustration of how we should read the Bible. We cannot wrench it from its historical setting. At the same time we should remember that 'the letter killeth, but the spirit giveth life' (2 Corinthians 3:6) and we must interpret what is peripheral by what is central. Paul's assertion of equality in Christ (Galatians 3:28) is more basic than instructions designed to meet a particular social setting.

1 TIMOTHY 3:1–7

'For the office of a bishop a man must be of blameless reputation . . . He must not be a beginner in the faith, for fear of his becoming conceited' (vv. 2 and 6, Phillips).

SMOKE SCREEN OF PRIDE. Lists of virtues required for various occupations—kings, generals, midwives—were current in contemporary Greek circles. Here Paul similarly describes the qualities required of a 'bishop'. In its original use this word denoted those exercising oversight in a local church, not those responsible for a group of churches in a whole area or diocese.

While acknowledging that the desire to hold office may be completely justified, the apostle is also aware of the dangers of ambition. Consequently this office must be closed to the new convert who might be tempted to conceit by such swift elevation.

The word translated 'lifted up with pride' means literally 'to wrap in smoke'. What an excellent description of the distorted outlook and isolation which pride brings!

Desire for success for its own sake, and not in order to serve, is always potentially unhealthy. Too often it compensates for failure in some more basic human responsibility. Arthur Guirdham maintains that 'ambition is a challenge thrown down by the personality to a universe it considers hostile.' We should certainly examine our ambitions to discover their motivation. As Dag Hammarskjöld observed: 'The wish to give everything is all very fine, providing you have succeeded in so enriching your soul that everything you have to offer is of value.'

1 TIMOTHY 3:8–13

'Deacons with a good record of service may claim a high standing and the right to speak openly on matters of the Christian faith' (v. 13, N.E.B.).

ONE WHO SERVES. A 'deacon' served as assistant to local leaders or travelling evangelists in the Christian community. Often he distributed the Church's charities and performed similar tasks. The Dutch theologian, J. C. Hoekendijk, claims that the word 'deacon' was originally without much glamour, meaning something like 'serving at tables' or 'functioning as a waiter'. When the Church entered the 'tunnel period', a period of almost a hundred years about which we have sparse information, we know what a deacon was. 'He entered the tunnel as a waiter, only to come out as an assistant to the bishop—a near-priest. He had been neatly clericalized. He had been removed from behind the backs of the table guests and been placed somewhere at the head of the table.' This, observed Hoekendijk, is symptomatic of the Church's reluctance truly to follow her Lord in humble service.

Mary Verghese, a young Indian Christian, became a student at the famous Christian Medical College at Vellore. When, for the first time, she went with a team who worked a mobile clinic she felt apprehensive. This meant entering a world she had previously seen only from a distance, the world of the poverty-stricken villagers. 'It was one thing having them come into her world of the hospital or of the same comfortable compound among the coconut trees. It was quite another to enter theirs'.

Is this not always the challenge of true service?

1 TIMOTHY 3:14–16

'Great beyond all question is the mystery of our religion' (v. 16, N.E.B.).

A MYSTERY. Paul pauses in making his list of practical proposals to consider the very reason for the Church's existence. Organization is of secondary importance to the faith it seeks to propagate. Besides this, Paul knew that practical affairs can get out of proportion unless constantly related to spiritual reality. So this chapter concludes with a lyrical quotation, probably from some early hymn or creed, exalting the achievement of Christ.

The Christian religion is here pronounced 'a tremendous mystery'. In Pauline usage this does not mean something beyond knowledge, but rather something once hidden and now revealed to those with spiritual discernment. Even this was no secret knowledge like that imparted to those initiated in the 'mystery' religions of the time. Rather, it was God's purpose in Jesus Christ to make universal the hope once confined to Israel. This mystery could be explained only in terms of God's love.

We are often concerned because our faith appears a 'mystery' in the more usual sense, at least to our unbelieving contemporaries. Nor must we cease to wrestle with this 'problem of communication'. Yet lives and actions can be eloquent even when speech falters. In the language of this epistle, it is a word to be trusted that it is not the task of believers to advocate a programme, but by the quality of their lives 'to create a mystery'—a mystery which can be explained only in terms of the grace of God.

1 TIMOTHY 4:1–5

'Everything God made is good, and is meant to be gratefully used, not despised' (v. 4, Phillips).

MORBID ASCETICISM. Unfortunately, religious people are usually less critical of commands to deny themselves than of encouragements to enjoy themselves. All of which is a sad reflection upon their view of the Deity.

This passage, however, makes it quite clear that there is a false asceticism. The prohibitions which the apostle condemned—against marriage and the eating of certain foods—probably arose from Greek views of the material universe as essentially evil. This emphasis was to trouble the Church persistently in the early centuries and, in fact, Christian teaching did become tainted with a quite unbiblical suspicion of the body. As E. F. Scott has commented, 'The question at stake is that of our whole conception of God. Are we to think of Him as grudging us our earthly life or are we to find in it a "proof of His presence and goodness?"'

Morbid self-denial can easily be detected: it fails to see the positive worth in the thing surrendered, at least for other people; it is obsessively concerned that others should make the same sacrifice; it is motivated by fear. Healthy self-denial is a free expression of love and does not underrate what is sacrificed, nor impose the same renunciation on others. It is wholly positive.

1 TIMOTHY 4:6–10

'By offering such advice as this to the brotherhood you will prove a good servant of Jesus Christ, bred in the precepts of our faith and of the sound instruction which you have followed' (v. 6, N.E.B.).

AIDS TO EFFECTIVE LIVING. The practical counsel contained in these verses has particular application for Christian leaders, but it is clearly not without value for believers generally.

First of all, it tells us how to teach others. We must constantly remind them of what they already know, in a spirit free of dogmatism and belligerence; people cannot be bulldozed into faith or bullied into unthinking acceptance of Christian dogma. They need the ministry of gentleness and patience, for only by such means can they be enabled to see for themselves.

Second, these verses tell us how to train for Christian warfare. Being athletes for God, we must keep ourselves in first-class condition, disciplined in body, mind, and spirit. Anything which blunts our senses and encourages spiritual stupor is to be avoided like the plague. A flabby mind is as disgraceful as a flabby body, and both drain the soul of its vitality. Avoiding, therefore, the danger of 'indulgent asceticism', an evil mentioned above, we should train ourselves in godliness, in goodness, with at least the same dedication as a sportsman preparing to win.

Finally, these verses tell us how to triumph in our Christian warfare. We must keep our eyes on the goal to which we are journeying, for its greatness will transform or make bearable the inescapable triviliality of much of life's routine. Indeed, such a vision will give significance to what is apparently meaningless, and sharpen our insight to perceive eternal values in the most surprising places.

1 TIMOTHY 4:11–16

'Think hard about all this, and put it into practice, and everyone will be able to see how you are advancing' (v. 15, Jerusalem Bible).

THOUGHT AND ACTION. Timothy was not necessarily a youth when he received this letter: the original Greek could indicate any age up to forty years old. However, he would be young compared to some of those he was called to instruct, and we must remember that ancient custom demanded that the less mature should defer to the wisdom of their elders. Perhaps some may think that they need parallel encouragement today not to be overawed by the young!

Paul's injunction, 'Make these matters your business and your absorbing interest' (v. 15, N.E.B.), includes a word which could mean meditate. Concentrated thought and vigorous action are seen as partners. Today, Christians are so concerned not to be guilty of religious practice divorced from life that they are in danger of surrendering their means of spiritual renewal. Yet as long as prayer, worship and meditation centre on God in Christ they must lead to action.

Roger Schutz, founder of the Taizé Community in France, writes words which breathe the spirit of this passage. 'Since it engages the whole man, contemplation of the God of Jesus Christ cannot lead to quietism. On the contrary, it moves us to bold action and rules out the possibility of lukewarmness. It commits us irrevocably to the race . . . The man whose course is directed by the vision of Christ knows where he is going. Two rules for running are interdependent and must always be observed: Forget that which lies behind, forget progression or regression, and fix your gaze attentively on Him who guides our faith.'

1 TIMOTHY 5:1–8

'You should make it clear that for a man to refuse to look after his own relations, especially those actually living in his house, is a denial of the faith he professes' (v. 8, Phillips).

LONG-SIGHTED LOVE. The lengthy section in this letter devoted to 'widows' has a twofold aspect: the responsibility of the

Church, and its individual members, toward widows; and the service widows render to the church. Probably a list was kept of widows in need, and something like an 'order' of widows may have existed who undertook visitation and in other ways assisted church leaders.

The principle laid down in this passage is that believers should care for the widows in their own family and not allow them to be a burden on church resources. 'Charity begins at home'—even though it should not end there.

There is a love which is so long-sighted that it cannot recognize need close at hand. Those so afflicted are moved by suffering in far lands, feel deeply about 'mankind', may even long to save 'souls'—but they do not love actual people. Jean-Paul Sartre describes a visit he made to a dogs' cemetery. The 'quavering oration which ran on from tomb to tomb' disgusted him because it reminded him of his grandfather's philosophy: 'Dogs know how to love; they are more affectionate, more loyal than men.' Adds the French novelist, 'When you love children and dogs too much, you love them instead of adults.'

The greatest danger in 'long-sighted' love, as in all sentimentality, is that it never recognizes its own deficiency of affection.

1 TIMOTHY 5:9–16

'I prefer young widows to marry again, to bear children, to look after their households, and not to afford our opponents any chance of reviling us' (v. 14, Moffatt).

CHURCH AND WORLD. Widows were not only recipients of church bounty; they also served the Christian community in a semi-official capacity. The argument here stated is that only older women should be encouraged in this ministry; younger widows would do better to remarry. The apostle obviously had in mind some instances when younger women visiting from house to house had caused slander. The word occasion (v. 14) is a military term for a 'base of operations'. J. B. Phillips translates, 'Some, alas, have already played into the enemy's hands.' This raises the whole question of the relationship between the Church and the world.

Tolstoy describes a man crossing a river in a boat. Half-way across the current grips him and he finds himself amid numerous other boats, the occupants of which are mostly gliding with the stream. Some have even thrown their oars away. Only a few struggle upstream. Just in time the man hears the distant thunder of rapids and begins rowing madly against the current. That current, Tolstoy says, is the tradition of the world, the oars are our freewill, the opposite shore is God.

While remembering society's fundamental opposition to Christ we need not tiptoe apologetically through the world, as though through God-forsaken territory. 'Jesus Christ is Lord.' Society does not recognize His lordship—but the Christian does. His rejection of the world's standards is not due to his fear of their paralysing power but to his commitment to Christ.

1 TIMOTHY 5:17–25

'Similarly some virtues are plain to see, while others, though not at all conspicuous, will eventually make themselves felt' (v. 25, Phillips).

UNSEEN VIRTUE. We are constantly tempted to over-simplification in our estimate of others, particularly if we have never recognized the complexity of our own personalities. Paul was anxious lest superficial assessments should lead to the choice of wrong men for leadership, and, equally seriously, the overlooking of promising candidates whose qualities were not glaringly obvious.

In similar vein Dag Hammarskjöld noted in his journal that distance often encourages superficial assessments. 'Take warning,' he wrote, 'from all those times when, on meeting again, we feel ashamed because we realize we had accepted the false simplification which absence permits, its obliteration of all those characteristics which, when we meet face to face, force themselves upon even the blindest.'

To encourage careful discrimination, the apostle reminds Timothy of how hidden faults and secret virtues both 'catch up' with us. The former aspect of this truth has frequently been emphasized at the expense of the latter. Moralizers all too often prefer the negative to the positive statement. There are virtues, like patience and courageous endurance, which are essentially unseen but produce a sure harvest. To keep one's eyes fixed upon Christ, refusing to be discouraged even by one's own failures, to get up again after each fall, never despairing of God's grace: this is a secret discipline which cannot ultimately fail.

1 TIMOTHY 6:1–10

'Loving money leads to all kinds of evil' (v. 10, Phillips).

BROKEN IDOL. The first Christian communities often included both slaves and masters. The relationship of equality within the fellowship could create problems back in the domestic context: hence the apostle's advice that Christian slaves should respect their Christian masters. Of course, the contradiction between what was true 'in Christ' and the degrading status of the slave in society could be solved, centuries later, only by the abolition of slavery.

The danger of wealth, we should note, was not in possessing it but being preoccupied with it. Loving money is possible to every social class. And once that idol has been raised in our hearts it can be destroyed only by drastic action, as witnessed by Christ's command to the rich young ruler.

An important development in the Franciscan movement took place when Francis invited 'lay' people to enter his family without leaving their homes and work. Tradition claims the first to join were Luca of Gianzi, a corn merchant, and his wife Bona. Luca had grown wealthy by hoarding grain until a bad harvest enabled him to sell at iniquitous prices. When he first heard Francis preach he became very uneasy and took his wife to listen to the poor man of Assisi. Sharing her husband's conviction she was soon laying her bangles and buckles at the feet of Francis. Together this couple gave away vast stores of grain, lands and farms. The shackles of materialism broken, they lived simply and honestly in 'the joy of the Lord'.

1 TIMOTHY 6:11–16

'But you, O man of God, must flee from these things, and strive for uprightness, godliness, faith, love, fortitude, and gentleness' (v. 11, Weymouth).

REACHING BEYOND OUR GRASP. Two striking contrasts appear in the apostle's charge to his son in the faith. Timothy is described as a 'man of God' as opposed to the man of material ambition described in the previous verses. A further contrast lies in the command 'flee these things; and follow after righteousness'. The second aspect of this injunction we will consider today.

The follower of Christ is more conscious of the heights to which he is summoned than of the depths from which he is saved. A parable is found in the world of artistic achievement. In *Duet for Three Hands* the pianist Cyril Smith explains why there are some of his own records he has never bothered to play. 'This is not because of any inverted pride on my part; it is a result of that performers' mentality which most of us share and which influences us to believe that it is only tomorrow's performance which matters, never yesterday's.'

Cyril Smith also tells a story about the sculptor, Auguste Rodin. Near the end of his brilliant life a friend entering Rodin's studio found him weeping over a statue. Amazed at the old man's grief the visitor remarked, 'But it is quite perfect.' 'I think so too,' came the reply, 'and that is why I am weeping.' Rodin was great enough a craftsman to know that further progress is impossible to him who is satisfied with present attainment.

1 TIMOTHY 6:17–21

'Avoid the godless mixture of contradictory notions which is falsely known as "knowledge"—some have followed it and lost their faith' (vv. 20 and 21, Phillips).

WITHOUT IDOLS. The novelist E. M. Forster pointed out that the difference between a character in a novel and a real person is that you know all there is to know of the former, whereas of the latter you can know very little. A constant temptation besetting religious thinkers is to claim 'knowledge' of God beyond what is humanly possible, so making God seem 'a fictitious character'.

When this letter was written 'knowledge' (gnosis) was fast becoming a key word in the pagan religions, and the gnostic sects which flourished as a result became the Church's principal rivals. Paul warns Timothy against this false teaching. Some, grasping at so-called 'knowledge', have lost their faith. The word agnostic now means a person who neither believes nor disbelieves in God. But Christians were the first true 'agnostics', refusing to claim the 'knowledge' which is possible only of material things, insisting that a relationship with the living God is possible only by faith.

Of course faith brings its own assurance, but this is not the result of having defined God. It comes from responding to the love which claims us in Christ and in our fellows. Faith is the one relationship to God which does not seek to make Him in our own image.

2 TIMOTHY 1:1–7

'For the spirit which God has given us is not a spirit of cowardice, but one of power and of love and of sound judgment' (v. 7, Weymouth).

LIVING WITH ZEST. How best could Paul encourage Timothy, his son in the faith, who was battling against false teachers and other insidious influences within the Christian community at Ephesus?

First of all, the Apostle spoke of his own implicit confidence in Timothy's faithfulness. To be the custodian of a person's trust and hopes is one of the most inspiring experiences in life. Far from encouraging pride and self-esteem, it humbles and fires every noble resolve. One of Dr. Barclay's students said to him: 'The trouble is that the minister I'm assistant to thinks I'm good. That's what frightens me, because I've got to work so hard to show him that he's right.'

Next, Paul reminded Timothy of his family tradition. He had a heritage that represented the practice of religion at its best. This did not, of course, guarantee Timothy's behaviour, but it surely strengthened him in his determination to be worthy of the family's revered name. If some of us lack such a heritage we can always help to create one.

Again, Paul reminded Timothy of his high calling and of the promises he had made at his public consecration to it. To know oneself appointed to a great work is to shun the trivial and inferior, and to feel the dignity of bearing vital responsibility; but always the dignity that expresses a sense of personal unworthiness and unmerited privilege.

Finally, the Apostle urged Timothy to possess his spiritual possessions. You have received, he says, the spirit of power, love, and a sound mind, qualities which the New English Bible names as strength, love, and self-discipline. And so have we! Then let us square our shoulders, and live with zest as the sons and daughters of God.

2 TIMOTHY 1:8–11

'Christ has completely abolished death, and has now, through the gospel, opened to us men the shining possibilities of the life that is eternal' (v. 10, Phillips).

ENLARGED HORIZON. After being condemned to death Socrates was asked how he would like to be buried. 'Any way you like,' the philosopher replied with gentle humour, 'that is, if you can catch me and I don't slip through your fingers.'

A twentieth-century thinker, W. MacNeile Dixon, also speaking from a position outside the Christian faith, asserted his belief in life beyond death. 'What could be less rational,' he asked, 'than that his pen and paper should be more enduring than the saint, that we should have Shakespeare's handwriting but not himself? Raphael's pictures but not the mind that conceived them? . . . A future list is, you think, unbelievable? . . . Well, I should myself put the matter rather differently. The present life is incredible, a future credible.'

It is not only Christians who believe in life beyond death but, as Paul makes clear in today's passage, the grounds of the believer's faith are unique. For him, it is not philosophical argument which opens up the wider horizon of eternity. 'Life and immortality' have been brought to light by the gospel; that is, by the good news of God's love and by the manifestation of that love in the life, death and resurrection of Jesus. In consequence, Christian discipleship is not a foolhardy way of life chosen by eccentrics; it is the path one would expect to lead to such a goal. As H. E. Fosdick wrote: 'When a man strips himself of all convictions about the future, he stops living altogether.'

2 TIMOTHY 1:12–18

'I know the One in whom I have placed my confidence' (v 12, Phillips).

PERSONAL BELIEF. Despite his unenviable situation as a prisoner anticipating martyrdom, Paul affirms his unshakable confidence. How much weaker his affirmation would have sounded had the apostle merely written, 'I know what I believe'. Instead, he reveals the deeply personal nature of his faith, 'I know whom I have believed'.

Believing in a personal God who has disclosed Himself in Christ, it follows that for Christians faith must be personal. 'We can get to know the properties of radium by suitable laboratory tests,' writes Murdo Ewen Macdonald. 'We can get to know what the moon is made of by building bigger rockets and space capsules and landing someone there. We can get to know a foreign language by studying its syntax and amassing its vocabulary. But we cannot get to know a person except by loving him, and there is no exception to this rule.'

Christian faith, therefore, must involve heart as well as mind. Philosophers have usually been suspicious of feelings and emotions, regarding them as obstacles on the path to pure truth. Their wariness is valid, however, only when they seek truth about objects, and then only if it is scientific truth they desire. Artistic appreciation, for instance, requires a totally different approach. Knowledge of God, particularly that which yields the sublime assurance Paul possessed, calls for commitment of intellect, emotions and will.

2 TIMOTHY 2:1–7

'Put up with your share of a hardship as a loyal soldier in Christ's army' (v. 3, Phillips).

SPIRITUAL COMBAT. The three illustrations Paul uses to encourage Timothy in Christian service—the soldier, the athlete and the the agricultural labourer—each carries a wealth of significance. While focusing upon the first we should note that the others are also examples of single-minded purpose. For instance, one commentator cites instances of athletes being required to swear an oath that they had fulfilled ten months' training before being eligible to enter a contest. In this way high standards of performance were ensured. Similarly, the hardworking farmer knew that slackness resulted in a poor harvest.

Paul was fond of military metaphors, probably because his own experience proved that Christian discipleship involved unremitting conflict. We recognize that warfare, which has never been glorious, was not then the indiscriminate horror it has now become.

Whether we find the metaphor 'soldier of Christ' congenial or not, we certainly cannot afford to forget we are engaged in real spiritual combat, and that this requires self-discipline and sacrifice. William James, the philosopher and psychologist, derived from his father the belief in an 'unfinished universe', one bristling with chance and possibilities, 'a universe in which both good and bad were real and eternally at war'. In James's view, wrote his biographer, Gay Wilson Allen, 'not the absence of vice, but vice there, and virtue holding her by the throat, seems the ideal state'. Christians do not share James's view that the outcome of this conflict is uncertain: we do agree with him that the combat is intensely real.

2 TIMOTHY 2:8–13

'There is no imprisoning the word of God' (v. 9, Knox).

FREEDOM MAN CANNOT DESTROY. What a graphic contrast Paul here portrays! An elderly apostle, still burning to preach the unsearchable riches of Christ, shut up behind bars: and on the other hand the conquering word of God which no man can imprison.

First consider the apostle. In the previous passage he had exhorted Timothy to endure hardness. He can now cite himself as an example. He is imprisoned as a common 'criminal', the only other time in which this word is used in the New Testament is to describe the 'malefactors' crucified with Jesus. Far too many exhortations to sacrifice have come from the lips of comfortably-placed speakers. Paul was not guilty of this inconsistency.

Cruelly cramped in his environment, Paul was utterly confident that the Word of God was unfettered. In the Bible the phrase 'Word of God' does not mean the Scriptures but, in the Old Testament, the living prophetic word; and, in the New Testament, Jesus Christ Himself either in His Incarnation or in the preaching of His church.

A pastor who worked in a country whose Government forbade all evangelism describes how Christians continued to witness. Butchers inserted Christian leaflets in the wrapping paper of meat they sold, children placed gospel portions in their teacher's coat pockets, printers went back to their presses late at night and ran off a few thousand copies of Christian literature. History confirms that, since the resurrection of Christ, men can no longer 'chain the word of God'.

2 TIMOTHY 2:14–21

'Try hard to show yourself worthy of God's approval, as a labourer who need not be ashamed, driving a straight furrow, in your proclamation of the truth' (v. 15, N.E.B.).

BY WORD AND DEED. Advising Timothy on how to deal with false teaching, Paul gives top priority to positive proclamation of the truth, always more effective than merely denouncing error and so entrenching people more deeply in their own positions. Like a skilful craftsman who competently handles his tools, Timothy is urged to show similar expertise in 'rightly dividing the word of truth' (A.V.). The Greek verb used here implies the idea of cutting: hence the N.E.B. translation, 'driving a straight furrow'. E. F. Scott suggests, however, that if a definite craft is indicated it is more likely to be that of a mason who hews stones and fits them together. 'So the teacher must fashion his message into a structure that will stand foursquare.'

We can easily translate this advice to a Christian teacher into everyday living. The gospel has never relied solely on verbal communication. Word and deed are equally essential. Richard Wurmbrand gives an illustration of the surreptitious distribution of Christian literature where overt evangelism is forbidden, and says, 'In any village or town, the Christians are the most well liked, beloved residents. When a mother is too ill to care for her children, it is the Christian mother who goes over and looks after them. When a man is too ill to cut his firewood, it is the Christian man who does it for him. They "live" their Christianity—and when they begin to witness for Christ people listen and believe—because they have seen Christ in their lives.'

2 TIMOTHY 2:22–26

'Avoid these futile and silly speculations, understanding that they only give rise to quarrels' (v. 23, Jerusalem Bible).

POINTLESS DISCUSSIONS. During our reading of Paul's first letter to Timothy we saw that abstract speculation, so fashionable at that time, was a real danger to the Church. The apostle's warning is equally valid today, yet how shall we distinguish 'foolish and ignorant speculation' from the legitimate, and sometimes controversial, search for new ways of communicating ancient truth? Timid thinkers are always ready to pin the label of 'foolish speculation' on any unconventional thinking which abandons their own timeworn clichés and flabby formulas.

'Foolish speculation' does not include the honest exploration of how the gospel may best be presented in each new age. Writing about religion and drama, W. Moelwyn Merchant has claimed that if the Church is to remain creatively alive, speculation must be pushed to the limits of orthodoxy, and this is frequently the vocation of dramatists, writers and artists. The test of all such work is this: does it enable us better to communicate the Christian gospel without reduction to the men and women of our age?

'Foolish speculation' for the Christian invariably betrays two characteristics. It does not centre in Christ or further illuminate His significance: indeed, it tends to suggest that the Incarnation was unnecessary. Furthermore, it does not lead to action. The energy which should be used in Christlike service is dissipated in controversy. H. E. Fosdick gave a fair warning when he wrote to a younger man: 'As I think on your inward tussle with the problems of religious faith, I do not want it to exhaust itself in speculation, without the clarifying, vitalizing influence of action'.

2 TIMOTHY 3:1–9

'They will keep up the outward appearance of religion but will have rejected the inner power of it' (v. 5, Jerusalem Bible).

THE DANGER OF FORMALISM. In his book, *Half-Way to Faith*, Lord Eccles records that the trustees of a museum were offered a tenth-century wooden crucifix, about three-quarters life-size and covered in paint. The villagers who had cared for the crucifix for a thousand years had painted and repainted it many times. When experts were asked whether the trustees should purchase the crucifix they replied that if the paint was carefully removed 'the cleaned crucifix was likely to astonish the trustees by its beauty, vigour and life, which had been partly concealed by the loving care of a thousand years'.

Paul's catalogue of the evils which would disfigure society in the 'last days' concludes with formal, powerless religion. How much this contributes to the other evils it is hard to say. What is certain is that lifeless religion can sometimes result from too many accretions which hide the pristine experience of Christ just as successive layers of paint encased the beauty of the crucifix.

Our parable can be taken a step further. The vigorous tenth-century carving 'had been partly concealed by the loving care of a thousand years'. The accretions which sometimes overlay essential Christian experience often began as expressions of devotion, and may even remain so for some. Periodically the Church has to undergo a process of simplification. So must the individual believer who desires to concentrate his limited energy on what is essential.

2 TIMOTHY 3:10–17

'Remember how you have known from childhood the sacred writings that can impart saving wisdom by faith in Christ Jesus' (v. 15, Moffatt).

THE PURPOSE OF BIBLE READING. Anthony Bloom, Archbishop of the Russian Orthodox Church in Great Britain and Ireland, hated Christianity in his youth. In order to check upon a certain lecturer's arguments he asked his mother for a New Testament, counting the chapters in each Gospel so as to read the shortest. Describing his experience he says, 'While I was reading the beginning of Mark's Gospel, before I reached the third chapter, I became aware of a presence. I saw nothing. I heard nothing. It was no hallucination. It was a simple certainty that the Lord was standing there and that I was in the presence of Him whose life I had begun to read with such revulsion and such ill will. This was my basic and essential meeting with the Lord. From then on I knew that Christ did exist.'

The primary purpose of the Bible, as in Anthony Bloom's experience and in this assessment of Paul's, is to create a living relationship with Christ. This is what saves a man from sin and from himself. It is not faith in the Bible, much less knowledge of the Bible, which saves; only that trustful relationship with God through Christ which the Bible so often, and so astonishingly, creates.

Yet how can reading of past events make possible a relationship with the living Christ? The answer is found in the work of the Holy Spirit. He makes Jesus our contemporary. Without Him Bible reading might make us students: it could never make us saints.

2 TIMOTHY 4:1–5

'Prove, correct and encourage, using the utmost patience in your teaching' (v. 2, Phillips).

THE VIRTUE OF PERSISTENCE. Paul's solemn charge to Timothy stresses the need for patient persistence in face of all discouragement and opposition. Other teachers may excite men by the novelty of what they say; Timothy must tirelessly expound the true riches of the gospel.

Patience is one of the great indispensables in Christian discipleship. Not only the teacher, but every believer must develop it in order to endure to the end. Communion with Christ does not become a living reality overnight; it is the fruit of persistence in prayer and openness to the movements of the Spirit. Robert Stroud, who during forty years in solitary confinement became an authority on the blood of birds, recorded his discoveries in a book. In the introduction he wrote, 'I probably do not know what I am talking about and have grave doubts about whether anyone else knows anything about the subject either; but . . . after 3,000 hours at the microscope, I pass that nothing on to you.' 3,000 hours at the microscope! That is the kind of dedicated persistence which makes a scientist. Can we hope that less patience will be required on the way of Christian discipleship?

Perhaps the area where patience is most demanded is with ourselves. Hence the wisdom of the remark of Seraphim of Sarov: 'Man must be lenient with his soul in her weakness . . . and suffer her failings as he suffers those of others, but he must not become idle, and must encourage himself to better things'.

2 TIMOTHY 4:6–13

'I have run the great race, I have finished the course, I have kept faith' (v. 7, N.E.B.).

NO AIMLESS RAMBLE. 'The human heart,' said Martin Luther, 'is like a millstone in a mill: when you put wheat under it, it turns and grinds and bruises the wheat to flour; if you put no wheat, it still grinds on, but then 'tis itself it grinds and wears away.' This contrast between purposeful and purposeless living could be endlessly illustrated.

Following his conversion Paul became a man with a goal. Life had new objectives. Therefore death, which he now believed imminent, was seen as an arrival, an achievement. Christ filled life with purpose and robbed death of its terror.

Whether we see life as purposive or view it as meaningless makes all the difference to our ability to tolerate frustration and react creatively to hardship. It is the difference between the millstone grinding wheat and the millstone grinding itself away. Nor is our decision to view life one way or the other merely personal preference. John Hick, a Christian philosopher, tells a parable of two fellow-travellers. One man considers himself on a pilgrimage to the Celestial City, and interprets the delights and hardships of the way accordingly; the other sees his journey as an aimless but unavoidable ramble. 'They do not entertain different expectations about the coming details of the road, but only about its ultimate destination. Yet, when they turn the last corner, it will be apparent that one of them has been right all the time and the other wrong.

2 TIMOTHY 4:14–22

'At the first hearing of my case no one came into court to support me ... But the Lord stood by me and lent me strength' (vv. 16 and 17, N.E.B.).

OUR CONTEMPORARY. 'Once at least in his life,' wrote Oscar Wilde, 'each man walks with Christ to Emmaus.' What the dramatist claimed was an occasional privilege for every man the saints experience as an abiding reality. Paul appears to record the desertion of his friends only in order to highlight the unfailing support of Christ. It was customary at a Roman trial for the defendant's friends to appear with him to give moral support, yet at the preliminary investigations into Paul's case, or at some earlier trial, the apostle stood alone—yet not alone. How are we to understand this sustaining sense of the presence of Christ shared by so many believers?

The experience is far more than the inspiring memory of past greatness. A man facing death for truth's sake may well be encouraged by the recollection of Socrates' courage; he cannot have Socrates beside him. A person suffering the injustice of racial prejudice may retain his dignity by recalling the example of Martin Luther King; he cannot have that great black leader at his side to help him endure the anguish. When a Christian affirms the presence of Christ he is adding his simple testimony to what the Church claims in the doctrine of the Holy Spirit.

It follows that Christ's presence is not registered mainly by our emotions. We do not always feel He is near. We affirm His presence by faith, live by this reality, and increasingly prove our trust is not misplaced.

THE EPISTLE TO TITUS

INTRODUCTION

Though we do not know as much about Titus as we do about Timothy, it is clear that in him Paul felt he had a man upon whom he could rely. Titus seems to have been of a practical turn of mind for he was given the task of organizing the collection for the poor in the Jerusalem church (2 Cor. 8:6). He was also charged with the organization of the church in Crete (Titus 1:5) and to show himself the kind of man whose instructions would be supported by his own Christian living (Titus 2:7).

Whether Paul's hope of spending the winter with Titus at Nicopolis (in the Roman province of Dalmatia) was ever realized we do not know (Titus 3:12). It is clear that the Apostle hoped to be released from prison (Phil. 2:24, Philemon 22). Certain traditional teachings support this, but certainty is impossible.

TITUS 1:1–4

'From Paul, a servant of God and apostle of Jesus Christ, marked as such by faith and knowledge and hope' (v. 1, N.E.B.).

THE BEST IS YET TO BE. Here are three essential characteristics of the slave and messenger of Christ.

First of all, he is a man of faith. But let us be clear what this means. Faith is not passive, the opposite of works or action. In his challenging book about Christian witness in the slums of East Harlem, Bruce Kenrick records a conversation between a minister of religion and the supporter of a Christian seeking election to the city council. Urged to advise his flock to vote for the Christian, whose programme of reforms was urgently needed in the district, the minister replied: 'If he's a man of God he'll win.' 'But doesn't God want our aid in helping him to win?' Again the minister replied, 'If he's a man of God he'll win.' 'But God doesn't take our place in the voting booths,' protested the supporter. Back came the imperturbable reply: 'If he's a man of God he'll win.' Concluded Mr. Kenrick: 'The man of God failed to win—as many men of God have seemed to fail. Perhaps he would have won with a few more votes from the Christian community.' No wonder the epistle of James insists that faith without works is a corpse!

Second, the slave and messenger of Christ is a man of knowledge. Now the biblical idea of knowledge is not simply the learning of facts. This is a Greek idea. In the Bible, knowledge means experience, not knowing about, but knowing, sharing a personal relationship and exploring ever more deeply its fathomless riches.

Finally, the slave and messenger of Christ is a man of hope. He does not merely hope for the best, hope that everything will work out all right, for his daily foretaste of glory assures him that, in the service of Christ, the best is always yet to be.

TITUS 1:5–9

'To exercise spiritual oversight, a man must be of unimpeachable virtue, for he is God's agent' (v. 7, Phillips).

CHRISTIAN BEGGARS. The Christians in Crete, some of them are mere 'babes in Christ', obviously had much to learn, and therefore the appointment of the right sort of leaders was of the utmost importance. They should be men, Titus was instructed, of integrity, of sound doctrine, and of pleasing personality; individuals in whom creed and character blended perfectly. But there was something else, representing a new and revolutionary idea.

The Christian leader was to be a 'steward of God'. In the ancient world the implication of this could not have been more clear. For a steward, a man of real authority and a custodian of great wealth, was the chief servant; he fulfilled his exalted office by being at the beck and call of everybody. This spirit, which found its perfect expression in Him who said, 'I am among you as One that serveth', is the hallmark of Christian leadership. Indeed, without it service of any kind becomes a sad contradiction. Yet how easily service in the name of Christ is offered without the spirit of a servant, the result of being that the unfortunate recipients are offended by patronage or self-conscious charity.

The only safeguard is the nurturing of Christian compassion, probably best accomplished in two ways—by talking to God about people before talking to people about God; and by remembering, preferably in contemplation of the Cross, that every Christian leader, however exalted his position, is, in the words of D. T. Niles, simply one beggar telling other beggars where to find food.

TITUS 1:10–16

'To the pure all things are pure, but to the corrupt and unbelieving nothing is pure' (v. 15, R.S.V.).

THE UNDERWORLD OF SOILED THINKING. Among the Christians at Crete were false teachers, one of whom was speaking the truth when he said: 'Men of Crete are always liars, evil and beastly, lazy and greedy' (v. 12, Phillips). The islanders were notorious for their readiness to cheat and lie for illicit gain. After their conversion to Christianity, some of them did not find it easy to throw off the influence of their old life, and they indulged in exciting heresy no less than in evil practices. Hence their need of strong leaders, men of character, sound doctrine, and dynamic personality.

The Christian community at Crete was like an island of truth surrounded by an angry sea of corruption; and its defences were further seriously threatened from within. For converts, their consciences not yet sensitive to the standards of Christ, were mistaking Christian liberty for licence, a common failing in the Early Church, or, going to the other extreme, were practising a fierce self-denial and reading into all things physical and material the misjudgments of their sick imaginations. Unavoidably people with soiled minds see everything in the twilight of their own impurity. With their suggestive talk, smutty stories, and hollow laughter, they spread contamination wherever they go; but people with pure desires—and they are pure only to the degree that purity is loved—escape much of this underworld and are impervious to the devilish insinuations of double-talk. Being simple (not simpletons) and innocent (not innocuous), they see and hear only what their passion for purity allows. They do not repress the unpleasant, but welcome into their secret lives only those things which are consistent with the mind of Christ.

TITUS 2:1–8

'In all your teaching, show the strictest regard for truth, and show that you appreciate the seriousness of the matters you are dealing with' (v. 8, Phillips).

ADVICE FOR ALL AGE-GROUPS. To counteract the influences threatening to overwhelm the little Christian community, Titus was told to instruct three distinct groups of believers, most of all by his strong example. The old men were to be told to practise self-control; the old women, self-sacrifice; and the young men, self-discipline. Now what was behind this rather 'profoundly obvious' counsel? Possibly the older men were taking advantage of their seniority and harshly dogmatizing against younger believers whose biggest sin was their youth. At all events the older Christians, apparently finding it difficult to be 'masters of themselves', were to be urged, to quote Moffatt, 'to be temperate, serious . . . sound in faith, in love, and in steadfastness' (v. 2).

The old women were to express their self-sacrifice predominantly in home-making, a task involving inescapable drudgery. They were to be a worthy example to the younger women, not least in their refusal to gossip away their time and other people's reputations. As Jesus illustrated in His parable of the unjust judge, a woman's main weapon, or one of them, is her tongue! What matters is how she uses it.

The young men, possibly wanting changes too radical and too

fast, were to be instructed in the art of radiant self-denial, the spirit that, apart from making a flabby body and a flabby mind impossible, silences criticism by the authority of its transparent goodness. Their defence against malicious accusations and sincere misunderstandings alike was to be the daily witness of a lovely life. Whatever our age, we are committed to the same ideals.

TITUS 2:9–15

Christians 'are to show themselves utterly trustworthy, a living testimonial to the teaching of God our Saviour' (v. 10, Phillips).

A DEADLY SIN THAT IS SOCIALLY ACCEPTABLE. The truth at the heart of this reading is summed up in the verse:

I'd rather see a sermon than hear one any day,
I'd rather one should walk with me than merely tell the way,
I can soon learn how to do it, if you'll let me see it done,
I can watch your hands in action, but your tongue too fast may run;
And the sermons you deliver may be very wise and true,
But I'd rather get my lesson by observing what you do.
For I may not understand you and the high advice you give
But there's no misunderstanding how you act and how you live.

One inconsistent believer probably does greater harm to the cause of Christ than a score of atheists. In the days of Titus Christians were contradicting their profession of faith by practising such crudities as laziness, insubordination and pilfering, failings reflecting the corrupt society in which they lived, and hardly likely to characterize the vast majority of modern believers, with 2,000 years of Christian civilization behind them. Christians today are tempted to deny their faith in ways more cultured than crude, more respectable than repulsive. They rarely steal—either money, their employer's time, or another man's wife—any more than they shout abuse or exploit positions of trust. Their worst sin is socially acceptable and almost invariably unrealized. It is the canker of the soul called apathy—drab, inoffensive, uninteresting, and deadly.

The only antidote, as Titus is urged to make clear with regard to the more obvious sins, is a growing awareness of God's unconditional and unmerited love revealed in Christ, an awareness best encouraged, as we have often noted, on bended knee at Calvary.

TITUS 3:1–7

'For we ourselves were once foolish, disobedient, led astray, slaves to various passions and pleasures . . . but when the goodness and loving kindness of God appeared He saved us' (vv. 3–5, R.S.V.).

APATHY'S INSEPARABLE COMPANION. We saw yesterday that the antidote to deadly apathy was a growing awareness of God's love in Christ. When this awareness transforms our knowing about the Cross into our realizing its unbelievable truth, an experience demanding the self-discipline of worship and work, the twin necessities of vital faith, we stop talking about what we must do for God and think only of what He has done for us.

From such a radical change of outlook there flows spontaneously the witness of a great gratitude. Without this spirit, which views the obligation (and sometimes the drudgery) of Christian service as a token payment of an unpayable debt, the believer becomes weary or proud in well-doing. The result is either self-pity or self-centredness. But when wonderment at the amazing and wholly undeserved mercy of God pulsates at the heart of personal religion, the burdens of Christian commitment grow wings and inspire songs of praise. As Henry van Dyke remarked: 'Thankfulness is the other side of mercy.' A great gratitude creates a great gentleness, even toward exasperating people, and defeats the temptation to hardness of heart, the inseparable companion of apathy.

TITUS 3:8–11

'But avoid stupid controversies, genealogies, dissensions, and quarrels over the Law, for they are unprofitable and futile' (v. 9, R.S.V.).

SAYING EVERYTHING AND DOING NOTHING. 'Christians', Titus is instructed to emphasize, 'should make it their business to practise virtue'; so reads the New English Bible alternative rendering of verse 8. The reason for this counsel is revealed in the following verse, which warns against the danger of making Christianity a subject for debate and not a way of life.

Innumerable believers have mistaken debate for devotion, and discussion for duty. They have made endless talking a substitute for faithfulness in service; and left problems solved in theory unresolved in practice. It is so easy to be outspoken about Christian principles and yet lacking in practical action. Some of us, for instance, who shout the loudest about racial discrimination, rarely, if ever, entertain a coloured person in our own homes. We possibly wax eloquent about the problems of old people, yet never visit the aged in our own neighbourhoods. With appropriate solemnity we help to pass outspoken resolutions at annual conferences, or applaud them when they are passed, and keep a discreet distance from the rough-and-tumble of effective action. Such empty gestures turn the Word made flesh into words, and the Kingdom of God into little more than a debating society. Unless our words are matched by deeds, we serve best by either keeping quiet or, much to be preferred, by learning to practise the truth.

TITUS 3:12–15

'And our people should learn to earn what they require by leading an honest life and so be self-supporting' (v. 14, Phillips).

OUR LIVING IS NEVER MORE NOBLE THAN OUR GIVING. Although we know so little about the two people mentioned by name in verse 13—Zenas and Apollos—the obscure reference to them reminds us of an important principle. It appears that they were about to leave Crete on a Christian mission, a mission involving the congregation to which they belonged in no little expense. To meet this and similar situations, Titus was to exhort every believer to strive for sufficient financial independence to make possible generous contributions to worthy causes. Evidence of each Christian's sincerity would be the extent to which he worked hard, not only to keep himself free of debt, but to be able to give increasingly to the Lord's work.

Our interest in missionary endeavour, as in any other form of Christian service, is never more than our financial commitment to it. When we really care, we seek ways and means, no matter how limited our financial resources, to give more and more This is one reason why the life of every humble follower of Christ, whatever the size of his bank balance, is characterized by an essential simplicity. The saintly John Fletcher, for instance, an intimate friend of John Wesley, lived on bread and broth that he might save money to give to the poor. Some Christians would not go to such extremes—and no one believer has the right to dogmatize about how much another should give—but the principle clearly emerges: we live for Christ only as much as we give sacrificially to His cause.

THE EPISTLE TO PHILEMON

INTRODUCTION

This short letter is unique because it was written to a single person, Philemon, and was concerned with the fate of a single person—the fugitive slave, Onesimus. The Apostle, on whose shoulders rested the care of all the churches, had a heart large enough to be interested in the welfare of a runaway thief (v. 18). The fact speaks for itself.

PHILEMON vv. 1–5

'Grace and peace be to you from God our Father and from the Lord Jesus Christ' (v. 3, Phillips).

UNMERITED LOVE. Philemon was not only the head of a Christian household; his house was a meeting-place of the local church. In extending his salutation to embrace all the believers who gathered in Philemon's house for worship, Paul uses two words which recur continuously in his writings—grace and peace.

In everyday speech 'grace' is usually applied to beauty of movement, form or manners. The graceful dancer, the graceful lines of a jet aeroplane and a gracious person all excite our admiration. 'Grace' is more often used in its adjectival or adverbial form than as a noun.

Theologically, 'grace' means either the free, unmerited favour of God, or a divine energy which sanctifies, strengthens and assists men to fulfil God's will. It was perhaps natural, but unfortunate, that it has most often received the latter emphasis. One definition of Thomas Aquinas was that grace is 'a supernatural something in man, coming from God'. Pursuing this line of thought some theologians increasingly thought of grace as a king of spiritual property accumulated by prayer or sacraments.

It is doubtful if Paul viewed grace in this way. Grace is God acting graciously, in pardoning our sins, in refining our personalities We would be saved many confusions if we insisted on relating our theological words to everyday usage, instead of allowing them to become a technical jargon.

PHILEMON vv. 6–10

'Accordingly, although in Christ I might make bold to point out your duty, yet, because of that same love, I would rather appeal to you' (vv 8 and 9, N.E.B.).

A FLEXIBLE APPROACH. This briefest of all Paul's letters, and a perfect gem of apostolic tact and graciousness, concerns Onesimus, a runaway slave who deserted the service of Philemon and may even have stolen his master's money as well. Probably aiming to lose himself in the crowded capital, Onesimus somehow came in contact with the imprisoned apostle at Rome, and acted as his personal servant. Paul now returns him to his master with the request that he may be forgiven and received kindly. The apostle speaks of Philemon's acknowledged benevolence and one commentator suggests that possibly the great earthquake at Colossae had already provided the wealthy Philemon with many opportunities to prove his generosity.

The apostle, therefore, bases his plea upon Philemon's reputation for kindness. He could equally well have used his apostolic authority and on occasions was swift to do so. Two reasons weighed against this. For one thing, loving action must be free and spontaneous or it easily becomes only a duty. Secondly, Paul knew the man to whom he was writing. Only rigid and unimaginative persons meet every single individual in the same manner, often making out of this unconscious 'necessity' a supposed virtue. Flexibility and variety of approach in human relationships are not signs of inconsistency; they prove we are sufficiently free from ourselves to appreciate the other's need and viewpoint.

PHILEMON vv. 11–16

'Once you found him a worthless character, but nowadays he is worth something to you and me' (v. 11, Moffatt).

HAPPY REVERSAL. The name 'Onesimus' means 'profitable' and we can well imagine Philemon's thought about the ironic misnaming of his slave. Paul anticipated this problem and it is with great delicacy and skill that he introduces the slave's name. He makes an untranslatable pun on the name Onesimus, saying, in effect, he 'whom I begot as truly Profitable'.

We have no difficulty in recognizing the Christian miracle of transformation in people dramatically converted. Elijah Cadman, for instance, was a light-weight boxer and joint-owner of the Rugby Boxing Saloon in his early days. Harsh training as a boy chimney sweep and vicious companions made him a trouble to the police as well as to himself. Converted in a Wesleyan meeting, Cadman later joined up with the Rev. William Booth and played a large part in making The Christian Mission into The Salvation Army. He never ceased to be a fighter; he did choose totally different opponents.

What of those Christians who can point to no such dramatic about-turn in their lives? Perhaps Paul's assessment of the change in Onesimus may help here. Once useless, but now truly useful;

this need not indicate a change from notorious vice to outstanding virtue. It does describe a process just as miraculous and thoroughgoing: a move from egotism to concern for others, from the pursuit of selfish ends to outgoing service, from possessiveness to generous liberality.

PHILEMON vv. 17–25

'If you feel he has wronged or cheated you put it down to my account . . . I, Paul, hereby promise to repay you' (vv. 18 and 19, Phillips).

AN APOSTLE'S IOU. This brief letter is all that remains to us of one of the 'hidden romances' of the New Testament. For the rest we are thrown back upon conjecture. We can safely assume that Philemon did as Paul hoped and forgave his slave, otherwise this letter would not have been preserved. But what happened to Onesimus afterwards? Did his master send him back to serve Paul, as the apostle seems to hint he might? (v. 13). Was Onesimus eventually freed?

In the years 107–117 the Bishop at Ephesus was named Onesimus and, if it seems unlikely that a slave should hold such position, we must remember that some slaves were more educated than their masters. Cyril H. Powell believes that Onesimus may have been responsible for first collecting together the letters of the apostle who presumably led him to Christ.

Finally, what shall we say of Paul's solemn IOU to repay Philemon the cost of his slave's defection? Presumably the apostle dictated this letter but, at the point where he pledges restitution, he takes up the pen to endorse his promise as legally required. However little the apostle expected Philemon to exact what was due to him, this is all so characteristic of Paul. He was like his Master in the infinite value he placed upon the individual, as well as in not expecting others to make sacrifices he shirked.

THE EPISTLE TO THE HEBREWS

INTRODUCTION

This Epistle makes more demands upon today's readers than any other part of the New Testament, with the possible exception of the Revelation of St. John.

First of all, the heading in our Authorized Version—'The Epistle of Paul the Apostle to the Hebrews'—is misleading. As the *New Testament Commentary* says: 'This improper inscription was added by some later hand'. Various alternative suggestions have been made over the centuries. One of the most intriguing was that of Harnack that the Epistle was the joint work of Priscilla and Aquila. Possibly A. B. Bruce was as wise as any when he declared it

> fitting that the author of an Epistle which begins by virtually proclaiming God as the only Speaker in Scripture and Jesus Christ as the one Speaker in the New Testament, should himself retire out of sight.

The aim of the author is to show to his fellow Jewish Christians that all that the Old Testament promised came to perfection and reality in Jesus. Particularly was this true of the manner in which Jesus opened up a new and living way to God. As the perfect priest He also provided in His own person the perfect sacrifice. Possibly none but a Jew could have so commended to Jews the right of Jesus to be acknowledged as the Christ.

Woven into the argument—especially towards the end of the Epistle—are words of encouragement addressed to any who might be wavering in their profession.

HEBREWS 1:1–4

'He is the radiant light of God's glory and the perfect copy of His nature' (v. 3, Jerusalem Bible).

GOD'S SON. This magnificent passage has been likened to a strong suspension bridge, spanning—so writes M. A. P. Wood—'the great chasm of man's tumultuous world, from eternity to eternity. One pier speaks of creation through Christ, looking back into a past eternity. The other speaks of Christ glorified for all future eternities.'

The writer contrasts the fragmentary glimpses of truth granted to Israel through the prophets with the full disclosure of God's nature in His Son. What does it mean to call Jesus the Son of God? Certainly not what the pagan world meant when it claimed that Heracles was the son of Zeus. It was Arius, the third-century heretic, who used the word 'Son' in this literal fashion, asking 'How can a son be as old as his father?' claiming thereby that Christ was not eternal.

In speaking of Jesus as the Son of God we assert His unique relationship with God and His divine likeness. The writer to the Hebrews uses two metaphors to illustrate this. One commentator has observed that 'as the rays of the sun reveal the glory of that celestial body and are identified with it, so Christ radiates the glory of God and is identified with Him'. The second metaphor is that of the seal which, when impressed upon soft wax, leaves the exact imprint of its inscription. In Jesus the very nature of God is perfectly imprinted upon the plastic material of a human life.

Of course, no analogy is perfect, but the writer is very certain that in Jesus 'the Word was made flesh'.

HEBREWS 1:5–14

'For God never said to any angel, "Thou art My Son; today I have begotten Thee"' (v. 5, N.E.B.).

DIRECT ACCESS TO GOD. Having stated that Jesus was superior to the prophets and that He was the fulfilment of all their hopes, the writer of *Hebrews* next asserted that Jesus was superior to the angels. At this time, belief in angelic beings was widespread and on the increase, the reason being that men could not conceive of human sinfulness having direct contact with God's holiness. So heavenly intermediaries seemed the obvious answer, a fact explaining why the author of these verses was anxious to underline a vital truth.

In Jewish thought—and this epistle was primarily for Jewish Christians—angels delivered God's messages to men, and communicated men's prayers to God; but Christ made direct access to God possible. There was now no need for angels, the Law, religious ritualism or human agencies.

God was known simply by taking Jesus into the heart and mind. Their name is legion who themselves erect unscalable barriers between themselves and God. They imagine that they need to *prove* their worthiness to receive forgiveness and enjoy fellowship with Him, and this they proceed to attempt with confessions of emotional self-hate (which they call repentance) and promises of costly faithfulness. Yet all the time, Christ, 'the stamp of God's very being', to quote the New English Bible, testifies to their unmerited and unconditional acceptance by God. We should stop fretting about our unworthiness and centre our thoughts on Christ's assurance of God's loving acceptance!

HEBREWS 2:1–9

'We ought, therefore, to pay the greatest attention to the truth that we have heard and not allow ourselves to drift away from it' (v. 1, Phillips).

THE PERIL OF DRIFTING. Many theories have been conceived about the group to which this letter was sent. William Manson suggested it was addressed to a group of Christian Jews who were part of the larger church at Rome. So attached was this group to the traditions and worship of the Old Testament that it tended to maintain the exclusiveness of Judaism, failing to recognize both the challenge and wealth of the Christian faith.

We see, therefore, why the author issues the grave warning of this passage. Having shown that the Son is far superior to angels he draws the obvious conclusion: the gospel of Christ must be equally superior to the law delivered by angels. The writer pleads with his readers to give the closest attention to the

Christian gospel for fear of drifting away. He uses a word which can apply to a ship carelessly allowed to drift past the harbour by a negligent mariner.

Retaining this same metaphor, we would say these Christians had carelessly gone off course, and were now back in old waters when they should be well set for a new destination. Is it not true of most of us that when we drift, we drift backwards in the direction of old habits? Our author offers one remedy to his original readers and us: the closest possible attention of mind and heart to Christ.

HEBREWS 2:10–18

'He also became a human being, so that by going through death as a man He might destroy him who had the power of death, that is, the devil; and might also set free those who lived their whole lives a prey to the fear of death' (vv. 14 and 15, Phillips).

A GREAT LIBERATION. Evelyn Waugh has ghoulishly satirized modern man's refusal to face the fact of death in his novel *The Loved One*. There a Californian funeral establishment arranges for the corpse to be skilfully restored to life-like appearance before being set in a prominent position and holding a 'reception' for its friends and relations. Sebastian Moore speaks of our life being set between the poles of sex and death, 'the ecstasy whence we come and the dissolution to which we go', and points out that both these realities have been feared, repressed and made subjects of secretive whispering. But whereas modern man has lost all reticence about sex he resolutely refuses to acknowledge death.

The writer to the Hebrews, now leading up to his main theme, claims that Christ has liberated believers from fear of death. By becoming our Brother, Christ fully shared our death. Because of His massive victory over sin and the grave He liberates us from the thraldom of these twin oppressors. As D. B. Taylor has said: 'If we wish really to become alive we must rise (with Christ) out of the dead body which we now inhabit, out of the dead world which surrounds us, and share His risen life. It is then that our dead bodies begin to live and our dead world begins to move in accordance with God's plan'.

HEBREWS 3:1–11

'Today, when you hear His voice, harden not your hearts as at the Provocation, on the day of the Temptation in the desert' (vv. 7 and 8, Moffatt).

THE NEW EXODUS. Moffatt gives the words provocation and temptation an initial capital letter because, in the Hebrew of Psalm 95, they are the names of two places—Meribah and Massah—where Israel refused trustfully to follow Jehovah to the Promised Land. The writer to the Hebrews compares Israel's journey under Moses to the new deliverance and exodus initiated by Christ. The Jewish Christians he addressed were in danger of repeating the error of their ancestors and, by clinging to the past, forfeiting the new freedom Christ had won for them.

The Catholic scholar Leenhardt writes about the tension persisting throughout the Old Testament between two tendencies which he describes as the Abrahamic motif and the Mosaic motif. The first emphasizes the need for Israel to be free, like Abraham of old, to abandon all past securities and follow God into uncharted territory. The second stresses Israel's need for laws and institutions to give her life definite shape, and exhibit God's way to the nations. Of course, Moses also led his people into unknown territory, but it was the Mosaic law that later represented the ideal of changeless stability. This tension is not confined to the Old Testament. We see it in the Church today, and even in our own lives.

How greatly we need divine guidance! Without it we timidly cling to outdated forms, or discontentedly embrace everything new, whatever its value. Yet if Christ leads us neither timidity nor discontent will dictate our path.

HEBREWS 3:12–19

'While that word "Today" still sounds in your ears, encourage one another, so that no one of you is made stubborn by the wiles of sin' (v. 13, N.E.B.).

ON THE MOVE TOGETHER. We have seen that to our writer the Christian community is involved in a new pilgrimage under its Leader, Jesus Christ. Perhaps his repeated emphasis on forty years was due to the fact that he was writing in the sixties of the first century A.D., something like forty years after the New Exodus of Christ's crucifixion and resurrection.

The command 'encourage one another' can be better understood if we consider the statement of Harvey Cox that 'this understanding of the Christian life as a journey appears time and again in Christian history, from St. John of the Cross to Dante's *Divine Comedy* to Bunyan's *Pilgrim's Progress* to Kierkegaard. Unfortunately it has often been individualized, whereas the earliest version was of a people moving together.'

While recognizing that every believer has his own exodus to make, his own pilgrimage to the Promised Land, we need this other emphasis of a community on the move together. Are we encouragers of our fellow-pilgrims, or concerned only about our own safe arrival? One of his contemporaries said of the great sixteenth-century missionary, Francis Xavier, that if any of the brothers were sad they had but to go and look at Francis to be made happy again. The Church today could do with a few more encouragers in its midst.

HEBREWS 4:1–11

'Let us then make every effort to enter that rest' (v. 11, N.E.B.).

BLESSED PROMISE. The writer to the Hebrews here concludes his comparison between the exodus under Moses and the new exodus under Christ. The aim of that first exodus, he claims, was that the people of God should enter into the divine rest. Yet, although under Joshua they achieved an end to their wanderings, they did not enter God's rest. That is why, centuries later, the psalmist was still making the same offer to Israel (v. 7). This means, claims the writer, that the offer is open even now; only unbelief prevents us experiencing the Sabbath-rest of God.

The assurance that there is 'a full and complete rest for the people of God' contains a blessed promise, particularly to those rent by internal conflict and wearied by moral strife. Words penned by The Salvation Army's second General, Bramwell Booth, express longings every believer has sometime shared:

O when shall my soul find her rest,
  My strugglings and wrestlings be o'er?
My heart, by my Saviour possessed,
  Be fearing and sinning no more?

We need to recognize, as one psychologist has said, that 'rest is found in what *is*, never in what *ought to be*'. As Paul, Martin Luther, and countless others have discovered, peace comes by resting in God's unconditional love for us. That is where we start—we go on from there to grow in grace. But we must experience God's infinite succour before we can face, in His strength, His infinite demand. Restless souls frequently know a great deal about God's demand but little of His succour.

HEBREWS 4:12–16

'Let us therefore approach the throne of grace with fullest confidence, that we may receive mercy for our failures and grace to help in the hour of need' (v. 16, Phillips).

CONFIDENT PRAYER. The main section of this letter, dealing with the High Priesthood of Jesus, begins at verse 14. Christ is uniquely fitted to be mankind's high priest, so bridging the gulf between man and God, for He has fully shared man's temptations without succumbing to sin. He can, therefore, sympathize with His weaker brothers while still being able to uplift them. This theme is worked out more fully in later passages. For the moment, we concentrate upon the immediate implication the writer makes.

Since God in Jesus has fully plumbed the depths of the human condition, bold prayer should be our constant resource. The invitation 'come' is in the present tense, suggesting that prayer will be no rare emergency exercise. For the Christian, 'the hour of need' (v. 16) will not be confined to his own personal crises; it will include his concern for others.

There can be no substitute for personal encounter with God. David Read has warned that 'if we concentrate our attention on what is called "God-talk"— that is, the statements we make about God, we shall never find that renewal of the Church, that revival of practical faith for which many on every side of the argument are seeking. Such real renewal comes not with talking *about* God but *to* Him . . . The latent atheism of our hearts can be fostered by endless discussion about God; it cannot survive the encounter of true prayer'.

HEBREWS 5:1–10

'Then, when He had been proved the perfect Son, He became the source of eternal salvation to all who should obey Him' (v. 9, Phillips).

PERFECT SYMPATHY. At this point we shall be helped by words which William Neil wrote in the preface to his commentary on Hebrews: 'I have written this commentary in a spirit of penitence. Hebrews was never a book which appealed to me very much as a student or even a teacher of Biblical Studies . . . Its general tone at first sight seems to be more remote from present day concerns than almost any other book in the New Testament.' That is likely to be our immediate reaction. Yet patient attention may enable us to share William Neil's discovery that 'once the key is provided there is not only a treasure house of insights into Christian faith but also a specific relevance to twentieth-century church life and thought which is startling'.

Two conditions were essential to the Jewish priesthood, claims the writer to the Hebrews: sympathy with human weakness and divine appointment. Both these conditions Jesus fulfilled. Particularly in Gethsemane Christ drained the cup of human agony and forsakenness. Making the same point today, we might point out that the 'self' is capable of either contraction or expansion. It may be thought of so narrowly as to be imprisoned entirely within our own bodies, or it may expand to embrace our family, friends and even larger sections of mankind. Jesus identified Himself with the whole race and is, therefore, the perfect revelation of the God who suffers in our suffering, rejoices in our joy and participates in our struggle.

HEBREWS 5:11–14

'Though by this time you ought to be teachers, you need someone to teach you the ABC of God's oracles over again' (v. 12, N.E.B.).

RETARDED SPIRITUAL GROWTH. Describing his early struggles with the philosophy of mathematics, Bertrand Russell says that his tutor finally gave him a book containing the gist of everything he needed. Yet, he says, 'I possessed the book for many years before I could make out what it meant. Indeed, I did not understand it until I had myself independently discovered most of what it contained.'

The writer to the Hebrews laments that his readers had conspicuously failed to assimilate the truths set before them in the gospel. Perhaps his digression at this point reflects his awareness of the demands he is about to make upon their understanding!

What caused the retarded spiritual development of the first readers of this letter? What is it, even today, which traps some believers in perpetual spiritual infancy? Mental laziness may partly be the answer to both questions. 'Religion is something different from mere strenuous thinking on the great religious questions, yet it still remains true (commented E. F. Scott) that faith and knowledge are inseparable, and that both grow stronger as they react on one another. More often than we know, the failure of a religion as a moral power is due to no other cause than intellectual sloth'.

An even more frequent cause of spiritual immaturity is failure to act upon what we do already know. Mental exercise is important: moral commitment imperative.

HEBREWS 6:1–8

'When you find men who have been enlightened . . . and who then fall away, it proves impossible to make them repent as they did at first' (vv. 4, 6, Phillips).

DISPROPORTIONATE REGARD FOR THE TRIVIAL. These strong words are related to the controversy surrounding the Early Church's attitude to lapsed believers. Under persecution many Christians denied their faith by burning incense to the Roman emperor. But when the persecutions died down, they came knocking on the doors of the Church hoping for readmittance. Some bishops refused to receive them, arguing along the lines of today's reading; others accepted them back after a period of penance. Though both Westcott and Manson hold that the situation here envisaged was 'hypothetical rather than real' we can and must take to our hearts the grave warning thus expressed.

It cannot be doubted that to play fast and loose with holy things ultimately makes repentance virtually impossible. The writer of *Hebrews* also emphasized a complementary truth—that such behaviour, often more flippant than flagrant, crucifies the Son of God afresh and puts Him to open shame. Nothing is more contradictory than a Christian with divided loyalties. Logan P. Smith was right when he said that, 'Those who set out to serve both God and Mammon soon discover that there is no God'; and many certainly give that impression. By their profane indulgence or cheap jesting, they bring the gospel to open shame, crucifying Christ afresh and progressively losing the capacity to repent. The first symptom of this soul condition is the absence of awe, which indicates a disproportionate regard for the trivial.

HEBREWS 6:9–12

'Beloved . . . God is not unjust to forget your work' (vv. 9, 10, Barclay).

WITH MERCY AND WITH JUDGMENT. John Wesley pointed out that this was the only place in this letter where the recipients were addressed as 'Beloved'. Though the previous words of warning had been stern enough, they were not to be received as the heartless rebuke of an unfeeling taskmaster, but as an expression of the tender concern of a loving father who, however deep His present disappointment, had not forgotten even the imperfect service of His children in the past.

One of A. J. Cronin's stories tells of a Christian nurse who went home to care for her aged but unbelieving father in his last illness. Concerned lest his daughter suppose that his atheistic convictions were in the least weakening, he said to her: 'Mind you, I still don't believe in God.' 'But, father', came the swift reply, 'He still believes in you.'

God does not scrub our name from His book of remembrance however deliberately we may ignore Him, or however repeatedly we may disobey Him. Nor does He fail to notice our weakest effort to do His will. Nothing could be of less significance than a cup of cold water. Yet, said Jesus, even a drink of water given in My name will be rewarded. This is one more reason why none of us need grow weary in well doing. Our labour in the Lord is not in vain.

HEBREWS 6:13–20

'This hope we hold as the utterly reliable anchor for our souls, fixed in the very certainty of God Himself in heaven' (v. 19, Phillips).

THE ASTONISHED JOY OF TRUE ADORATION. God's promise to Abraham, that through him all the families of the earth should be blessed, was confirmed by an oath, thereby doubly binding the Eternal to fulfil His word. The ancient patriarch waited twenty-five years for the birth of his son Isaac, a son in whom naturally he vested all his hopes for the greater fulfilment of God's promise. This came true in and through Jesus Christ, who explains and justifies every believer's sure and certain hope. But hope of what? Life beyond the grave? Yes, but more than that.

This hope, the 'anchor for our souls', is the assurance that in Christ we have direct and immediate access to God in this life. Before the coming of Jesus, the Holy of holies, stood for the presence of God, a place veiled and entered only by the High Priest once a year. On these annual occasions the people trembled for his safety, fearing that God's holiness would react in wrath against human sinfulness. But now, claimed the writer of *Hebrews*, because of what Jesus was and did, the veil was ripped aside and the door into God's presence thrown wide open to all.

To people taught to believe in a distant God whom they approached through elaborate ceremonialism, and then only fearfully, this was breathtaking news; and their living experience of it, resulting in ever deepening communion with God, inspired the astonished joy of true adoration.

HEBREWS 7:1–10

'He is like the Son of God. He remains a priest for ever' (v. 3, Jerusalem Bible).

THE TIMELESS CHRIST. What meaning can we find in our author's view that Melchizedek was a kind of prototype of Christ? To the writer to the Hebrews an air of timelessness surrounds this enigmatic figure from the dawn of Israel's history. Appearing abruptly upon the stage he equally abruptly disappears. His name, 'king of righteousness', and title, 'king of peace', are recorded. 'That is all; no name of father or mother, no pedigree, no date of birth or death; there he stands, eternally, a priest, the true figure of the Son of God' (v. 3, Knox). Of course, our writer is using an 'argument from silence' which would be inadmissible today but was legitimate by the contemporary standards of Rabbinic exegesis. In any case, the point he makes is equally appropriate today. Jesus is a historical figure, but He possesses timeless significance.

Those living in countries steeped in Christian tradition tend to associate the gospel with venerable buildings, long-practised customs and an ancient heritage. In fact, in a fast-changing world these are sometimes more hindrance than help. Yet Christ Himself is unencumbered by tradition: He is always relevant. The despair portrayed by modern novelists, the violence of idealists who cannot find an ideal, the desperate alternatives of international co-operation or racial calamity: all these form a setting in which the Man from Nazareth is as urgently relevant as He was in the first century.

HEBREWS 7:11–19

'Now this commandment is replaced by something better—the hope that brings us nearer to God' (v. 19, Jerusalem Bible).

A NEW PRIESTHOOD. The vast difference between the Jewish priesthood and the priesthood of the mysterious Melchizedek was that the former depended on hereditary rights, the latter upon an inherent greatness. Jesus, says the writer to the Hebrews, was like Melchizedek in that His priesthood depended upon no automatic transference of priestly powers, but 'from the power of indestructible life within' (v. 16, Phillips).

The writer claims therefore that the Levitical priesthood, and with it the whole Mosaic law, is annulled. This is indeed a bold assertion, but he quotes the psalmist (110:4) to substantiate his claim that the Melchizedek priesthood had been dormant only while the Levites held sway.

The Jewish priesthood failed in its primary purpose to bring men into a living relationship with God. Access to God, comments William Barclay, is prevented by two barriers: fear and sin. 'So long as man is terrified of God he can never be at home with God. Jesus came to show men the infinite tender love of the God whose name is Father—and the awful fear is gone. We know now that the one thing God wants us to do is to come home, not to punishment, but to the welcome of His open arms.' While we fear God we cannot love or trust Him, so fear is as much a cause as a result of sin. This vicious circle Christ destroys, so opening the door to reconciliation and trustful fellowship.

HEBREWS 7:20–28

'His power to save is utterly certain, since He is living for ever to intercede for all who come to God through Him' (v. 25, Jerusalem Bible).

ONCE AND FOR EVER. Continuing to illustrate the superiority of Christ's priesthood, the writer to the *Hebrews* here introduces a genuinely new note. Unlike all other priests, the sacrifice Christ offers is Himself (v. 27). His priesthood is unique also in that without end He offers intercession (v. 25). What is the link between Christ's sacrifice made 'once and for all', and His unceasing intercession?

Some early fathers contrasted Christ's human and divine natures, implying that the completed sacrifice was linked with one, while the perpetual intercession was an aspect of the other. This distinction is closed to us for it destroys the unity of Christ's personality.

The link between Christ's sacrifice and His heavenly intercession is His undying love. His offering of an unreserved obedience to God leaves nothing to be added. Calvary was the one perfect sacrifice. Christ's continued intercession reminds us that the love which prompted such a sacrifice can never die. In the unseen world Christ still gives Himself in ceaseless spiritual ministry for man. This is the element of truth recognized by one of Ibsen's characters who asks, 'Where is He now? What if *that* at Golgotha, near Jerusalem, was but a wayside matter, a thing done, as it were, in the passing? What if He goes on and on, suffers and dies and conquers again and again, from world to world?'

HEBREWS 8:1–6

'He is the minister of the sanctuary and of the real tabernacle—that is, the one which the Lord has set up and not man' (v. 2, Phillips).

ONE TITLE AMONG MANY. Although Ibsen is rated as one of the five greatest dramatists of history, few have attempted to imitate him. This, said Una Ellis-Fermor, was because 'like Shakespeare, he affected his contemporaries by the stimulus and inspiration of his example, not by the conventions which found schools'.

Far more than is recognized by ardent system-weavers, the same is true of Jesus Christ. The diversity of thought among New Testament writers shows men of different outlook each being variously inspired by one personality. Hence the uniqueness of the letter to the Hebrews.

The titles applied to Jesus in the New Testament—including the one we are now considering, the High Priest—were in current usage. Perhaps, when we apply a title to Jesus, says Geoffrey Ainger, 'we should always ask the question, Who else claims it? If the answer is, nobody, then we may suspect that the use of such a title involves a wrong way of speaking about Jesus.' Contemporary titles—like the Outsider, the Representative, the Revolutionary, the Freedom Fighter, the Servant—may help to convey what Christ means for men today. Excellent advice for the evangelist, this cannot exempt the believer from seeking to penetrate the New Testament witness to Christ. A timeless reality is enshrined in His Priesthood—He alone reconciles us to God. But we must never dissociate any of His titles from the Man revealed in the Gospels.

HEBREWS 8:7–13

'I will set My laws in their understanding and write them on their hearts; and I will be their God, and they shall be My people' (v. 10, N.E.B.).

WHY ARE WE RELIGIOUS? The quotation in this reading of Jeremiah 31:31–34 in itself indicates that the Old Testament recognized the need for a new covenant. The old one, written on tablets of stone, was inadequate and waiting to find its completion in something better, written on human hearts.

Fellowship with God always involves the secret places of a man's life. External conformity to devout practices is no substitute, and certainly no compensation, for heart religion. When Jeremiah and later Ezekiel wrote of the inwardness of the new covenant, they were doubtless thinking of the heart of stone which replaced the heart of flesh in an Egyptian mummy; on one such tablet found in a Pharaoh was an inscription asking his heart not to give him away on the Day of Judgment. An optimist indeed!

Our religion is what we do in our private lives. It is, in other words, the reason why we are religious. Under the old covenant men obeyed the Law in fear, even in terror of God's displeasure.

But under the new covenant they were to obey Him from hearts full of love and holy desire; not for what they could get out of Him, but for Himself alone. As Augustine prayed in the fourth century A.D.: 'Give me Thine own self, without whom, though Thou shouldest give me all that ever Thou hast made, yet could not my desires be satisfied.' The degree to which we share this petition is the depth of our personal religion.

HEBREWS 9:1–10

'Both gifts and sacrifices are offered and yet are incapable of cleansing the soul of the worshipper' (v. 9, Phillips).

SUFFERING LOVE. Influenced by Greek thought, some Jewish philosophers distinguished between heavenly 'patterns' and earthly counterparts. To our writer the furnishings of the tabernacle all had eternal significance, though most modern readers are relieved when he adds, 'This is not the time to go into greater detail about this' (v. 5, Jerusalem Bible).

The old worship had to be superseded because it failed to liberate from guilt or renew character. Why was this? A Japanese theologian, Kazoh Kitamori, contrasts men's response to the message of God's love with their being overwhelmed by the realization of God's pain. The Levitical sacrifices showed God's love, for they were His gracious provision; Calvary manifested God's pain, and this touches the sinner and the sufferer at far deeper levels.

In his poem *High and Lifted Up* Studdert Kennedy compares God's glory perceived by Isaiah with His love exposed on the Cross. There is no doubt which strikes the more profound chord.

God, the God I love and worship, reigns in sorrow on the Tree,
Broken, bleeding, but unconquered, very God of God to me.
All that showy pomp of splendour, all that sheen of angel wings,
Was but borrowed from the baubles that surround our earthly kings . . .
Thou hast bid us seek Thy glory, in a criminal crucified.
And we find it—for Thy glory is the glory of Love's loss,
And Thou hast no other splendour but the splendour of the Cross.

HEBREWS 9:11–14

'He offered Himself without blemish to God, a spiritual and eternal sacrifice' (v. 14, N.E.B.).

OBEDIENCE OR REBELLION. The great obstacle to our understanding of sacrificial language today is the persisting idea that sacrifice deflected the anger of a wrathful god. Whatever may be true of pagan religion, or even primitive Jewish rites, this was not the belief in later Hebrew practice. James Denney, who expounded a truly evangelical doctrine of the Atonement, insisted, 'God is not conceived in this Epistle, or in any part of the New Testament, as a malignant or hostile Being who has to be won by gifts to show His goodwill to man ... Atonement is not something contrived, as it were, behind the Father's back; it is the Father's way of making it possible for the sinful to have fellowship with Him.'

Christ is both perfect Priest and unblemished Sacrifice (v. 14). How does this reconcile us to God? There can be no trite answer to this question, for every age and, in some sense, each believer finds new depths of meaning in the Cross. One helpful line of thought recognizes that 'sin and sacrifice are eternal opposites' (F. D. Maurice). Sin is rebellion against God: the sacrifice of Calvary was full, complete obedience unto death. If man is to be won back from alienation he must not only see an example of perfect obedience, he must make that obedience his own. This the Christian can progressively do as he meditates upon Christ's passion and lives in fellowship with Him.

HEBREWS 9:15–22

'One might almost say that by Law everything is cleansed with blood. No blood shed, no remission of sins!' (v. 22, Moffatt).

COSTLY SACRIFICE. We have seen several valid reasons why this letter is obscure to modern readers, but there is one further difficulty which should give us pause to think. This writer saw sin as a problem of vast magnitude. Do we find his thought difficult because of our diminished sense of sin? We rightly rejoice that modern man refuses to be enslaved by false guilt about his own humanity, but man's alienation from his fellows and from the Source of his being is still his greatest problem, whatever terms we use to describe it.

God's answer to the problem of man's sin was to establish a new covenant or relationship. Under the old covenant, the writer points out, sin was nearly always cleansed by blood-sacrifices. Now a new, trustful relationship with God is made possible by Christ's shed blood.

'We make sacrifices,' wrote P. T. Forsyth, 'and costly ones, which yet do not draw blood from us. They do not come home. They do not go to the very centre of our life. They do not touch the nerve or strain the heart . . . But when we speak of the blood of Christ we mean that what He did drew upon the very citadel of His personality and involved His total self. The foundations of His great deep were broken up . . . The love of God is only shed into our hearts in the shedding of that most precious blood.' William Booth and P. T. Forsyth were in step when the Founder of The Salvation Army said: 'Take away the Cross, and the river of our peace would cease to flow; the joy of our faith would come to an end'.

HEBREWS 9:23–28

'For Christ has entered, not that sanctuary made by men's hands which is only a symbol of reality, but heaven itself, to appear now before God on our behalf' (v. 24, N.E.B.).

A BARRIER TO GOD'S FORGIVENESS. This reading, the main points of which we have previously noticed, provides us with the opportunity to continue our meditation.

Forgiveness is usually costly, sometimes almost unbearably so, but the sacrifice of Christ reveals the extent of God's outreaching forgiveness towards us. From His side, the way is clear for our reconciliation, for true forgiveness not only pardons the past, but seeks with unyielding goodwill the restoration of every broken relationship. Without such restoration, forgiveness is conditional and therefore artificial.

A major barrier between ourselves and God's forgiveness is our own unwillingness to forgive. And we have no right or reason to withhold forgiveness, a fact clearly implicit in Albert Schweitzer's confession: 'I must', he said, 'forgive the lies directed against myself because my own life has been so many times blotted with lies; I must forgive the lovelessness, the hatred, the slander, the fraud, the arrogance which I encounter since I myself have so often lacked love, have hated, slandered, defrauded, and been arrogant.'

This spirit of ungrudging forgiveness is the spontaneous expression of self-acceptance. It is when we live in an unreal world, refusing to accept the truth about ourselves, that resentment and disappointment poison the secret springs of our souls and encourage self-pity. The answer is to explore afresh the reality of our own forgiveness in Christ.

HEBREWS 10:1–10

Jesus says to God: '"Sacrifices and offerings, whole-offerings and sin-offerings, Thou didst not desire nor delight in"—although the Law prescribes them—and then He says, "I have come to do Thy will". He thus annuls the former to establish the latter' (vv. 8–9, N.E.B.).

THE SACRIFICE OF OBEDIENCE. The words above are part of Psalm 40. 6–9, the whole of which the writer of *Hebrews* puts into the mouth of Jesus. His purpose was to make abundantly clear that God wants, not the offering of animals, but the sacrifice of obedience. It was this that the death of Jesus most powerfully revealed, and it leads us to a conclusion we frequently overlook.

We are saved, not by the extent of Christ's sufferings, but by the depth of His obedience. The Apostle Paul stated the truth concisely: 'He became obedient unto death, even the death of the Cross.' Times without number, the prophets of the Old Testament declared the futility of sacrifice that was out of harmony with the intentions of God. For He does not want our sacrifice, but our obedience that often leads to sacrifice, even to death; it is the obedience that concerns Him. The ancient people of Israel sacrificed animals and sometimes even their own children in their attempts to keep or gain God's favour, but this was of no avail when such offerings were intended to replace, not express, their obedience to God's will.

The sacrifice of Jesus, on the other hand, involving indescribable suffering, was the outcome of His perfect obedience to God; and this indicates, as nothing else can, that what He looks for first of all, and what makes possible the fulfilment of His purposes, is not how much we sacrifice for His cause, but how much we obey Him.

HEBREWS 10:11–25

'Since we have a great High Priest set over the household of God, let us draw near with true hearts and fullest confidence' (vv. 21 and 22, Phillips).

NOT CUT OFF. Theodore Ferris suggests a modern parable to illumine one aspect of the Atonement. The *Queen Elizabeth* found a drifting sailing boat, lost and rudderless on the Atlantic. The big ship could not restore to the small boat the things lost through folly or misfortune: its rudder and compass. It could, and did, inform it of its position and put it in contact with coast-guard services. So, says Dr. Ferris, Christ 'saves me from sin . . . and by that I mean being cut off from the heart of existence. He somehow throws out a lifeline to me when I need it most. I may not be saved from the mistakes I continue to make or the individual sins I commit, but I am not cut off from the heart of life.'

The writer to the Hebrews leads us along what to modern readers is a rather tortuous route. Yet his destination is luminously clear. Christ died that we might confidently approach God, and not be 'cut off from the heart of existence'. Whether we think of the Cross in terms of a sacrificial offering, or in some other way, what matters is the life of communion it opens up. This is real to many who have not studied the theology of the Atonement. Conversely, we may have faultlessly grasped the theology without enjoying the experience.

HEBREWS 10:26–39

'Do not then throw away your confidence, for it carries a great reward' (v. 35, N.E.B.).

TREASURE NOBODY CAN SNATCH. Urgent warning and simple encouragement are linked in this passage just as they were in chapter six. The 'sin beyond pardon', as previously noted, is no ordinary backsliding but determined and unabated rejection of God's grace. As T. H. Robinson has commented: 'If a man were to insist—with full knowledge (that must always be borne in mind)—on casting God away, then God Himself would be impotent, for He could "save" such a man only against his will, and that would mean a violation of the law of personality'.

Encouraging his readers to hold fast to their Christian faith the author reminds them of a previous persecution in which they bravely endured confiscation of goods. In contrast to this he exhorts them, 'Don't throw away your trust now.' Material wealth may be snatched from us: spiritual treasure only we ourselves can throw away, or inadvertently let slip. When a man loses his confidence in God he loses his most precious possession.

In this same vein Polycarp, the Bishop of Smyrna who was martyred in A.D. 155 or 156, wrote to the church at Philippi. 'Let us therefore hold constantly to our hope, and to the guarantee of our uprightness, that is, Jesus Christ, who carried the burden of our sins in His own body on the Cross . . . let us be imitators of His endurance, and if we suffer for His sake, let us glorify Him . . . Stand fast in these things, and follow the Lord's example, steadfast in faith and immovable.'

HEBREWS 11:1–7

'Now faith means putting our full confidence in the things we hope for; it means being certain of things we cannot see' (v. 1, Phillips).

VISIBLE AND INVISIBLE. One man defined faith as 'living by the noblest hypothesis'. His emphasis upon 'living by', rather than just 'believing in', would be approved by New Testament writers. The writer to the Hebrews, however, certainly held that faith involved more than a noble hypothesis. The contemporary thought of his time, as has already been noted, held a doctrine of two worlds: one unseen and spiritual, the other visible and material. Naturally this writer saw faith as that spiritual faculty which enabled a man to lay hold upon the unseen, eternal world. Through our five senses we perceive the physical universe; by faith we grasp the world of the spirit.

The weakness of this view for us today is that it suggests that atheists are hard-headed realists who believe only what they see, while Christians persuade themselves of the existence of another unprovable universe. The truth is, of course, that both atheists and Christians look out upon one universe and interpret it differently. The unbeliever's position is as scientifically unprovable as the Christian's.

Faith is as much the spiritual vision enabling us to penetrate beneath surface appearances as the faculty discerning another unseen world. We do not believe the visible world is the sum total of reality, but we do hold the universe to be one. Biblical faith, as our author shows once he begins using Old Testament illustrations, is as much concerned with discerning meaning in the midst of this life as with what lies beyond its borders.

HEBREWS 11:8–12

'It was by faith that Abraham obeyed the summons to go out to a place which he would eventually possess, and he set out in complete ignorance of his destination' v. 8, Phillips).

HOW TO STRENGTHEN FAITH. This old patriarch possessed the Land of Promise in faith, but never in reality. To the end of his days he remained a stranger in Canaan and even had to buy a bit of land to be buried in. Yet he never stopped believing or venturing, which is the proof of faith. 'Merely to hug a creed and take no risk', wrote Dr. J. H. Jowett 'is no more faith than to hug a time-table is to take a journey.'

The only way to get faith is to exercise it. George Matheson learned this hard lesson in the early years of his ministry. Far too many people of the multitudes blessed by his hymns, notably, 'O Love that wilt not let me go' and

Make me a captive, Lord,
And then I shall be free,

fail to realize that, as the shepherd of the faithful in the highlands of Scotland, he lost his own faith and wanted to resign. But his elders would not let him go. They told him that he was a young man and, given time, would yet solve his theological problems. He remained, preaching as much vital Christianity as he could believe; and his faith deepened and matured.

Someone once said: 'It is often easier to act yourself into a new way of thinking than to think yourself into a new way of acting.' In other words, live faith until you have it! There is no other way. To wait for proof—of emotion or understanding—is sometimes to wait for ever, but to act on the assumption that Christianity is true (which is faith) is progressively to know its reality.

HEBREWS 11:13–22

'They [the patriarchs] only saw them far away and hailed them' (v. 13, Moffatt).

GOD'S PROMISES. The twofold nature of faith—grasping unseen realities and penetrating beneath surface appearances—are both illustrated in this passage. Faith inspired concrete down-to-earth action; it also created hope for 'a better country altogether, nothing less than a heavenly one' (v. 16, Phillips). So this author interpreted the stories of the patriarchs.

They maintained their enthusiasm in the face of disappointment by the clarity of their vision. Having set out as pilgrims, they never looked back, finding inspiration to persist by lifting their eyes from the often gloomy present to the ultimate fulfilment of God's promises. They refused, unlike some of us, to isolate the immediate contradictions of faith—and how vicious these can be—from the fullness of their belief in God's utter dependability.

People lack the conviction that inspires persistency because their vision is too self-centred. Their concern is not the cause they serve, but personal recognition and comfort. The result is that all their dreams belong to the past, a past for which they pine with sick longing. But the true believer is homesick for God, fired to greater exploits of faith in this world because of his awareness of the next, and because he knows that his noblest hopes, though frequently postponed, are never cancelled. Cautious faith finds confirmation only of its own pessimism, but adventurous faith finds more of God.

HEBREWS 11:23–31

'Ill-treatment with God's people he preferred to the passing pleasures of sin' (v. 25, Moffatt).

GOD'S MINORITY. In the Bible, faith is never only an individual phenomenon even though some men exhibit faith beyond their fellows. Faith also concerns the community of faith, 'the people of God'. So with Moses: the solitary encounter with Jehovah in the desert led him to identify himself with the oppressed Hebrew slaves, a decision which must have appeared utterly quixotic to all his contemporaries. If Jewish tradition is correct, Moses had real prospects of gaining the throne of Egypt, a situation reflected in the legend of the infant Moses throwing Pharaoh's crown upon the floor. To the author of this letter Moses' decision manifested the piercing vision of faith which saw in an impoverished and dispirited rabble a nation which would eventually bear God's revelation to the world.

A similar choice probably faced this writer's first readers: to remain within the boundary of Judaism, a religion legally recognized by the Roman authorities, or to be whole-heartedly Christian and risk persecution. In most countries in the western world we do not face the same threat today. But, claims E. F. Mascall, 'a state of affairs in which an almost total disregard of the Christian religion goes with a genuine goodwill towards the religious establishment seems to me to be too irrational and unstable to endure.' How much does our loyalty to Christ depend upon this 'general goodwill'? Are we prepared to be in a despised minority?

HEBREWS 11:32–40

'Others were tortured to death, disdaining release' (v. 35, N.E.B.).

FAITH'S ENDURANCE. Someone has described a diamond as a piece of coal which stayed on the job. Unlike a man, it had no choice!

In today's passage the author rapidly summarizes his Roll of Honour, passing from the era of the Judges to the heroic struggle of the Maccabeans (in the inter-testamental period) against Greek attempts to paganize their religion. One of the most moving characteristics of those 'ill-treated by a world that was too evil to see their worth' (v. 38, Phillips) was their endurance, their disdain of an easy escape from suffering. Although here applied to martyrs, living one's faith calls for endurance as surely as dying for it.

Mary Styles, a Salvationist missionary nurse, was called out one night to attend a chief's wife in childbirth. Friends attempted to prevent her accompanying the rather fearsome looking Zulu who called for her. On arrival she found the chief hoping that, after many disappointments, this birth would present him with a desired heir. In an atmosphere both tense and threatening, Mary quietly carried through her task to a successful conclusion. The chief had his heir and his admiration of the nurse who trekked through the night with a known murderer was immense. 'Not accepting deliverance' (v. 35) can be applied to a thousand situations where Christians must choose between loyalty to Christ and easy compromise.

HEBREWS 12:1–3

'Surrounded then as we are by these serried ranks of witnesses, let us strip off everything that hinders us . . . and let us run the race that we have to run with patience, our eyes fixed on Jesus .' (vv. 1 and 2, Phillips).

BOTH SAVIOUR AND EXAMPLE. The word 'witness' in this letter invariably means 'one who bears witness', not a spectator. We who run life's race are to look for encouragement to these 'serried ranks of witnesses', just as supremely we look to Christ. The writer is not making a statement one way or the other about those who have died 'looking on' at those still completing their course.

We need to consider what the writer might have said in order to be shaken from easy familiarity with these verses. For instance, a race calls for energy and enthusiasm, but the quality demanded is —patience. Not the short, sharp burst of the sprinter but the plodding endurance of the long-distance runner is required for the Christian life.

'In the advance to self-mastery', said Roger Schutz, 'it is important to keep our eyes fixed, not on details, progression or regression, but on the goal: Christ Jesus.' It is noteworthy that here the Cross of Christ is linked with joy. Two common attitudes to His passion—pity and anger—are equally unprofitable. Despite the Master's command to the women of Jerusalem, 'Weep not for Me,' all too many hymns stimulate pity. Indignant censure of those responsible for the crucifixion also encourages us to consider ourselves mere spectators. Only when we glimpse the joy for which Christ endured the Cross, do we become fruitfully involved; then the Crucified becomes both Saviour and Example.

HEBREWS 12:4–13

'Discipline always seems for the time to be a thing of pain, not of joy; but those who are trained by it reap the fruit of it afterwards in the peace of an upright life' (v. 11, Moffatt).

GOD'S LOVING DISCIPLINE. In facing trials of faith, the believer, says the writer of *Hebrews*, should remember three things.

First, he should recall the greater sacrifice of other Christians and thereby see his own discomfort in its right perspective. Second, he should, above all, recall the example of Jesus who despised the shame of the Cross, making its pain and humiliation an opportunity to prove His eager loyalty. And third, he should accept adversity as God's loving discipline. 'The trying things,' said Fénélon, 'which you fancy come between God and you, will prove means of unity with Him, if you bear them humbly. Those things that overwhelm us and upset our pride do more good than all that which excites and *inspirits* us.' G. K. Chesterton was even more positive when he said: 'I believe in getting into hot water; it keeps you clean.'

To say that adversity is God's loving discipline is not to suggest that He necessarily sends it. But accepted as such, He uses it to train the soul. 'The best way out is always through,' wrote Robert Frost; and this is the Christian's triumphant outlook in face of trials of any kind. He refuses to walk round them, wallow in self-pity, or endure in stoic silence. Rather he wonders what God is trying to say to his soul and, throwing himself upon divine resources, so lives that from the other side of the challenge, he is free of shame or regret.

HEBREWS 12:14–17

'Let it be your ambition to live at peace with all men and to achieve holiness' (v. 14, Phillips).

PEACE-MAKING. The pursuit of peace, to which the author urges his readers, is sometimes misdirected so that it actually fosters conflict. For instance, there is the cruel practice of allowing a person with a grievance slowly 'to come to the boil' without creating opportunity for candid discussion. This is wrong even if the grievance, from our point of view, is imaginary. Here present peace is bought at the price of future explosion—for which the wrong person often feels guilty.

Similarly peace is often sought by refusing to articulate our disagreements. 'In my house people never talk to me about unpleasant things', says a characer in Ibsen's *The Wild Duck*. To which the reply is, 'No. That I can readily believe.' Some households which are superficially peaceful are actually hotbeds of repressed resentment.

We need to recognize the vital distinction between the merely peaceable and the peace-makers. John Oman made this very clear: 'You can see who the peacemakers are by the account of what happens to them precisely because they are not the peaceable, because they do not accept things as they are . . . generally obeying the prudent maxims which ensure a quiet life. On the contrary, like all true guardians of the peace, they are resolute, uncompromising fighters against every disturbing, disruptive force. And that means they are foes of all evil, for all evil is disturbing and disruptive.'

HEBREWS 12:18–29

'Be sure you do not refuse to hear the voice of God!' (v. 25, Phillips).

THE HOME THAT BECOMES A PRISON. Breaking free from one's family background, which is perhaps necessary for everyone in varying degrees, is well described by a character in Laurens van der Post's *A Face Beside the Fire*. It is not, he says, 'just a matter of walking out of one's home and slamming the door behind one. One does not walk out so easily from the house, the solid and cunningly fortified building, the labyrinthine courtyard that the family has built in the mind, spirit and emotions, in the very sinews, nerves and reflex of its members . . . Indeed, this breaking down of prison doors . . . is perhaps one of the more truly heroic tasks of life.'

With magnificent poetry and symbolism the writer to the Hebrews contrasts the oppressive terror of Sinai with the exultant glories of the new age initiated by Christ. Commented William Neil: 'With every word he strikes a nail into the coffin of the old régime'. He saw that the 'home of the spirit' in which his readers had lived—the Judaism of law and ritual—could now become a veritable prison-house.

Stephen Neill once said that it seemed to him 'that every new Christian group, perhaps every individual in his progress to fullness of faith, has as it were to live through all the successive stages of revelation.' We ourselves will know whether our faith has proved to be a liberation of the spirit or is still a burdensome encumbrance.

HEBREWS 13:1–9

'Jesus Christ is always the same, yesterday, today and for ever' (v. 8, Phillips).

SEEING CHRIST TRULY. In a *Punch* cartoon some explorers were being met by a missionary dressed, incredibly, in dog-collar, black coat and trousers, wringing his hands and saying, 'I'm afraid there's been a terrible mistake'. The reason for his consternation was depicted in the background—a tribal dance in full swing around a totem pole carved with dog collar, black coat and trousers.

The tendency to create God in our image extends even to the Second Person in the Trinity, successive ages emphasizing different aspects of Christ to the point of distortion. During the Constantine Empire, artists portrayed Him as Pantocrator, or Ruler of the universe, in huge mosaics on church ceilings. As the empire weakened, pictures of Jesus became less regal, more human. The agonizing figure on the Cross has sometimes become so central as to exclude all others. Certain periods presented a 'Christ' so fierce that the cult of His mother alone gave an element of tenderness to Christianity; in other ages the popular figure was woefully effeminate.

The truth our writer proclaims to combat various 'strange doctrines' is not therefore as simple as it seems. Jesus Christ is eternally the same. But how can we ensure we see Him truly? First, by recognizing how prone we all are to mould a 'Christ' after our own desires. Then by constant recourse to the Gospels, read imaginatively and with open mind, relating each passing episode to that central revelation of His character, the Cross. Lastly, by allowing the Spirit of Christ Himself to clarify our vision.

HEBREWS 13:10–17

'Let us go to Him, then, outside the camp, and share His degradation' (v. 13, Jerusalem Bible).

FINAL OPTION. The Israeli writer, Shin Shalom, depicts a Palestinian villager who so loved the woman he married that he treated her differently to local custom. 'He did not harness her to the plough, neither placed the grindstone in her hand nor sent her after the cattle to collect their droppings, and all the villagers rebuked him and embittered his life . . . He became a figure of fun and mockery until he conformed to normal behaviour and became a husband in his nation like all other husbands.'

It requires almost superhuman strength to be different, yet the writer to the Hebrews claims that just this resolve is required of his first readers. Detailed interpretation of today's passage varies according to the view taken about the identity of its first readers. According to the one here followed, the author is calling Jewish Christians to show their loyalty to Christ more decisively and openly. On any reckoning the challenge is to Christian non-conformity, to a willingness to be misunderstood and rejected with Christ.

One commentator likens this passage to the end of a symphony when a theme we thought exhausted suddenly reappears in a new startling crescendo. So here, the choice between ancient, settled traditions and following Christ in the sole security of faith has been presented in great detail. Now, starkly, a decision is demanded: and we also have our answer to make.

HEBREWS 13:18–25

'May God, the author of peace, who has raised our Lord Jesus Christ from the dead, that great shepherd . . . grant you every capacity for good' (v. 20, Knox).

THE CARING CHRIST. A nineteenth-century traveller, H. B. Tristram, told of addressing a Cingalese congregation. 'I unfortunately chose the subject of the Good Shepherd,' he wrote. 'My interpreter told me afterwards that not one of my hearers had even seen a sheep or knew what it was. "How then," I asked, "did you explain what I said?" "Oh," he replied, "I turned it into a buffalo that had lost its calf, and went into a jungle to find it'."

At an emotional level, urbanized man finds the title 'Shepherd' little more evocative than 'High Priest'. Translating the phrase 'that great shepherd of the sheep' for our contemporaries, we might look for a member of what have been called 'the helping professions'—a doctor, social worker, probation officer—whose concern for individuals is deep and practical. We could choose someone like Dame Lilian Barker, one-time Governor of girls' Borstal homes and women's prisons. Her zeal to change conditions—beautifying drab surroundings, humanizing institutional routines, introducing interesting pastimes—was matched only by her interest in each person in her care. 'Miss Barker loved us all,' said one of them, 'but she loved the naughty ones best.'

No matter what language we use to express this truth, and no matter how much circumstances may seem to deny it, Jesus shows to us the God who cares, and who pays the price of caring.

THE EPISTLE OF JAMES

INTRODUCTION

This is not a letter to a particular church like that 'to the Romans', nor yet a private letter similar to the one addressed to Philemon, but consists of a series of general exhortations to Christian living. It has been traditionally attributed to James, the Lord's brother, (Galatians 1:19) and leader of the Jerusalem church (Acts 15:13).

In thought this Epistle is close to such Old Testament prophets as Amos and Micah with their demand that religion be related to life. James insists that any formal acknowledgment of Jesus as Lord must be supported by obedience to His two great commands (Matthew 22:34–40). 'Faith that doesn't show itself by good works is no faith at all.'

JAMES 1:1–8

'When all kinds of trials and temptations crowd into your lives, my brothers, don't resent them as intruders, but welcome them as friends' (v. 2, Phillips).

FACE DIFFICULTIES BRAVELY. This letter, addressed to 'the Twelve Tribes dispersed throughout the world' (v. 1, N.E.B.), may have been intended for Jewish Christians scattered abroad or for Christians generally. If the latter, the 'Twelve Tribes' would be a figurative term meaning the new Israel, or the people of God. The writer begins his homily by reflecting on the way in which trials and difficulties, if borne with courage, both reveal and produce fortitude.

An Arab and an Englishman once proposed to race their horses against each other. All went well with their arrangements until it came to deciding the length of the race. The Englishman suggested an hour. The Arab would agree to nothing less than three days! An hour's race would reveal nothing of the stamina of a horse, he urged. James affirmed that trials and temptations test the stamina of a man; but more than this, if accepted with courage, they produce character. And as character is what counts more than anything else, difficulties have a positive usefulness.

We may not rise to the prayer of George Whitefield, 'Lord Jesus, if Thou seest me nesting, put a thorn in my nest', but we can try to accept the thorns without resentment. Difficulties met in this way increase our self-understanding, and this is the basis of all growth. They deepen our sympathy with others, so equipping us better to serve them. They help us to rely upon God.

JAMES 1:9–11

'The wealthy brother must find his pride in being brought low' (v. 10, N.E.B.).

WHERE LIFE'S TRUE VALUES LIE. There is a marked emphasis on practicalities in this down-to-earth letter, and in this brief section James deals with the merits and demerits of poverty and wealth. He does not condemn the rich man *ipso facto*, but does point out clearly the spiritual dangers of wealth, even going so far as to say that it is the 'brother in humble circumstances' who 'may well be proud that God lifts him up' (v. 9, N.E.B.). The point is that true riches must be assessed in spiritual and not in material terms. This is a truth to which both the Bible and human experience point again and again. Yet, incredibly, it is a truth which men seem slow to learn.

We who are followers of the Christ who had 'nowhere to lay His head' are sometimes deceived into thinking that success is measured by the kind of salary we command, the type of home we live in and by our future material prospects. Perhaps many of our anxieties, our feverish activity and our half-conscious envy of other people and their achievements show that we have not really grasped that it is the depth and beauty of the inner life that really counts.

Christians, of all people, should learn the 'true place of riches and the place of true riches'.

JAMES 1:12–18

'A man's temptation is due to the pull of his own inward desires, which can be enormously attractive' (v. 14, Phillips).

HOW TO DEFEAT TEMPTATION. To say that life's difficulties can become occasions through which God teaches us precious lessons is not to say that God sends the difficulties to us. Sometimes, in an attempt to escape the responsibility for our own failures, we say God sent trials that proved too much. But God does not send temptations, a truth James hastens to press upon his readers. Can we seriously think that the God and Father of our Lord Jesus Christ would set out to trap us, His children, into sin? Temptations come to all, of this there is no doubt, and God does not cushion us against them. But whether we go under or rise above them is a matter largely of our choosing, though to help us find the way of victory He offers His strengthening and keeping grace. Again, this we may have if we choose.

The power of temptation lies in its appeal to our own secret, selfish desires and impulses. When we yield to them we place our feet on the slope of spiritual defeat. It is better, therefore, that we pray that God will refine our desires than that He will deliver us from the temptation which we have permitted to take hold. The latter prayer will not go unheard; but often at that late hour our will is so weakened that we cannot give God the co-operation necessary to ensure the positive answer. To pray for our desires to be purified is the better way to defeat temptation.

JAMES 1:19–27

'It is for us men to be ready listeners, slow to speak our minds, slow to take offence; man's anger does not bear the fruit that is acceptable to God' (v. 19, Knox).

THE ART OF LISTENING. In the early Christian gatherings there was much greater freedom for individual participation than in the formal worship of later ages. Sometimes this freedom was abused by those who were all too eager to make their voices heard. They wanted to teach but were unwilling to learn. James urges his readers to be ready listeners. Only the truly receptive have anything of value to say to others. Let us develop this truth in two directions.

True evangelism involves listening as well as speaking. In his book, *The Quaker Contribution*, Harold Loukes writes, 'Mission is not message, but meeting; not preaching but encounter, in which listening is as much an act of love as speaking.' He cites John Woolman's attitude to the Indians: 'That I might feel and understand their life, and the Spirit they live in, if haply I might receive some instruction from them, or they be in any degree helped forward by my following the leadership of truth among them.'

The sympathetic listener exerts a ministry of untold value to people in trouble. How often we miss the chance to help because we are too intent on what we have to say. A prayer by Michel Quoist powerfully illustrates this:

> I have just hung up; why did he telephone?
> I don't know . . . Oh! I get it . . .
> I talked a lot and listened very little.
>
> Forgive me, Lord, it was a monologue and not a dialogue.
> I explained my idea and did not get his;
> Since I didn't listen, I learned nothing,
> Since I didn't listen, I didn't help,
> Since I didn't listen, we didn't communicate.
>
> Forgive me, Lord, for we were connected,
> And now we are cut off.

JAMES 2:1–7

'Don't ever attempt, my brothers, to combine snobbery with faith in our Lord Jesus Christ!' (v. 1, Phillips).

THE SIN OF SNOBBERY. In his autobiography, Father Joe of Poplar describes his call to the Anglican priesthood. He came from a very impoverished family and when he went to the vicarage his poor appearance led to a sad rebuff. Describing the vicar, Father Joe writes, 'He was tall and fine-looking, the perfect gentleman. He didn't shake hands, though. He said, "What do you want?" I told him who I was and very, very quietly I said I felt I was called to the ministry. He looked down at me from a great height, for he had the advantage of the vicarage doorsteps as well as his own six-foot odd. He said, "How interesting," and I think he said "Good morning." Anyhow, he shut the door.'

Snobbery made an early entry into the Christian Church, according to this reading. We must recognize this sin for what it is, the retreat of the insecure. Those who fear genuine encounter with other people create distinctions which either cut other people off altogether, or allow only the relationship which exists between superior and inferior. Snobbery can even infect service for others so that we gain secret satisfaction from looking at others from the height of our supposed superiority. Many a philanthropist, with a reputation for loving his fellows, is incapable of relationships based on equality.

Class distinctions should hold no place among the followers of Christ. The worth of every man should be recognized for what he is, not what he has. As God in His grace has freely accepted us, so should we freely accept others.

JAMES 2:8–13

'If you continue to allow snobbery to dictate your attitude to other people, you are committing a sin (v. 9, Barclay).

HOW WE SHOW OUR LOVE TO GOD. James, like the Apostle Paul (Galatians 5:14; Romans 13:8–10), held that the law, 'You must love your neighbour as yourself' matters above all others. Jesus did not quite say that. He said that the law to love your neighbour as yourself was second only to the command to 'love the Lord your God with all your heart, with all your soul, with all your mind, and with all your strength' (Mark 12:30, N.E.B.). There is no contradiction. The New Testament writers were not saying that love for men made love for God irrelevant. They rather saw love for men as an expression of love for God. And so it is. We cannot express our love for God save in our love for those who are themselves the objects of the divine love.

Though Christians are right to address words of adoration and devotion to God, words of themselves cannot be enough. Even if they do not become mere pious mumblings (and there is always the danger that they may!) their true worth is seen only in the outreach of love. The trouble with most of us is that though we may make loud claims to 'love the world for Christ's sake', we find it difficult to love individuals. This is well expressed by Charles M. Schulz in one of his famous 'Peanuts' cartoons. One of his quaint characters, Linus, tells his sister that he wants to be a doctor. She says, 'You could never be a doctor! You know why? ... because you don't love mankind, that's why!' And Linus answers emphatically, 'I love mankind: it's people I can't stand!'

We must learn—and this reinforces what is said above—to love people: awkward, difficult, even dirty people; people who are not 'our type' and who do not share our views. When we try we are growing in love to God.

JAMES 2:14–26

'What use is it for a man to say he has faith when he does nothing to show it?' (v. 14, N.E.B.).

BELIEF AND BEHAVIOUR. It was the emphasis of these verses that caused Martin Luther to call this 'an epistle of straw'. But the great reformer was mistaken in regarding this teaching as a contradiction of Paul's fundamental doctrine of justification by faith. Paul held that a man cannot earn salvation by works: and with that James would have agreed. James contended that a man's faith in Christ will find expression in how he lives; and Paul would not have quarrelled with that. The great Apostle to the Gentiles said, indeed, that faith worked by love; and did not Jesus Himself teach that a tree is known by its fruits? Christianity is not merely the holding of certain views, though what we believe is important. Belief must be translated into behaviour.

A Christian whose manner of life contradicts his profession is likely to turn people away from Christ. This is what David (Lord)

Eccles found. He writes in his book *Half-way to Faith*, 'My doubts were increased by the difficulty I had to recognize a professing Christian by his behaviour. I looked round among my believing friends and acquaintances for signs that their faith influenced their conduct. Perhaps I had bad luck for the experiment was a failure and what made it particularly depressing was that some of the most unselfish and honourable men, as far as I could tell, had no religion in them, and certainly never went to church except as a social function.'

How far does the way we live accord with what we say we believe?

JAMES 3:1–5

'All of us often go wrong; the man who never says a wrong thing is a perfect character, able to bridle his whole being' (v. 2, N.E.B.).

WOUNDING WORDS. A black minister whose life had been shattered by his wife's death went to see H. E. Fosdick who spent two hours trying to help him. As the man left he said to Fosdick's secretary, 'He has put the stars back into my sky.' If this is what words of encouragement can accomplish it is equally true that unkind and thoughtless expressions can cloud the brightest day. As is mentioned below, James writes very feelingly about 'sins of the tongue'. 'His language is more than picturesque; it reads like a transcript of bitter experience' (Moffatt).

We need to guard against hurtful and damaging speech but we also need to recognize its origins in our personalities. 'Watch your own speech', said George Eliot, 'and notice how it is guided by your less conscious purposes.' One psychiatrist noted that he was tempted to make unkind remarks to his wife when he was already feeling guilty about his neglect of her or some other failure. Any compulsive urge to criticize, ridicule or find fault ought honestly to be scrutinized. Does the potential victim of my spite make me feel guilty, or inferior, or arouse unpleasant memories? Does he represent a part of myself which I despise? Am I secretly jealous of him?

To learn to control the impulse to hurtful speech is good. To grow in self-understanding so that such immature impulses become less and less frequent is even better.

JAMES 3:6–12

'Out of the same mouth come praises and curses. My brothers, this should not be so' (v. 10, N.E.B.).

WATCHING OUR WORDS. A homely rebuke was once administered to an able preacher of the gospel. 'Sir,' said one of his flock, 'you light a very good candle on Sunday, but put it out all the week.' The minister spoke eloquently from the pulpit, but his words out of church did not accord with his Christian profession.

At first thought we might feel it odd that James devotes a section of his letter to the use of the tongue, but a little reflection will convince us just how right he was. It is a sad fact that from the same mouth come blessings and curses; that the same tongue can heal and destroy, inspire and depress, purify and pollute. A man, like the unworthy preacher, speaks with courtesy and gentleness in one place, and in another—chiefly, perhaps, with his family—he is impatient and ungracious. A woman cruelly maligns the character of one to whom she had previously spoken with grace and charm. There is something unnatural about this, as unnatural as for a stream to pour out both fresh and foul water, or as for a tree to produce different kinds of fruit. 'This', says James, 'should not be so.'

It is our plain Christian duty to take his words to heart and to keep a guard on the words we use. Our surest guarantee that we do not offend in this matter would be to use only those words we should want Christ to hear. And as your words are controlled by our thinking, our aim should be to guard carefully the door of the mind.

JAMES 3:13–18

'The wise are peacemakers who go on quietly sowing for a harvest of righteousness—in other people and in themselves' (v. 18, Phillips).

GOD'S TEMPO. Wisdom was greatly admired in the ancient world. Unfortunately, it was often confused with facility of speech and an ability to argue the latest philosophical fashion. To James, wisdom was a moral quality showing itself in modesty and spiritual perception. Growth of character was the wise man's ambition. If this was to be achieved two things were essential: patience and goodwill towards others.

The man who aims at spiritual growth and development must take account of what William Purcell called 'the majestically unhurried tempo with which God works'. The seeds we sow in our gardens grow a long time in darkness before they push their shoots up into the sunlight. Much of our growing is done in darkness, or in what Evelyn Underhill called 'the night shift', when we seem to make little progress and God seems absent. We must 'go on quietly sowing'—the harvest will be sure.

The man who seeks spiritual growth must keep the soil of his inner life free from the poisons of resentment. Strife, bitterness and jealousy have nothing in common with true wisdom (vv. 15 and 16). Doctors have now discovered how great a part resentment plays in some illness. They are sometimes tempted to ask a patient, '*Who* is the matter with you?' Animosity and resentment also block personal growth. Consequently these emotions must be kept in our conscious minds, not buried in the unconscious, and healing from them must be sought in a deeper experience of God's love.

JAMES 4:1–7

'He gives us grace potent enough to meet this and every other evil spirit, if we are humble enough to receive it' (v. 6, Phillips).

THE BLIGHT OF EGOTISM. What is the source of quarrelling and ill-feeling among Christians? asks James. Outward strife originates within the individual human heart, particularly in the jealous envy of other people's gifts and possessions. The word 'murder' in verse 2 is almost certainly due to a copyist's error: in Greek the omission of only one letter changes 'envy' into 'kill'. James asserts that selfish craving, which is the essence of worldliness, destroys fellowship and even poisons the prayer life of the Christian.

Self-centredness destroys fellowship. The quarrels which rend communities are rarely caused by conscious differences of opinion but by jealousy, fear and love of status. Even when self-centredness does not lead to strife it prevents real community. Writes A. B. Starratt, '. . . when the egocentric man says, "I love you," what he means is that you give me a thrill—"I get a kick out of you"—"you do something to me"—and other expressions of self-satisfaction through the instrumentality of others. You have heard a guest leaving a party use the traditional expression, "I enjoyed myself." This is all that the egocentric man can do—enjoy himself. He becomes an emotional cripple who is unable to enjoy anyone else.'

Self-centredness also poisons prayer. It makes prayer an attempt to 'use' God for our own ends: such an attempt is obviously doomed. Yet James has an encouraging word to add. Though God refuses to answer selfish prayers He never withholds His grace, and it is His grace which can defeat the egotism to which all of us are prone.

JAMES 4:8–12

'Humble yourselves before God and He will lift you high' (v. 10, N.E.B.).

WHEN WE MUST POCKET OUR OWN OPINIONS. In the early years of this century A. G. Gardner published a series of character sketches of prominent men of his time. In one of them he wrote, 'Lord Curzon would have been a great man if he could occasionally have forgotten Lord Curzon ... He dwells in a house of mirrors! Wherever he turns he meets the dazzling reflection of himself.' Such self-esteem, readily noticeable in a man in public life, is not rare in people of all levels of society. It is an attitude alien to the Christian spirit and should not be found in the believer.

In a book entitled *The Layman and his Conscience*, Ronald Knox imagined the case of a Christian who had lost to someone else a job for which he himself was hoping. The writer asked: What ought to be the interior attitude of the Christian in that situation? Ought he to be humble enough to believe the other man the better candidate, if necessary in defiance of the obvious facts? Or ought he to make an act of faith that he must have been the better candidate in spite of appearances? Or ought he to retain the belief that he was the better candidate himself, but thank God other people didn't realize it and so have inflicted upon him a welcome humiliation? The last-named attitude, said Ronald Knox, sounds terribly priggish, but he put it that way to emphasize that 'humility doesn't always call upon us to revise our opinions; it may call upon us simply to pocket them.'

To be put in the wrong when we know we are in the right; to

carry blame that belongs to another; to have our advice overridden and to have to follow what we believe to be a mistaken policy—and to do it all in simplicity, without bitterness or despair—this, suggests Ronald Knox, takes a man who is humble with the humility of Christ.

JAMES 4:13–17

'How do you know what will happen even tomorrow?' (v. 14, Phillips).

THE LESSONS OF UNCERTAINTY. An entry in John Wesley's journal, written when his immediate programme was uncertain and he was waiting at Chester for a favourable wind to take him to Ireland, reads: 'I find it useful to be in such a state of suspense, wherein I know not what will be the next hour, but lean absolutely on His disposal, who knoweth and ruleth all things well.' James would have approved the spirit of this entry, contrasting as it does with the presumption of those he rebuked who planned the future without regard to the will of God or the uncertainties of life. What James urges is not a morbid preoccupation with possible disaster, but a realistic attitude to the future made possible by faith in God.

Realizing the future is uncertain not only teaches us trust in God, it helps us properly to value the present. To be obsessed with future plans may mark our failure to appreciate present blessings or our evasion of present duties. Evelyn Underhill wrote of the 'sacrament of the present moment' in which God meets us 'in the midst of time, with the clock ticking, the engagement-book bristling, the tube running a two-minute service and every new edition of the paper recording some new movement, new sin, new sorrow of the restless world.' The form in which God comes to us in the 'sacrament of the present moment' may be baffling indeed. But if we miss Him in the now how can we be sure we will more easily recognize Him in the future?

JAMES 5:1–6

'You have picked out just what you wanted like soldiers looting after battle' (v. 5, Phillips).

SELF-DEFEATING GREED. This scathing attack against wealthy exploiters of the poor sounds like Amos or Micah.

Originally it may have been part of a sermon addressed by James to a mixed audience. Its tone suggests that it was poor Christians who were being oppressed by Jewish or pagan land-owners. J. B. Phillips, in his translation, vividly describes the rapacious rich as acting 'like soldiers looting after battle'.

The greedy acquisition of material possessions is a self-defeating form of selfishness. Far from being a calculated decision to 'look after number one' it is blind even to its own real interests. Of course, this is true of all selfishness. James reminds the wealthy that the moth and the rust will destroy all that they have valued. What a pity they were so impoverished in the treasures which endure!

We must distinguish selfishness from the legitimate love of self. The former is the worship of a false self, seen in competition with other selves, whose gain must be their loss. This 'dark idolatry' brings no true happiness. Nobody envies Stanley Spencer's state of mind when he said, 'I am so interested in myself that I would like to give my whole time to it. I don't want to lose sight of myself for a second.' Happily for him he did sometimes lose sight of himself, even if only when painting. Legitimate love of self, the kind implicit in the command to love your neighbour as yourself, starts out with a different picture of the self—a self which needs other selves and can find fulfilment only in satisfying and out-going relationships.

JAMES 5:7–11

'You have all heard how Job stood firm, and you have seen how the Lord treated him in the end' (v. 11, N.E.B.).

SPINELESS SUBMISSION OR POSITIVE PATIENCE? The exhortation to patience which James directs at his readers was not a call to resign passively to the inevitable. His reference to Job shows that, for Job did not submit unquestioningly in face of his many trials. He firmly voiced his protests at life's dealings with him as he struggled in agonies of doubt and perplexity. Though he did not lose his faith in God, he had to fight for it every inch of the way.

Patience is sometimes mistakenly equated with a weak and reluctant submission to that which cannot be avoided. In the words of William Barclay, the patience which was ascribed to Job was 'that gallant spirit which can breast the tides of doubt and sorrow and disaster and still hold on, and come out with faith still stronger on the other side'.

In a sermon entitled, 'The Incomplete Virtue of Resignation', James Reid said that he saw 'life's inevitable hardships and sorrows as the conditions in which we have to seek the will of God'. This means not merely bowing our heads to the sorrows; not simply holding on in face of seeming Godforsakenness; not just refusing to deny our faith that God is love though a hundred stark facts would persuade us He is not. It means trying to shape our lives in the shadow of the cross which, though not God-sent, we have to bear. And it means through it all, displaying the courage and faith we see in Jesus and which are the hall-mark of the saints. This is the positive, purposeful patience to which we are called.

JAMES 5:15–20

'My brothers, if anyone wanders away from the truth, and someone turns him back again, I want you to know that the man who turns a sinner back from his wandering way will save that sinner's soul from death, and will draw a veil over a host of sins of his own' (vv. 19, 20, Barclay).

DOING THE TRUTH. Throughout this letter the writer has been eminently practical. For him the reality of faith is proved by how a man lives. In these closing verses, where James deals with the Christian's duty to try to lead a straying believer back to Christ, he uses the expression 'if anyone wanders away from the truth', and once more underlines the practical nature of a great Christian concept. Christian truth is not merely an intellectual exercise, something a man accepts with his mind. It has moral implications; it is that to which a man gives his life; it is something from which a man can wander. We might say, then, that a man not only accepts or believes Christian truth, he also does it.

Let us apply this fact to our own Christian living. I may say that since God has touched my life I love people. Yet this means next to nothing unless I translate that love into practical terms by meeting John or Mary (and not simply people) at the point of their need, and unless I am willing to involve myself in their urgent and perhaps even desperate concerns.

Christian discipleship is not merely a verbal avowal of love for

God and men; it is putting that love into action in the difficult arena of human experience. To do this effectively is to do it without a hint of patronage or any sense of superiority. It must be an unselfconscious consequence of our deep caring. This is doing and not simply agreeing with the truth.

THE FIRST AND SECOND EPISTLES OF PETER

INTRODUCTION

Accepting that Silvanus (5:12) acted as an efficient secretary, there is little reason to query the traditional authorship of Simon Peter, the leading spirit among the Twelve, of the first Epistle that bears his name.

The message itself was addressed to believers in Asia Minor, now part of Turkey, and was intended both to instruct and to strengthen them in their faith. All that Peter said about the need for Christian steadfastness amid persecution is heightened by the fact that, according to tradition, he himself was soon to suffer for his loyalty to his Lord.

Scholars are more hesitant to attribute this second letter to the Galilean fisherman. This epistle was not included in the canon of A.D. 170, the first official list of the books of the New Testament. Even John Calvin questioned whether the Apostle Peter would ever refer to his fellow Apostle Paul in the terms employed in 2 Peter 3:16.

Nevertheless, by whomsoever written, the Epistle has its value as a timeless protest against those who looked on the grace of God as providing them with an excuse for sinning. 'I dread every approach of antinomianism,' wrote John Wesley. The author of 2 Peter would have agreed with him.

1 Peter 1:1–2

'Chosen in the foreknowledge of God the Father, to be sanctified by the Spirit, to give their allegiance to Jesus Christ and be sprinkled with His blood' (U.2. Knox).

CHOSEN TO OBEY. To be chosen by God is both an honour and a responsibility, which explains why those who are most used in His service are also the most humble. Robert Raikes, prominent Sunday-school pioneer, once led a young friend to the spot in a back street in Gloucester where he had been inspired to start his first school.

Deeply moved, and reverently uncovering his head, he said, 'Pause here. This is the spot on which I stood when I saw the destitution of the children and the desecration of the Sabbath. As I asked, "Can nothing be done?" a voice answered, "Try." I did try, and see what God has wrought. I can never pass by the spot where the word *try* came so powerfully into my mind without lifting up my hands and heart to Heaven in gratitude to God.'

We, too, have been chosen 'according to the foreknowledge of God' and for a basic twofold purpose: to be sanctified or consecrated by the Holy Spirit; and for obedience to Christ. This latter truth is illustrated by reference to the 'sprinkling of blood' ceremony associated with the covenant relationship between Israel and God (Exodus 24:1–8). The covenant was valid only as Israel obeyed. Christ's blood was shed for us, but the intimate relationship with God this makes possible is contingent upon our obedience. As Stephen Neill wrote: 'The commands of Jesus are never polite recommendations; they demand obedience, albeit it is recognized that true obedience is precisely that which man is his own strength is unable to render.'

1 PETER 1:3–9

'You are guarded by the power of God operating through your faith' (v. 5, Phillips).

FACING ADVERSITY. 'The things that try us most', wrote Robert Rainy to Alexander Whyte, 'are the experiences which are the most indispensable of all for us.' Such wisdom is hard to believe, and harder to act upon, particularly when trials actually come. Persecution, called by Peter 'the trial of your faith', was expected by the Christians to whom this letter was addressed. How were they to meet it? The Apostle, by now a veteran of the spiritual battlefield, gave them rich encouragement:

If adversity would prove their faith (v. 7), it would also prove God's keeping power (v. 5). When Polycarp, saintly Bishop of Smyrna, was about to be martyred, he stopped his persecutors nailing him to the stake at which he was to be burned alive. 'It is unnecessary,' he said. 'He who gives me strength to endure in the flame will enable me to stand firm.'

God's power and our faith can still do the seemingly impossible. Imprisoned by the Nazis, a German pastor declared: 'I will somehow hold out physically, no matter how long it may last.' But he knew that more than human resolve was required. 'During these years', he continued, 'in sheer terror we may sometimes have felt as though we were falling into the bottomless abyss. . . . But there is a power that sustains us; we are borne up by God the Father's everlasting arms.' For every experience in life we should heed John Wesley's dictum: 'The power of God is there; use it.'

1 Peter 1:10–12

'The prophets of old did their utmost to discover and obtain their salvation' (v. 10, Phillips).

REVELATION. 'An atheist I never was,' wrote Charles Kingsley to someone in mental perplexity, 'but in my early life I wandered through many doubts and vain attempts to explain to myself the riddle of life and this world, till I found no explanation was so complete as the one which one had learned at one's mother's knee.' Kingsley found the truth, despite his doubts, because he never stopped seeking for it.

God reveals Himself only to the diligent seeker (v. 10). Far too often we complain that spiritual revelation never comes, without recognizing the reason why—our moral and mental dilatoriness. Observed Albert Einstein, 'There is such a thing as a passionate desire to understand, just as there is a passionate love for music. This passion is common with children, but it can vanish as they grow up.' Explaining Einstein's greatness, Antonina Vallentin, his biographer, commented, 'This passion never left him.' Nor should ours to know more and more of God.

God reveals Himself always through the Spirit of Christ (v. 11). He indwelt the O.T. prophets and inspired them to speak even more than they themselves could realize of His sufferings and glory; and still He alone makes God real to us, for where there is beauty and truth and aspiration, there is the Spirit of Christ. Could this fact, that revelation comes most readily to the diligent seeker whose mind is saturated with the gospels, explain our lack of insight and conviction?

1 Peter 1:13–16

'Be holy in every detail of your lives, as He, whose servants you are, is holy' (v. 15, Basic English).

HOLY LIVING. Peter has some down-to-earth advice, all in verse 13, about how to live victoriously.

We need to 'gird up the loins' of our mind. Unless oriental robes were neatly folded and tucked into a girdle, they wrapped themselves about the outdoor wearer's legs, seriously impeding his progress; and this was the picture Peter had in mind when he told his readers to 'gird up the loins' of their mind. (Probably he would have urged us to 'roll up the sleeves' of our mind.) Slovenly thinking and noble living never go together. Our thought life, our imagination, our secret affections, of which other people possibly know nothing, could explain our spiritual malnutrition. (Holiness means health, wholeness.)

We need to 'be sober'. A man can be intoxicated by more than alcohol, which is one reason why we say that some people are sober-minded, meaning that they have stability and balanced judgment. 'Be on your guard', exhorted J. H. Jowett, 'against everything which is creative of heaviness, and which may put your senses into a perilous sleep.' Stupor of soul is a dangerous condition.

We need to 'hope to the end'. Now this is not the same as being hopeful or hoping for the best. It means seeing present trials in the light of future glory; of making every decision against the background of God's ultimate judgment. Some people see no farther than the end of their nose; their vision rarely extends beyond the immediate. One frequent result is their early gain at the cost of ultimate disaster. We must seek to live in the light of our eternal hope.

1 PETER 1:17–25

'See that you do love each other . . . from the heart' (v. 22, Phillips).

Each verse in this passage is noteworthy. 'Reverence' seems the most helpful translation for 'fear' (v. 17), so long as this attitude is not limited to our behaviour during public worship, but is related to the whole of life. Remembering the cost of our redemption—'the price was paid in precious blood' (v. 20, N.E.B.)—it is not an unworthy emotion to fear lest we be disloyal to Him who died for us.

The Revised Version (both here and elsewhere) translates 'conversation' as 'manner of life'. As with 'citizenship' in Philippians 3:20, the word stood for behaviour rather than speech.

V. 20 reminds us that the Cross stands in human history for a fact that is eternal. The Cross marked no new stage in God's redeeming purpose but laid bare His eternally loving heart.

Finally, the Christian life must be marked by love that is genuine (v. 22). Backslapping is no substitute, for that can be an exercise in deceit. As C. E. B. Cranfield has commented: 'If we do not love the brethren, then all our talk about obedience, fear of God and holiness, is so much humbug.'

1 Peter 2:1–5

'Like newly born children, thirst for the pure, spiritual milk to make you grow up to salvation' (v. 2, Moffatt).

SPIRITUAL GROWTH. Christian discipleship can exist only as a 'function of pilgrimage'. In other words, growth is essential. Indeed, few things are more pathetic or ominous than stunted spirituality. Knowing this, the Apostle, characteristically with his feet on the ground, makes a twofold emphasis:

To 'grow up' in Christ demands fierce renunciation (v. 1). Notice which sins are specifically mentioned:

'Every trace of ill-will and deceitfulness, your affectations, the grudges you bore, and all the slanderous talk' (v. 1, Knox).

'All evil and deceit, all pretence and jealousy and slander' (v. 1, Phillips).

The list is formidable, but nevertheless 'respectable'! Apparently Christians have often had more trouble with sins of the spirit than of the flesh. The Apostle, like his Master, knew that envy and a gossiping tongue could be more difficult to overcome, and therefore more spiritually serious, than drunkenness and gambling. We must take this insight to heart.

To 'grow up' in Christ demands disciplined Bible study (v. 2). Peter refers to the 'milk' and Paul to the 'meat' of the word, each of them to underline an essential of spiritual development. If we have 'tasted that the Lord is gracious' (v. 3), says Peter, we shall want to renounce every hindrance and nourish our faith on the word of God. But this works the other way too. If we practise a healthy renunciation and give adequate attention to our Bibles, our spiritual palates will become increasingly sensitive.

1 Peter 2:6–10

'Chosen generation . . . royal priesthood . . . holy nation . . . peculiar people' (v. 9).

UNITED WE STAND. All four phrases come from the Old Testament. These descriptions of the Israel of race are taken over by the Israel of grace—the Church of Christ.

Two truths are thus suggested. One is the continuity of the work of God. The old Israel and the new are one, with an unbroken history, for the saints before Jesus came, like the saints after His coming, lived by faith in the living God. This is one of the arguments of Paul—see his reference to Abraham in Romans 4:10–12 and in Galatians 3:6–9—as it is of the writer of the letter to the Hebrews (11:8 ff.). 'All the old titles of God's people now belong to you' (v. 9, J. B. Phillips). 'Brothers, we are treading where the saints have trod.'

The other truth is the unity of God's people. On this point J. W. C. Wand has written: 'Peter's scattered readers now feel through membership of the new Israel a unity which they did not possess before. The Gentiles among them had never had it, and the Jews among them had lost it when their nation forfeited its special position by rejecting the Christ. Both have now achieved a vigorous sense of nationhood through the new faith which they hold in common.'

Jointly, they are God's 'peculiar people'—which does not mean His eccentrics or His queer folk, but His very own. Believers the world over belong to God—and must therefore remember whose they are and whom they serve.

1 Peter 2:11–17

'Free men, but the liberty you enjoy is not to be made a pretext for wrongdoing; it is to be used in God's service' (v. 16, Knox).

FREEDOM TO CHOOSE SLAVERY. For numerous reasons, early Christians were slandered and finally viciously persecuted. Peter here tells them that such antagonism is best answered by noble living. It should again be noted that the word conversation (v. 12) means more than verbal exchanges. It refers to a person's whole conduct, every aspect of his living, which says the Apostle, should be honest, a word translated by Phillips as 'good and right'.

A danger is that Christians, misinterpreting the meaning of their new-found freedom in Christ, should use their liberty as 'a pretext for wrongdoing', failing to see that they are free only to choose to be slaves. Paradoxically this choice alone guarantees true freedom, a truism the world is taking a long time to learn.

When in 1957 Bishop Ordass of Hungary, then recently released after six and a half years' detention for his faith told his story, he used the third person, describing himself as 'an aging disciple of Jesus Christ'. Then came an unforgettable sentence: 'He would like to say that when he was in bondage, in the most literal sense of the word, Christ gave him royal freedom.'

'I used to think', wrote Father Andrew, 'that liberty was freedom to get what I wanted. I know now that liberty is freedom to give what God wants and what my neighbour needs.'

1 Peter 2: 18–25

'If when you do right and suffer for it, you bear it patiently, this is an acceptable thing with God' (v. 20, Weymouth).

THE ACCEPTANCE OF SUFFERING. The majority of first-century believers were slaves, and Peter had a special word for them. Slavery was undoubtedly an evil, but the social and economic life of the Mediterrranean world was based on slavery, and any revolt by slaves against their lot would have been mercilessly crushed. One such revolt headed by Spartacus, himself an escaped slave, was so crushed in 71 B.C. The New Testament does not defend slavery but, in the context of the times, counsels the Christian slave how he is to behave.

In the Christian community slave and freeman were brothers together. This is how Paul bade Philemon receive Onesimus. Serving a heathen master, the slave could link his undeserved sufferings with those of his Lord who, though He 'thought it not robbery to be equal with God . . . took upon Him the form of a servant' (i.e. a slave). Peter thus linked together the highest of ideals with the most menial form of human existence.

The word translated 'bishop' (v. 25) is an interpretation of the idea of 'shepherd', for its primary meaning is 'one who watches over others'. The R.S.V. and the N.E.B. use the word 'guardian'. From a life of wandering the readers of this letter had found their way into the security of the fold of Christ.

1 PETER 3:1–7

'You are not to adorn yourselves on the outside . . . but inside, in the heart, with the immortal beauty of a gentle, modest spirit, which in the sight of God is of rare value' (vv. 3–4, Moffatt).

WINNING UNCONVERTED LOVED ONES. These verses, concerned with the relationship between husband and wife, have a much wider application; for here is guidance about the attitude of the Christian toward the unconverted, particularly unconverted relatives.

In the ancient world, a man owned his wife in much the same way as he possessed his cattle and plough. If he changed his religion, then automatically his family changed theirs. But for a wife independently to change her religion was unheard of; hence the plight of the converted housewife whose husband did not share her faith.

Peter advises that such a woman's first responsibility—without forswearing her new found faith—is to be a good wife. She should be characterized by submissiveness ('voluntary selflessness'), purity and 'reverent behavour', resulting in what William Barclay finely calls the 'silent preaching of a lovely life'.

Likewise, the husband has obligations. He should be understanding, gentle, and look upon his partner as a spiritual fellow heir. Anything less will mean that his prayers are hindered (v. 7), for nothing stands between a man and his prayers more than broken or strained relationships. It should be impossible, for example, for a man to be a good Christian *and* a difficult husband. Froude's phrase about Carlyle—'gey ill to live wi''—ought not to apply to any believer.

1 PETER 3:8–12

'You should all be of one mind living like brothers with true love and sympathy for each other, generous and courageous at all times' (v. 8, Phillips).

PITY OR CONTEMPT? Apart from our individual lives, the fellowship to which we belong should be marked by such qualities as unity ('all of one mind'), compassion, love, pity, courtesy, forgiveness and dauntless goodwill. Knox translates verse 9: 'I would see you tender-hearted, modest, and humble, not repaying injury with injury, or hard words with hard words, but blessing those who curse you.'

Consider today the essential nature of Christian pity. In *The Private World of Pain*, Grace Stuart, almost a lifelong sufferer from arthritis, makes this revealing comment: 'We receive too much of that coin of pity whose other face is contempt. Contempt—and yet perhaps not always quite contempt. Should one say, rather, an urgent, unconscious need to see someone else as in any way down in order that the looker-on may feel himself to be in some way up? Our fond belief that we do not kick a man when he is down may have as one of its functions the concealment of the fact that we need people who are down in order to have someone to kick.' Later she refers to those who 'need their pity of us, their morbid interest in us, for unhappy ends of their own'. Here speaks a woman who obviously has suffered at the hands of well-meaning but insensitive 'sympathizers'.

Pity does issue in sympathy, but never in sentiment; it is costly, often making severe demands. Indeed, easy pity is really the contempt of which Grace Stuart rightly complains. We must make time to ponder the masculine compassion of Christ which always expressed itself, through His vicarious suffering, in sensitive caring.

1 PETER 3:13–16

'Be ready at any time to give a quiet and reverent answer to any man who wants a reason for the hope that you have within you' (v. 15, Phillips).

HOW TO TESTIFY. Peter's guidance about how to witness for Christ is as valid today as ever:

The Christian should be 'ready' to witness. This refers not only to specific preparation, but to the spirit in which the believer faces daily responsibility. A man is ready to witness, not because he has the right words formulated in his mind, but because he has secretly maintained 'the spiritual glow' (Rom. 12:11, Moffatt). Such an individual is never 'caught on the hop'.

The Christian's witness should be reasonable. He is called upon to give a reason for the hope within him. This does demand intelligent reading and hard thinking; but in these days of the paper-back no Christian can be excused for not being informed about his faith.

The Christian's witness should be given with 'meekness', rendered 'gently' by Moffatt and 'courteously' by Knox. We can be forthright without raising our voices and becoming bigoted, dogmatic or intolerant. Conviction loses none of its winsomeness or authority by being 'quiet', the word used by Phillips, meaning gracious and patient.

The Christian's witness should be given with 'reverence'. There is a danger that testimony can become cheap, slick, a matter of little more than words. A believer called upon frequently to witness at open-air meetings, for instance, can merely talk, not testify. The element of wonder should be safeguarded in testimony; this will help to avoid argument or theological wrangling.

1 PETER 3:17–22

'Christ Himself died . . . to bring us to God' (v. 18, Goodspeed).

BROADER THAN THE MEASURE OF MAN'S MIND. Once again the Apostle links the undeserved suffering which a believer may be called upon to endure with the suffering of Jesus. He suffered 'the just for the unjust'. Then we, His followers, cannot reject what He accepted.

There follows the difficult passage about 'the spirits in prison'

(v. 19). Perhaps it is not unfair to say that 'the descent of Christ into Hades' is a subject for the painter or the poet rather than for one who is limited to sober prose. It was supposed that those who perished in the Flood were among the worst of sinners, but if they heard the word of saving grace, then there is hope for all men. This could be one way of expressing the truth that the Cross looks both backward and forward, as befits Him who is Lord of time.

Of course there is mystery here that we do not—perhaps cannot—fully understand, but this could be Peter's way of saying—

> The gates of brass before Him burst,
> The iron fetters yield.

The phrase in the Nicene Creed, 'He descended into Hell', is one way of proclaiming the truth that there is no prison house of evil habit from which a man cannot be delivered if he will call upon the name of the Lord. This was the faith of the Early Church—and is ours as well. Jesus is mighty to save from the uttermost—to the uttermost.

1 PETER 4:1–6

'He that hath suffered in the flesh hath ceased from sin' (v. 1).

PAINFUL CONQUEST. Peter is possibly suggesting that physical suffering purifies the soul. More likely, however, he is stating Christian idealism, as distinct from general Christian attainment. 'When we speak of "conquering ourselves"', said Bishop F. R. Barry, 'we mean entering by conquest a land which was always ours, but is not yet won.' This sin-free experience should remain the aim of every believer, if only to overcome the danger of lowered standards being accepted as 'normal'.

Realistic identification with Christ demands heroic and painful renunciation. The Apostle doubtless had in mind converts from paganism making a radical break with their past, to accept the challenge of Christian discipleship. The step could never be easy, for it involved probable ostracism and certain self-crucifixion.

This principle remains. Whatever the believer's background, when the rule of self ends and God's rule really begins, sacrifice and pain are never far away. But such dedication results in sin losing its hold and increasingly its appeal, which means that temptation loses much of its sting. As Brother Roger commented in his *So Easy to Love*: 'Try to keep at the still centre of your soul where God is. This is the best way to keep the desires in order. They will grow to be like God's—or perhaps it would be nearer the truth to say that you will only desire what God wants you to desire.'

1 PETER 4:7–11

'Serve one another with the particular gifts God has given each of you, as faithful dispensers of the magnificently varied grace of God' (v. 10, Phillips).

MOTIVE. With insight into the wiles of 'respectable' human nature, Peter admonishes: 'Be hospitable to each other without secretly wishing you hadn't got to be!' (v. 9, Phillips). He knew that purity of motive was more important than *doing* the expected thing. And this is the emphasis he again makes in verse 11, which is concerned with preaching and serving 'behind the scenes'. Christian activity so conveniently provides opportunities for the unconscious parading of oneself; pride is then fed and the people to whom one 'ministers' are silently humiliated. Stephen Neill has aptly commented that 'as long as a man remains the centre of his world, everything, religion included, can be used in his service, to minister to his own self-realization, his own sense of dominion'.

The remedy is found in v. 10. We must see ourselves as 'stewards of the manifold grace of God'. In the ancient world, stewards were numerous. They acted on behalf of their respective masters, knowing that none of the things over which they had control belonged to themselves. Custodians of other people's goods, they served only for their benefit, never their own. Any other motive left them open to easy temptation. So Peter writes: 'One of you preaches, let him remember that it is God's message he is uttering; another distributes relief, let him remember that it is God who supplies him the opportunity; that so, in all you do, God may be glorified through Jesus Christ' (v. 11, Knox). That motive alone makes a Christian's service acceptable.

1 PETER 4:12–16

'If a man suffers for being a Christian, be need not be ashamed, he should rather glorify God for that' (v. 16, Moffatt).

EASY PEACE. The 'fiery trial' to which Peter refers did burst upon these early believers. An explanation was sought for the fire of Rome, and Nero diverted suspicion from himself by accusing the little-understood Christians. They were hunted like rats and, when caught, became the victims of the emperor's mad ravings. Tacitus records the grim story: 'They died in torments and their torments were embittered by insult and derision. Some were nailed on crosses, others sewn up in the skins of wild beasts and exposed to the fury of dogs, others again, smeared over with combustible materials, were used as torches to illuminate the darkness of the night.' Yet incredibly they died rejoicing. One of them greeted her violent end with, 'This is my coronation day'; her spirit was typical. They were not 'ashamed' (v. 16), but counted themselves happy (v. 14) to be 'reproached for the name of Christ'.

These verses say four things about the suffering of believers: (i) there is nothing surprising about such a fact; (ii) its purpose is to test the reality of the believer's faith; (iii) it is a sharing of Christ's suffering; and (iv) it should be a cause for rejoicing. As has been said: 'Joy is the crown of all Christian virtue, the surest token of sanctity . . . In the face of persecution not prudence, nor patience, nor even dedication, but joy is the final mark of the Christian soul.'

1 Peter 4: 17–19

'Let those who by the will of God are suffering trust their souls to Him, their faithful Creator, as they continue to do right' (v. 19, Moffatt).

DAILY PREPAREDNESS. Judgment must begin at the house of God, for the most privileged must always bear the greatest responsibility. This was something the people of Israel never fully learned; they allowed their 'election' by God to foster both national pride and bigoted contempt for all non-Jews. The Apostle here explains how believers, without morbid self-centredness, can prepare themselves for unavoidable judgment.

They should 'commit the keeping of their souls' to God (v. 19). This is, of course, a daily committal, as Leslie Tizard vividly realized during final weeks of suffering from a fatal disease. 'It means', he wrote, 'to do that bit of my task which is within my power today, without worrying about whether I shall be able to finish it, and leaving it in God's hands to make what use of it He can. It means bearing the day's sufferings, if suffering there is to be, in the strength that the day brings, without worrying about how I shall endure the more severe trials that may come, but believing that "as thy days, so shall thy strength be".' God is able to keep us from falling. Then let us trust Him to do it!

They should continue their 'well doing', rendered by Phillips as 'go on doing all the good they can'. Those who live each day as though it were their last, cramming it simply with good deeds in the name of Christ, are ready always for judgment. Such people do good because they are good.

1 PETER 5:1–4

'Carry out your charge as God would have it done, cordially, not like drudges, generously, not in the hope of sordid gain; not tyrannizing, each in his own sphere, but setting an example' (vv. 2–3, Knox).

CHARACTERISTICS OF SERVICE. In what spirit do we serve Christ? The answer is not necessarily obvious, for, unhappily, the habits of years, though loyally maintained, can lose the essential spirit that initially fired them. In today's verses, the Apostle focuses four characteristics which, apart from outlining a minimum standard for the aspect of leadership under consideration, should mark every expression of Christian service.

We must serve 'willingly' (v. 2). Few things are more contradictory than a half-hearted Christian. Yet how difficult it is to maintain enthusiasm and a willingness to serve in any capacity! Unless we are careful, we find ourselves doing only what we enjoy or cannot decently avoid.

We must serve the cause of Christ and not for personal gain (v. 2). When we—our interests and our wishes—become more important than the Kingdom we profess to serve, our witness degenerates; and our selfishness is no less selfish because it has 'religious' associations.

We must serve with humility (v. 3). To minister to others without patronage, without making them feel 'small' or embarrassed, or lording it over them, is possible only to the man who remains at heart a slave of Christ.

We must serve as an example (v. 3). Before we complain about the indifference of 'our young people' we should recognize that they are largely reflections of our own spirituality. Parental inconsistency in religion cannot produce filial spiritual zeal; casual 'evangelical' leaders cannot inspire enthusiastic 'evangelical' followers. We must prayerfully ask ourselves whether our example is helping or hindering others in their search and service for God.

1 PETER 5:5–11

'Throw the whole of your anxiety upon Him, because He Himself cares for you' (v. 7, Weymouth).

HUMILITY. In *Christian Holiness*, Stephen Neill recalls: 'Over nearly forty years there comes back to me a beautiful description of a preacher returning from the University Church at Oxford with a bulky manuscript under his arm, bursting with pride because he had just preached so excellent a sermon on humility!' Well might Peter write: 'God resisteth the proud, and giveth grace to the humble. Humble yourselves therefore under the mighty hand of God.'

Humility is not self-depreciation. To under-estimate oneself is just as wrong as personal over-estimation. Christian initiative and daring have been stifled far too often in the name of humility, falsely conceived. 'Self-confidence is essential, self-sufficiency is disastrous,' said E. J. Tinsley in a broadcast. 'Self-confidence means proper acceptance of ourselves as we are; self-sufficiency is to persuade ourselves that we are what we can never be.'

Humility flows from honest self-knowledge. 'The truly humble man', said Alexander Whyte, unconsciously illustrating his own words, 'is he who has gone down deep into himself, and who abides there, and walks with God there.' Shortly after a prominent citizen in Edinburgh had been imprisoned, and the whole city was aghast at the scandal, Dr. Whyte walked into his vestry one Sunday morning as the bells were ringing for church. He turned to his assistant and said, 'Do you hear those bells? He hears them in his prison cell this morning. Man, it might have been me!' Such a person, a tower of strength to others, always feels the need to cast himself upon God's mercy; hence his strong serenity.

1 PETER 5:12–14

'I am sending you this short letter . . . to stimulate your faith and assure you that the above words represent the true grace of God. See that you stand fast in that grace' (v. 12, Phillips).

A HARD LESSON. The 'holy kiss', a sign of respect and affection, was for centuries a part of Christian fellowship and worship.

This greeting was customary in the ancient world, as witness, for instance, Christ's observation that such a courtesy was not shown to Him in the house of Simon the Pharisee (Luke 7:45); and His words to Judas, 'Betrayest thou the Son of Man with a kiss?' (Luke 22:48). But the practice, obviously open to abuse and suspicion, gradually fell into disuse.

Silvanus (v. 12) was the Roman form of the name of Silas (Acts 16:37), sharer of many of Paul's missionary travels. On this occasion he acted as a secretary to Peter, the one-time Galilean fisherman, and to this fact scholars attribute the excellence of the original Greek.

This generous disciple is remembered primarily as the helper of men who were greater than himself. But though, as in the preparation of this letter, much was owed to him, yet he was content to take second place. It is not always easy to serve without getting the credit, to contribute to the work of another and yet remain in the background. Yet this is the very essence of Christian service for its only motive is the glory of God. Those who so work for the Kingdom can be encouraged by the fact that every orchestra has to have its quota of *second* violins.

2 PETER 1:1–4

'Grace and peace be yours abundantly, as you gain fuller knowledge of God, and of Christ Jesus our Lord' (v. 2, Knox).

FINDING GRACE AND PEACE. All of us need grace and peace. In other words, we need to be more gracious and serene, despite life's sometimes hectic round. This common aspiration is indicated by the popularity of books about resolving inner tensions, facing strain with poise, and finding peace of mind. The trouble is that many people are searching in the wrong places.

Grace and peace only deepen as we gain a 'fuller knowledge of God'. During a fierce storm at sea, twenty-six Moravian missionaries simply continued their worship. On board was John Wesley who, though an ordained minister, was petrified. 'Were you not afraid?' he later asked one of the missionaries. 'I thank God, no,' came the quiet reply. 'But were not your women and children afraid?' inquired Wesley. 'No; our women and children are not afraid to die.' That conversation further confirmed to Wesley the poverty of his personal knowledge of God, and fired his search for more light.

The Christian is called to conflict, but never to conflict within himself. We must realize that inner confusion is never avoided by our seeking for peace of mind. Serenity is always a by-product of 'fuller knowledge of God, and of Christ Jesus our Lord'. With this as the central quest of life, other things will take care of themselves.

2 PETER 1:5–11

'See that your faith carries with it real goodness of life' (v. 5, Phillips).

FRUITFUL STABILITY. These verses continue the above thought about the need for spiritual progress. True, we cannot work for our own salvation, which is always God's unmerited gift, but we can and must work out our own salvation; and this involves strenuous effort on our part—'do your utmost from your side', translates Phillips (v. 5).

The list of virtues to be claimed by faith and won is formidable. Look at these, as presented by Moffatt: resolution, intelligence, self-control, steadfastness, godliness, brotherliness and Christian love. We have to grow in these qualities; and if we do, two things are promised:

We shall never be 'unfruitful' (v. 8). In this same verse is 'barren', which is rendered 'idle' in the margin (A.V.); and unrealized idleness, according to Ronald Knox, is one of the besetting sins of middle-aged discipleship! Let us be on our guard, too, against any shallow evaluation of fruitfulness, remembering that our responsibility is to obey God. The consequences of that obedience are in His hands.

We shall 'never fall' (v. 10). One reason is obvious enough: we shall have the insight of pure hearts (v. 9). This promise 'you will never slip' (Barclay's translation) is only for those who 'do these things'; the qualities outlined are not merely to be admired, but practised. Lip service is a dangerous form of hypocrisy and imperceptibly deadens the soul.

2 PETER 1:12–15

'For this reason I shall always persist in reminding you of these things, although you know them and are steadfast believers in the truth which you already possess' (v. 12, Weymouth).

FORGETFULNESS. Pearl Buck, the American novelist, was talking to a German lady shortly after World War II. They discussed the Nazi atrocities, and the German said, 'Let's forget about the war as quickly as possible.' 'No, let's never forget about it,' replied the writer. 'Let's learn how it happened so that it can never happen again.'

The Apostle knew the danger of easy forgetfulness. Some things it is better deliberately to forget; others it is needful constantly to recall. Realizing this—for familiarity has always tended to breed contempt—Peter saw the necessity for reminding Christians of what they believed, and of the truth they already possessed; which is one reason why regular public worship is vital. We need reminding!

Tell me the story often,
For I forget so soon.

As we muse upon old truth the fire is rekindled. Our need is not for a new gospel, but for new insight and renewed enthusiasm. We must more often 'call to remembrance' the centralities of our faith and our spiritual origins.

2 PETER 1:16–21

'The word of prophecy was fulfilled in our hearing! You should give that word your closest attention, for it shines like a lamp amidst all the dirt and darkness of the world, until the day dawns, and the morning star arises in your heart' (v. 19, Phillips).

LOOKING FOR GOD. Happy the believer who can speak with the authority of personal experience! 'It was no fabricated fables that we followed', wrote Peter, 'when we reported to you the power and advent of our Lord Jesus Christ; we were admitted to the spectacle of His sovereignty' (v. 16, Moffatt).

We too can share this insight by taking heed unto the 'sure

word of prophecy', which means that we must study our Bibles and master accredited Christian teaching. Holy men of old spoke as they were moved by the Spirit; but their words needed to be interpreted; and the history of the Church painfully illustrates how often this interpretation was biased, the expression of unconscious prejudice and pride, or even personal animosity.

Throughout the centuries, nevertheless, devout scholars have given their 'closest attention' to what the Epistle here calls the 'word of prophecy'; and their consequent teaching remains remarkably consistent, which is a safeguard for us against private interpretation. Though it is wrong to be enslaved by orthodoxy and tradition, it is stupid to ignore either of them. Yet how often we are tempted to do just this in protest against our drab and second-hand spiritual experience? The answer is not to look for a more exciting and spectacular interpretation of Christianity. It is to heed—steadfastly to centre our minds upon—the old and yet ever new truths of our faith.

2 PETER 2:1–3

'There will be teachers of falsehood who . . . will have many eager disciples, through whom religion will be brought into disrepute' (vv. 1–2, Weymouth).

TEST OF ORTHODOXY. These verses help to amplify the above comment. 'False teachers', guilty of private interpretation at variance with apostolic teaching, were misinforming unsuspecting minds and therefore encouraging sub-Christian living (v. 2). Our doctrine must be sound; but let us be sure that we understand the meaning of this term. 'In the New Testament', says Wayne E. Oates in *Religious Factors in Mental Health*, 'the word translated sound (Titus 1:9) means health-giving or, in other words, a teaching that is hygienic.'

Holy living is the one infallible pointer to 'sound' teaching. There are bound to be different interpretations and emphases within the universal Church, but these are not important, nor do they necessarily contradict each other, so long as they contribute to holy living. Beware of the believer whose 'orthodoxy' makes him harsh, intolerant and quick to judge. He who said of Himself 'I am the Truth' was never contemptuous of sincere unbelievers, only of those whose closed minds made them hostile to any point of view not their own.

Christian belief is more a way of life than a cold acceptance of 'correct' words defining that belief. This does not mean that doctrines and creeds are unimportant; we have already seen that false teaching results in false living. But it does mean that our beliefs are vital only in so far as they assist holiness of life.

2 PETER 2:4–11

'You can be sure that the Lord knows how to rescue truly religious men from trial' (v. 9, Barclay).

JUDGMENT. When in his early teens Albert Schweitzer was being prepared for membership of the church, his pastor lamented that the youth was approaching the step with 'indifference'. Yet Schweitzer himself has since revealed that even in the preparatory studies he was so weighed down by the seriousness of the spiritual issues involved that 'he felt himself sick'. How often our judgment of others is similarly misinformed! God makes no such mistakes.

His judgments are as sure as they are inescapable (v. 9). This is the truth about which Peter is concerned: 'false teachers', like more obvious 'evil doers', are also under God's judgment, despite any appearance to the contrary. His love does not deny His justice. We must realize that because God loves us, He can neither let us go nor let us off. To do otherwise would be to make us pampered and self-pitying; and to make our worship of Him impossible.

His judgments are concerned with character, not prestige. These 'false teachers' were winning converts and cheap notoriety; their preaching was 'successful'. But see how the Bible describes them: they are self-opinionated; and, translates Phillips, 'they think nothing of scoffing at the glories of the unseen world'. Perhaps we too need to pray, in words from John Baillie's *Diary of Private Prayer*: 'Help us to see the vanity of the temporal and the glory of the eternal'; for much of our sinning stems from our spiritual blindness.

2 PETER 2:12–16

'Such men . . . sneer at what they cannot understand, and will soon perish in their own corruption' (v. 12, Knox).

PLEASURE. It is hard for us to realize that these objects of Peter's fiery denunciation were actually parading themselves as Christian teachers, representatives of the truth! 'Their technique of getting what they want', translates Phillips (v. 14), 'is, through long practice, highly developed.' Self-will often wears religious garments, just as numerous expressions of piety are motivated by self-seeking. These verses will surely help us to understand ourselves better if we allow them to suggest one searching question: from what do we derive our greatest pleasures in life?

Thomas Aquinas once said, 'No man can live without pleasure. Therefore a man deprived of the pleasures of the spirit goes over to the pleasures of the flesh.' Are not most of the sins we commit an attempt to gain from the flesh what can only be satisfied by the spirit? We excuse our lack of zest by telling ourselves (and others) that we 'need a change', that we 'have been overdoing it lately'; and possibly we are right. Yet more likely our basic trouble is an unconsciously neglected spiritual life, for which nothing, least of all indulgence of any kind, can compensate. We need always to seek the pleasures of the spirit rather than to avoid the sins of the flesh. The former takes care of the latter and solves many other personal problems as well.

2 PETER 2:17–22

'These men are like wells without a drop of water in them, like the changing shapes of whirling storm clouds' (v. 17, Phillips).

EMPTY NOISINESS. Continuing his invective against these 'false teachers', Peter strikingly outlines a number of their characteristics. To consider only the first of these—they were spiritually empty (wells without water').

Thomas Merton somewhere refers to the 'empty noisiness' of some people's laughter; such individuals are noisy because their characters are hollow, a fact also revealed by their faces.

'Few things are more striking', said the late Dean Inge of St. Paul's, 'than the change which comes over even the outward appearance of a man or woman between youth and old age, according to whether he or she has or has not a fixed purpose which is being carried out day by day. The face of the man who has found his work shows, in each decade and his life until the failure of his powers, increasing strength and dignity, and even beauty; while the man who lets himself drift shows in every line of his face that his will has been overpowered by disorderly impulses or has simply abdicated.'

Could this explain why Albert Schweitzer was nominated during his lifetime by America's top calendar artists as having 'the most interesting face in the world'? This much can be said: the Christian who thinks he can pass off his own shallow spiritual experience as one of great depth is fooling no one but himself.

2 PETER 3:1–7

'I have tried to stimulate you, as men with minds uncontaminated by error, by simply reminding you of what you really know already' (v. 1, Phillips).

CYNICISM. This passage speaks of the dangers of cynicism. Peter is answering these 'false teachers' who for two main reasons scornfully reject the belief in the second coming of Christ. They argue that the promise self-evidently has not been fulfilled; and that, though Christians have already died, life continues much as before (v. 4). We can almost hear their sneering mockery as they refute this important teaching of the Early Church.

When God's promises are delayed or not fulfilled in the manner anticipated, faith can so easily turn to scepticism and finally to cynicism. Wrote W. R. Niblett in *Christian Education in a Secular Society*, 'Cynicism (sometimes the refuge of bright young critics) is little but an anti-rolling device for those spiritually at sea.' Aging Christians are far more likely to become cynical at heart than publicly to renounce their faith, for life tends to make the most gracious of people worldly wise and hard. Only constant watchfulness, unhurried 'looking unto Jesus', can prevent the strong simplicity of our faith from giving way to the corroding influence of materialism.

In the reading below we see how Peter answered these scoffers (v. 3). Meanwhile we should remember that throughout the New Testament the Second Coming is made a motive for present purity of life.

2 PETER 3:8–13

'The Lord . . . bears patiently with you, His desire being that no one should perish but that all should come to repentance' (v. 9, Weymouth).

GOD'S MERCY. The scoffers' twofold denial of Christ's second coming was answered by Peter in characteristically forthright terms. The universe, he explains, is not like a machine which God has started and left to run itself. Sometimes He intervenes in judgment! Once He did so by water; the next time would be by fire (vv. 5–7).

The second part of the Apostle's answer comes in this particular reading. Men must learn that for God time does not exist; with Him a thousand years are as a day (v. 8). Further, the delayed Second Coming is not an evidence of God's dilatoriness or indifference, but of His patience and mercy (v. 9). He is 'long-suffering to us-ward, not willing that any should perish'.

'Trying to make men good is indeed a weary, disheartening business,' said William Booth. 'I wonder why God has not given the world up long ago!' True, but incredibly He hasn't. The danger is that, like the scoffers of Second Peter, we mistake His mercy for His weakness or the easy condoning of our unrighteousness. The love of God, as has earlier been mentioned, can neither let us go nor let us off; and this also can be a motive for present purity of life. A healthy regard for God's judgments puts steel into a believer's loyalty.

2 PETER 3:14–18

'Be eager to be found by Him unspotted and unblemished in serene assurance' (v. 14, Moffatt).

THREE QUALITIES. The writer here calls upon the massive influence of Paul to underline that the delayed Second Coming is not an evidence of God's indifference, but of His forbearance. The fearful possibility of wrong interpretation is further illustrated by reference to Paul's epistles; and we know how often his teaching about liberty in Christ was made an excuse for licence, and unmerited grace a reason for fleshly indulgence. The true Christian, concludes Peter, should be marked by certain qualities:

He should be watchful (v. 17). Seeing how some individuals twist the Scriptures to suit their own ends (v. 16), the sincere believer must guard against similar self-deceit, against making the searching moral demands of the New Testament conform to his second-rate living.

In my youth I set my goal
  Further than the eye could see.
I am nearer to it now—
  I have moved it nearer me.

He should be steadfast (v. 17). When Sir Walter Scott was dying he asked his friend, J. G. Lockhart, to read to him. 'From what book?' asked Lockhart. 'Need you ask?' was the reply. 'There is but one.' And when Scott had listened to the fourteenth chapter of the gospel of John he commented: 'That is a great comfort'. In the security of Christian truth he was held steadfast.

He should be growing in grace (v. 18). As Jesus said, the good man hungers for righteousness as a starving man hungers for food; and he seeks with such intensity because he has already found.

THE JOHANNINE EPISTLES AND THE EPISTLE OF JUDE

INTRODUCTION

That these writings were known to the Early Church from the middle of the second century is confirmed by the writings of Polycarp and Papias (say A.D. 150) and Irenaeus (d. A.D. 202), and from the middle of the third century the author of the fourth Gospel and the first Epistle has been regarded as one and the same.

John's purpose in writing was twofold – to affirm that the Christ of God was none other than the historic Jesus of Nazareth and, secondly, to emphasize that the truth that 'God so loved the world' could not be separated from the command 'Love one another'.

The second Epistle repeats for the benefit of a particular Christian community—'the elect lady' of v. 1—the main points elaborated in the first Epistle.

The third Epistle is an interesting and illuminating commentary upon the tensions which arose in the Early Church between a settled and an itinerant ministry.

Jude is considered to have been one of the brethren of our Lord, and his letter is a stern denunciation of certain heretical and immoral teachers who were infecting the life of the Church. In modern parlance, Jude did not pull his punches.

1 JOHN 1:1–4

'This message about what we have seen and heard we pass on to you, so that you too may share in our fellowship . . . so that joy may be yours in full measure' (vv. 3, 4, Knox).

PROCLAIMING FROM EXPERIENCE. These four verses, a single sentence in the original Greek, present, in C. H. Dodd's words, 'a grammatical triangle', but the modern translations help to make plain what, in the A.V., is not at all clear. Several of these (Barclay, Knox and Today's English Version among them) commence with the main subject, the Word of Life, which, in the original, does not appear until the end of the lengthy verse 1. John says that he is writing about this Word of Life, Christ Himself, whom he had actually seen, heard and, indeed, touched, for he wants his readers to be able to share the fellowship and joy which knowing Christ brings. This passage is a Prologue in the true sense, briefly introducing what is to follow in four short chapters.

Without any preamble the writer immediately refutes a current heresy which held that Christ did not really become man, but only appeared to do so. Knowing Him as he did, John could bear witness to the reality of Jesus Christ.

Here we come to the heart of the urgent business in which all Christians are—or should be—engaged: not simply that of ourselves saying 'Yes' to Christ (though how vital that is!), but of proclaiming Him to others. How this should be done in our rapidly-changing world is a matter which the Church must take very seriously indeed. But this much is true: the gospel can be proclaimed most effectively from the standpoint of personal experience. It is the man who can say, like John, 'Listen to me. I have seen Him, heard Him and I know Him', who is likely to get a hearing. When Daniel Webster was asked what was his strongest argument for Christianity, he said, 'An old aunt in the Hampshire hills'.

1 JOHN 1:5–10

'If we say we have no sin in us, we are deceiving ourselves' (v. 8, Jerusalem Bible).

RIGOROUS EXERCISE. In *The Gospel according to Peanuts* there is a cartoon in which Lucy shouts after the retreating Charlie Brown, 'The whole trouble with you is that you won't listen to what the trouble with you is!' We sympathize with Charlie Brown. We too dislike being told where we go wrong. Yet this same reluctance to admit our faults may lead us to 'flatly deny God's diagnosis of our condition and cut ourselves off from what He has to say to us' (v. 10, Phillips).

Confession is indispensable to spiritual progress, for a false picture of ourselves is the greatest obstacle between us and God. Yet, wrongly practised, confession is self-defeating. Karl Rahner, the Jesuit theologian, underlines one difficulty when he writes, 'We never know where we or the world with its history should be forgiven; we can never say with an absolute judgment: There is sin, it happened right there.' Because we can never be truly objective about ourselves, or properly assess the degree of our freedom and responsibility, confession which attempts to measure our guilt (or even exaggerate it) is futile. The kind of confession that leads to spiritual growth examines particular deeds or omissions only to gain insight into what we are. This is a far more rigorous exercise and can be carried through only in deep certainty of God's love and mercy.

1 JOHN 2:1–6

'Here is the test by which we can make sure that we know Him: do we keep His commands? (v. 3, N.E.B.).

DO WE KNOW GOD? There is so much in today's short passage which calls for comment. There is the tenderness of the approach. 'My dear children', John writes, revealing the concern of the true pastor, who, though he has to give correction will, in William Barclay's phrase, 'love them into goodness'. Then, with very few words, he goes to the heart of the universal human malady, which is sin, and shows where its remedy lies: in forgiveness and cleansing through Christ. He proceeds to outline the test of Christian experience—here our principal thought. The phrase John uses in this connection is knowing God, and the test of whether that knowledge is authentic is: do we obey His commands?

Men may claim to know God in an intellectual sense, as did the ancient Greeks. They believed they could find God by reason, thought and argument. The Bible consistently teaches, however, that God can be known only as He reveals Himself. Men cannot, by searching, find out God (Job 11:7). Furthermore, because He reveals Himself as holy and good He requires holiness and goodness in those who say they know Him.

This, we may think, is a tall order, until we learn, as J. P. Love says, that His demand for our willing obedience does not mean 'the laying down of some cold rule of practice, but rather an insistence that the forgiven heart is ready to do the will of Him who forgave'. It cannot be too difficult to obey One whose love for us has been so unmistakably proved.

1 JOHN 2:7–11

'If a man claims to be in the light, and at the same time hates his brother, he is still in the dark' (v. 9, Barclay).

KNOWLEDGE AND LOVE. The heretical teachers John was opposing in this letter were making claims to be 'in the light'. By this they meant they had been enlightened with some kind of superior knowledge. They were the Gnostics. John's reply to them was that any claim to live in the light of which he was writing, would be proved genuine only by love for other people. John insists that this light (knowledge) and love go together. We have already noted that knowledge of God has moral consequences; now we see it should also have social consequences.

There was nothing new in the command he was giving to them, said John; the Old Testament law required love for one's neighbour. But the command was new in the sense that Jesus gave it a depth it had never before been seen to possess. In the parable of the Good Samaritan, for instance (Luke 10:25–37), He showed that the term neighbour means not simply those in the family circle, or the people next door, or those to whom we are naturally drawn, but all men everywhere. So His followers' love will be universal. He also taught that their love will stop at nothing, but go on loving whatever the cost.It will be unconditional.

Love like this is far from easy. It involves a deep sensitivity to others, an awareness and understanding of human need, a sincere appreciation of the good in others, patience with their failings, and willingness to forgive. H. F. Lovell Cocks wrote that this love is not 'sentimental gush, but a steady will to serve in spite of all discouragements'. We cannot manufacture it for ourselves. It has to be given us—and will be given us—by God Himself who is love.

1 JOHN 2:12–17

'That world is passing away with all its allurements, but he who does God's will stands for evermore' (v. 17, N.E.B.).

LOVE OF THE WORLD. John's statement, 'Anyone who loves the world is a stranger to the Father's love (v. 15, N.E.B.), appears odd when put alongside that well-known verse in John's Gospel, 'God loved the world so much that He gave His only Son' (3:16, N.E.B.), and an earlier verse which says 'And God saw all that He had made and it was very good' (Genesis 1:31, N.E.B.).

We must be careful to understand what the writer of our epistle meant by 'the world'. He did not mean the lovely things of nature, nor the world of unbelievers. Christians may certainly take pleasure in the beauty God has made and which, we have seen, He Himself called 'very good'. And they make a sad mistake in trying to separate themselves from non-Christians, for there is nothing Christlike about a 'holier-than-thou' attitude.

What John meant by 'the world' was that order of life which is organized apart from God; the world of false gods, false values and false standards; what C. H. Dodd described as 'human society organized apart from God'. Love of the world is a spirit, an attitude. As Kenneth Grubb has written, 'its motto for progress is "forward", never "upward". Its goal is success, not holiness'. This writer goes on to define unworldliness as being also an attitude of soul which 'sets God always before the eyes and fearlessly seeks to carry out His judgments in personal, social and practical life'. It has been suggested, however—and this is our 'point to ponder'—that our apparent 'unworldliness' may simply disguise the fact that we don't want to be involved. How is it with us?

1 JOHN 2:18–23

'To deny the Son is to be without the Father; to acknowledge the Son is to have the Father too' (v. 23, N.E.B.).

KNOWING GOD IN CHRIST. John believed in the moral and social consequences of the Christian gospel, for he wrote that the Christian is proved to be 'in the light' by his pure living and his brotherly love. But he would not have subscribed to the saying, 'It doesn't matter what you believe, so long as you try to do good.' True belief is important, as this reading makes abundantly plain. And for John true belief centred in Jesus as the revelation of God.

John refers to those who were denying this as 'antichrists'. They had seceded from the Christian fellowship and were claiming superior spiritual knowledge. They were not denying God, only that He could not have lived in the world in human flesh. Therefore, they said, Jesus could not have been the Christ. And this, as it has been put, is the master-lie.

'God was in Christ' is the indispensable factor of Christianity. Karl Barth wrote, 'The Church is not "of the opinion", it does not have "views", convictions, enthusiasms. It believes and confesses, that is, it speaks and acts on the basis of the message based on God Himself in Christ. How true this must be becomes obvious after a moment's thought.' Can we have confidence in Jesus' words if we deny His unique relationship with God? Does His claim to be the Way, the Truth, and the Life, and His invitation to men to 'Come unto Me' mean anything if He is not the divine Son of God?

'In Christ,' says Oliver Tomkins, in an arresting phrase, 'we are let in on the character of God', and knowing what God is like we find it not difficult to trust and obey Him.

1 JOHN 2:24–29

'Remember to live continually in Him' (v. 28, Phillips).

DOWN-TO-EARTH ADVICE. We will have noticed already how frequently this letter echoes the Fourth Gospel in its references to light and darkness, eternal life, the 'new commandment' and the Holy Spirit. Here we encounter another familiar theme in the command, 'Abide in Him' (v. 28), with its allied injunction to allow the Christian teaching to 'abide in you' (v. 24).

Living in Christ may appear to be a thoroughly mystical enterprise, beyond the capacities of hard-boiled, down-to-earth people. This is why we are grateful that Jesus linked so closely our need to abide in Him with allowing Christ's words to abide in us. Living in Christ, as W. B. J. Martin said, 'is within the grasp of all of us. It does not mean swooning back into the "arms of Jesus", but letting the strong, realistic, God-centred thought of Jesus correct and guide our thoughts which, alas, are often fantasy-thinking, wishful thinking, childishly self-centred thoughts'.

The result of this way of life, John claims, will be a joyous confidence (v. 28). This boldness marked out the early Christians as they confronted their powerful opponents; it characterized the unique assurance with which they approached God in prayer; it made them long for the coming of Christ as eagerly as sleepless watchers await the dawn.

1 JOHN 3:1–3

'This we know: when Christ appears, we shall become like Him, because we shall see Him as He really is' (v. 2, T.E.V.).

CHILDREN OF GOD. A modern translation is necessary in order that we get the full impact of the first verse for, unfortunately, the A.V. omits a vital phrase: 'And so we are!' The N.E.B. translates, 'We were called God's children, and such we are'. And the Living New Testament has, 'He allows us to be called His children—think of it—and we really *are*!' To have the name 'God's children' is wonderful enough. But it is more than a matter of a name; it is—John stresses—a glorious fact. Thus the rich love of God for us is conveyed in the simplest terms possible. He is our Father; we are His children.

This, it should be noted, indicates the relationship which is established when men respond to the approach of God to them. All men are the creation of God: but it is by grace they become children of God. William Barclay suggests that the two English words paternity and fatherhood convey this difference in relationship. 'Paternity describes a relationship in which a father is responsible for the physical existence of a son . . . Fatherhood describes an intimate, loving, continuous relationship in which father and son grow closer to each other every day.'

This father–son relationship makes for confidence in the present.

We are God's children now, and our present trials should always be seen in this context. Is our Father likely to let us down in the midst of our need? Further, this relationship establishes our confidence for the future. 'We can't even imagine what it is going to be like later on' (v. 2, L.N.T.), wrote John. Whatever the future may involve, we can be sure that its glories and joys will surpass our highest expectations. 'The best is yet to be'.

1 JOHN 3:4–13

'A child of God does not commit sin' (v. 9, N.E.B.).

NEITHER COMPLACENT NOR INDIFFERENT. The verse quoted above appears to be a flat contradiction of John's earlier assertion, 'If we claim to be sinless, we are self-deceived' (1: 8, N.E.B.). This apparent conflict is resolved, first, when we recognize that the original Greek implies that a child of God does not habitually, or persistently, keep on sinning. It does not rule out occasional failures. Secondly, in these two parts of his letter John addresses two different heresies. 'The former (wrote Neil Alexander) tells the complacent, convinced of their moral perfection: "You are deceiving yourselves." The latter tells the morally *indifferent*, convinced that their super-humanity as "children of God" placed them above the moral law: "No Christian makes a steady habit of sin"'.

Both the complacent and the indifferent evade the challenge of moral growth and development. But so do those who harp on endlessly about their sins. The New Testament alternative to complacence and indifference is not constant self-accusation. A woman in one of Janice Elliot's novels tells another character, 'You blame yourself too much. There is something very simplifying about guilt. It is very much more difficult to be honest.' The Christian would add to this insight that, beyond the acknowledgment of our guilt, and even beyond the more difficult achievement of self-knowledge, there must lie the steady attempt to live in fellowship with Christ. There lies our hope of moral growth.

1 JOHN 3:14–18

'We know that we have crossed the frontier from death to life because we do love our brothers' (v. 14, Phillips).

LOVE MUST BE EXPRESSED. To equate hatred with murder, as John does here, may well seem extreme. Black and white contrasts, however, which ignore all the varying shades of grey in between, serve a useful purpose when moral issues have become blurred and indistinct. It may provide a salutary shock to recognize that hatred and murder at least belong to the same family.

Even more helpful is John's claim that hatred means death for the one who hates, and love means life. Instinctively, we tend to safeguard our security by restricting the area in which our love flourishes. It is dangerous to care too deeply and too widely. Yet to withhold ourselves from others is death; to give ourselves freely is life.

John insists that love, if it is genuine, must show itself in deeds. In one of her books, Iris Murdoch describes a coloured woman who, in her childhood, had been 'brutalized by unhappiness into a condition which resembled mental deficiency'. The irony of this tragedy lay in the fact that she had been surrounded by people who insisted that God loved her. 'The brisk women had taught her this very early on, turning her over as it were to God when they had, as they usually had, other things to do.' Talking about God's love, or even feeling loving, is no substitute for expressing love in action.

1 JOHN 3:19–24

'If we live like this, we . . . can reassure ourselves in the sight of God, even if our own hearts make us feel guilty' (vv. 19 and 20, Phillips).

COMPLETE ASSURANCE. The assertion 'God is greater than our conscience' (v. 20, N.E.B.) is open to two interpretations, one challenging and the other comforting. The grammatical construction of the original Greek makes it impossible to determine whether John stressed God's greatness 'because He is more merciful than our heart, or because He is more rigorous in His judgment upon us'. Of course, both emphases need making at different times to different people. The self-righteous need reminding that an easy conscience is by no means an indication of holiness: the self-blaming need to learn to rest in God's love, not their own sorry achievements.

Is it possible, without being morally insensitive, to have assurance before God, to gain what A. E. Whitham called 'a peace as far above contentment as contentment is above disquiet'? In *The Practice of the Presence of God,* Brother Lawrence said 'that when he had failed in his duty, he only confessed his fault, saying to God, "I shall never do otherwise, if You leave me to myself; 'tis You must hinder my falling, and mend what is amiss." After that he gave himself no further uneasiness about it.' This assurance is born, not only of a trust in God's mercy, but of confidence in His sanctifying grace at work in our lives.

1 JOHN 4:1–6

'You can recognize the Spirit of God by this: every spirit which confesses Jesus as the Christ incarnate comes from God' (v. 2, Moffatt).

GOD IN CHRIST. Once again John stresses the importance of right belief. Those who were insisting that the humanity of Jesus was not real, but only an appearance, were revealing that they were not of God, but of 'the world'. They were 'antichrist'. Such teaching as theirs robbed the Christian faith of its corner-stone—belief in the incarnation. Take this away and Jesus becomes an impostor, He has no power to be man's Saviour, and God is remote from human life. Yield the incarnation and what is distinctively Christian is taken from our faith. Wrote J. S. Whale, 'The Christian Church . . . stands or falls with the conviction which originated it, namely that Jesus Christ is nothing less than God's redeeming gift of Himself to sinful men'.

What does this mean for us as we seek after God, and as we attempt to translate our faith into human compassion?—all of which we find so difficult at times. It means that God understands us: the incarnation signifies His involvement with the kind of problems we have to face and the kind of temptations with which we have to do battle, for He was 'touched with the feelings of men's infirmities, Himself a Man of Sorrows and acquainted with grief'. If the incarnation does not mean this, it means nothing at all.

But it also means that God can do something for us we could never do for ourselves. 'Personally present and redeemingly active' in Jesus, God comes to save us when, without Him, we should perish. We need to see in God the compassionate Jesus, and in Jesus the mighty God.

1 JOHN 4:7–13

'God is love' (v. 8, N.E.B.).

ALL THAT GOD IS. Here we have one of the simplest, most beautiful and most profound summaries of the Christian gospel. Like a mountain towering in splendour even above a whole range of awesome companions this passage transcends much of the rest of the New Testament.

The truth 'God is love' needs safeguarding from two misunderstandings. It is not the same as saying 'love is God'. Yet once this Christian assertion is detached from its Christian anchorage in the life, death and resurrection of Jesus Christ it becomes all too easy to fall into just this confusion. D. W. D. Shaw cites the 'Flower Power' movement as an example of those who wanted to base their lives upon love, to regard love as 'god' for them. But when 'love is God' replaces 'God is love', love easily comes to mean merely 'what an individual or group happens to find congenial or thinks that it needs'.

Secondly, we need to see how much richer is John's great assertion than the weaker claim 'God is loving'. The latter could mean that loving was only one of God's many activities, to be placed alongside His creating, ruling and judging. 'God is love' means that there is no divine action which does not originate in His infinite compassion. Love is not simply one 'of the faces of God': all that God is, is love.

1 JOHN 4:14–21

'We love because He loved us first' (v. 19, N.E.B.).

WHERE CHRISTIAN COMPASSION BEGINS. Gotthold Hasenhüttl wrote of a married woman who had given up everything for her husband but was aware that she did not have his love in return. 'But I only want him to be happy,' she said, 'even if I myself am unhappy, even if I am rejected again and again personally. I will go on persevering a whole lifetime because I love him and because I know that without me he is lost like a child.' The writer adds, 'On her leaving me I could only answer, "You are a truly great woman"'.

This story perfectly illustrates the Christian love of which the New Testament speaks, the love that is absolutely independent of the worth, or the response, of the person loved. It is Christlike love which persists in spite of every rebuff. The question is: How is it possible to love like this?

John, now drawing together the various strands of his argument, gives us the answer: 'We love because He loved us first.' The woman who gladly gave her unreciprocated love must have drawn from deep personal resources created by having been loved by someone, perhaps in her early years, perhaps in her religious experience. Here the insights of psychology and theology coincide: nobody can love who has not been loved. The dynamic of Christian compassion lies in the gospel of God's love for us.

Evelyn Underhill's comment on this truth was that 'God loves, not tolerates, these wayward, half-grown, self-centred spirits, and seeks without ceasing to draw them into His love. And the first fruit of His indwelling presence . . . must be at least a tiny bud of charity breaking the hard and rigid outline of our life'.

1 JOHN 5:1–12

'This is He who came with water and blood: Jesus Christ. He came, not by water alone, but by water and blood' (v. 6, N.E.B.).

BAPTISM AND THE CROSS. With the words quoted above John sought to refute a particularly dangerous heresy, linked with a Gnostic named Cerinthus. The Gnostics could not conceive of God come in the flesh, and least of all could they think of Him becoming involved in suffering and death. So Cerinthus, a contemporary of John, taught that at the baptism the divine Christ descended upon Jesus the man, and He was thus enabled to exercise His unique ministry in the world. At the end, however, the divine Christ left the human Jesus, and He was crucified simply a man.

Against this grave error of thinking and teaching John loudly raised his voice. Jesus Christ, he wrote—notice his use of the full title in verse 6—came not only 'by water', but also 'by blood'. That is to say, both the baptism and the crucifixion of Jesus were essential parts of His Messiahship. Not only was God in the life of Jesus, He was also in His death.

It is perhaps because they want a religion that is free from effort and pain, that men too easily baulk at the idea of a suffering God. Yet the glory of the incarnation is that Christ's humanity was real and not a pretence, that He fully entered into the human situation and plumbed the very depths of human sorrow. This means that God is not aloof from us, not indifferent to our sorrow. He understands all we have to bear. As General Orsborn wrote:

Present He is in all men's woes,
Upon a world-wide Cross is hung;
And with exceeding bitter throes
His world-embracing heart is wrung.

1 JOHN 5:13–15

'This letter is to assure you that you have eternal life . . . if we make requests which accord with His will He listens to us' (vv. 13, 15, N.E.B.).

TWO CERTAINTIES. In the closing verses of his letter John states some of the certainties of the Christian faith. Here we look at two of them. There is the certainty of eternal life which means (commented G. H. C. Macgregor) not simply 'a future promise, but a present possession of the believer, in virtue of that act of faith which had put him in touch with the realm of "the eternal"'. It is the life of God within a man now, and signifies not only quantity, but quality.

Then there is the certainty that God hears and answers the prayers of His children. Most of us find prayer difficult, many of the difficulties being within ourselves. We forget that prayer has to be developed and mastered; and we try also to form patterns of prayer unsuited to us, and find it all very hard. Don Chapman, a great teacher of prayer, used to say, 'Pray as you can and don't try to pray as you can't.'

But all our concentration and effort will be wasted if we do not have in mind the truth John is pressing on his readers: God hears and answers our prayers. John does give, however, the vital element of all successful praying: we must ask 'according to His will'.

The trouble is that so much of our praying is dictated by what we want. Have we then to suppress our desires and pretend to want something other than that which our selfishness craves? Of course not; dishonesty is no firm basis for prayer. What we must do is make our selfishness the subject of our prayers, until at length we discover God's will and are possessed by the desire to do it gladly.

1 JOHN 5:16–21

'My children, be on the watch against false gods' (v. 21, N.E.B.).

IDOLATRY IN BELIEVERS. Without a doubt the first two verses of today's reading present us with a problem. What is the 'deadly sin' of which John writes and which, he suggests, puts a man beyond the prayers of the Church? It must be the man who deliberately defies God, who glories in his sin and has no regrets about his sin who is guilty of the 'deadly sin'. This kind of sin is 'unto death' because there is no repentance, and without repentance there can be no forgiveness. Not that God is ever unwilling to bestow forgiveness, but the unrepentant man is unable to receive it.

John's final word (v. 21) was a terse warning to avoid contamination by pagan society. It was also a warning to guard against accepting the false ideas of God which heretical teachers were spreading. The warnings still apply. Men in an affluent society may so easily become obsessed with success, money or pleasure, to the exclusion of God, and that is certainly idolatry. Equally serious is the tendency of some believers to continue to hold immature and therefore false ideas of God—also a deadly form of idolatry.

It is sad enough to witness intelligent and militant unbelievers who years ago abandoned immature ideas of, say, the universe, attacking concepts of God they should also have long left behind. But it is sadder still to witness Christians of many years' standing (note: standing, not growing!) whose infantile ideas of God are revealed by their immature approach to life and events.

Only intelligent application to the Bible's portrayal of God in Christ will help us to cast away idols of this kind.

2 JOHN 1–8

'The love of which I am speaking consists in our living in obedience to God's commands' (v. 6, Weymouth).

LOVING PEOPLE WITH OFFENSIVE VIEWS. The Elder, writing with the authority of an apostle, addresses his letter to the elect lady, meaning either an individual or a church, probably the latter. The fact that some of the 'lady's' children were 'walking in truth' clearly implies that some of them were not; despite their Christian profession, they were not obeying the 'new commandment' to love one another (v. 5).

In other words, 'walking in truth' is simply an adventure in Christian loving, in caring at depth. Some zealots defend the truth, or seek to, in a most belligerent spirit, apparently not realizing that their very attitude is a betrayal of their cause. The truth rarely needs defending; more often it needs living. But when its defence is called for, the absence of love is fatal. Christian history is marred by the exploits of people who have fought for the truth in unloving ways; as though differences of viewpoint or emphasis were justification for discourteous behaviour, and sometimes much worse!

Dogmatism, like intolerance, its near neighbour, is usually a sign of uncertainty, which means that harsh and loud words, often described as 'righteous indignation', reveal more confusion than conviction. 'Walking in truth' makes harmonious relationships possible even between people whose interpretation of the truth varies. For they love each other (in the New Testament sense of seeking each other's highest good with unyielding goodwill) more than they hate each other's views.

2 JOHN 9–13

'The man who goes back, who is not true to Christ's teaching, loses hold of God' (v. 9, Knox).

WHEN TOLERANCE IS HALF-INDIFFERENCE. The problem behind the writing of this letter was created by wandering preachers (either *apostles*, who had direct links with the earthly life of Jesus, or prophets). Normally they remained for one or two days, receiving hospitality from local believers, but some of them were taking advantage of this generosity; worse still, they were teaching heresy, which was particularly serious for small Christian communities already battling against virtually overwhelming odds. John the Elder's advice appears to contradict the truth we considered above: that we must love people more than we hate their mistaken views. Such false prophets, he said, should be ostracized—snubbed on the streets and turned away from places of Christian hospitality.

In the *Moffatt Commentary*, C. H. Dodd wrote: 'It is possible that the boycott of heretics was the only policy that could have succeeded in preserving the distinctive witness of the Church. . . . Yet we must doubt whether this policy in the end best serves the cause of truth and love. . . .' However, Dodd agreed that 'good-humoured tolerance which is more than half-indifference' does not really come to grips with serious error; and this is the implicit concern of John's letter.

So here is the principle which love alone can obey: only the strength of the charity of God is capable of dealing with the errors of men.

3 JOHN 1–14

'Never let evil be your example, dear friend of mine' (v. 11, Phillips).

TRUTH WILL OUT. In this private letter to an influential Christian, mention is made of three men—Gaius, Diotrephes and Demetrius.

Gaius, to whom the Apostle is writing, has become renowned for his gracious generosity to visiting evangelists. But, more than that, he has earned a reputation for faithfulness. Note particularly verse 2, in which John wishes that the man's body may be as healthy as his soul. This is a thought worth pondering. What exactly is the condition of our inner life? The health of our bodies is often outside our control, but the state of our souls has to do with our own volition. The word 'prosper' means 'to make a good voyage'.

Diotrephes is a very different character, and the thought of his disloyalty to Christ offends the Apostle. Diotrephes is a lover of the limelight, he has tried to challenge John's authority; he has refused hospitality to missionaries; and with a high hand presumed to put devout men like Gaius in their place.

Then there is Demetrius, through whose life the truth shines. He is universally honoured and receives the Apostle's commendation.

The prospect of a visit from John is likely to be differently assessed by these three men. Diotrephes will be 'odd man out', perhaps receiving publicity that he will not welcome. Life has a way of catching up with us. 'Truth will out', we say. Whether or not in this life—without doubt ultimately!

JUDE 1–4

'From Jude, servant of Jesus Christ and brother of James, to those whom God has called, who live in the love of God the Father and in the safe keeping of Jesus Christ' (v. 1, N.E.B.).

GOD'S GRACE IS FREE, BUT NEVER CHEAP. This letter was to have been an exposition of fundamental Christian teaching, but dangerous heresy within the Church caused the writer urgently to change his plans. Certain believers, mistaking their liberty in Christ for licence, were craftily justifying their indulgence of the flesh: where sin abounds, they argued, grace much more abounds. Some even denied that indulgence of any kind was sinful, claiming that nothing was evil until it was thought to be so. They failed to realize that though the grace of God would never be denied to any seeking soul, it was never to be presumed upon.

Basically their trouble was that, to quote Phillips's translation, they refused to 'recognize their only master, Jesus Christ our Lord'. This refusal expressed itself in a denial of Christ's divinity and the claim that He was either little more than a phantom or merely one of many intermediaries between God and man.

We have previously noticed that wrong thinking, even pious wrong thinking, leads to sin; for what we receive into our minds we take into our lives. Holy living is, therefore, impossible without straight thinking; and this means that we are wise to soak our minds in Christian teaching. For to wander down the 'side turnings' of doctrinal speculation is to become, at best, a fervent devotee of the trivial.

JUDE 5–11

'Such men sneer at the things they cannot understand; like the brute beasts they derive knowledge only from their senses, and it serves to corrupt them' (v. 10, Knox).

SANCTITY AND SELF-DISCIPLINE. These debasers of the truth regarded themselves as advanced leaders; as leaders, not corrupters, of the Church. So Jude referred to the history of Israel to illustrate that even the guidance of God was no guarantee of immunity from disaster. The people of Israel, led to the borders of the promised land, failed to enter through unbelief. Certain of the angels, privileged to enjoy the courts of Heaven, rebelled against God, and were cast out. Sodom and Gomorrah likewise suffered the consequences of their self-chosen ways.

The reference to Michael (v. 9) is taken from the Assumption of Moses—known by scholars as a piece of extra-canonical apocalyptic literature written in the early part of the first century—where the devil is described as claiming the body of the Hebrew leader on the ground that he was a murderer (Ex. 2:11). Though this was blasphemy to Michael, all he said was: 'The Lord rebuke thee'.

By contrast, the heretical ministers whom Jude was denouncing showed what manner of evil men they were by abusing even the good men who withstood their erroneous teaching. These false teachers ridiculed what they did not understand, and were in the grip of the one power that ruled their lives—their physical appetites. Self-indulgence blinds men to the truth—hence the need to remember Paul's advice about keeping the body under.

JUDE 12–16

'These are the men who complain and curse their fate while trying all the time to mould life according to their own desires. They "talk big" but will pay men great respect if it is to their own advantage' (v. 16, Phillips).

HOW NOT TO BE A CHRONIC GRUMBLER. In his fierce invective against the despoilers of the peace of the Church, Jude likened them to hidden rocks which threatened to wreck the fellowship meals known as love feasts. Then he described them as clouds which shed no rain, to trees which bore no fruit, to waves that deposited only scum on the shore, and to stars without any fixed orbit which were a danger to the heavens.

He further described these leading church members as chronic grumblers who sought only their own ends and stooped to any device to secure them. They even presumed to make 'spiritual' judgments (v. 19) though they themselves were the most unspiritual of men.

The saintly Raymond Raynes provided the antidote to this troublesome spirit. 'What is required of us', he said, 'is to obey. Most of the complainings, criticisms, mutterings, natterings would disappear if we would get back to the simplicities of our faith. The dear Lord loves us, and the best way of showing our love to Him is by faithfulness in daily life.'

JUDE 17–25

'There are some doubting souls who need your pity; snatch them from the flames and save them' (vv. 22–23, N.E.B.).

THE DAILY SACRIFICE OF A LOVELY LIFE. The false teachers, dominated by their physical impulses, sought to deny or excuse their depravity by mocking at goodness and ridiculing the self-disciplined. Such influence naturally caused division within the Church. The faithful, on the other hand, built their lives upon the foundation of Christian truth, and were characterized by prayer in the Holy Spirit (meaning freedom from devout self-centredness), loving obedience to God, and purposeful waiting for the day of Christ; the assaults of evil, though often devastating, were recognized for what they were—the death throes of a desperate enemy.

Jude next reminded the faithful that their Christian duty was to seek the redemption of the unfaithful; and to seek it with compassionate urgency. Exactly how this was to be done was dependent upon the attitude of the unfaithful themselves: some would have to be enlightened in discussion, an approach presupposing the ability of the faithful to give a reason for the hope that was in them; others, on the brink of plunging to destruction, were to be helped in time (their name is legion who have taken the wrong turning in life because of the procrastination of people who professed to care); and yet others of the unfaithful, more pathetic than wicked, and more to be pitied than blamed, were to be treated with gentleness and encouragement.

Jude concluded his letter with a wonderful doxology: God was to be accorded glory, majesty, power and authority, all in thankfulness to Him who could save and keep His people from falling.